AF553471

Local Governance

The Institute of Social Sciences

The Institute of Social Sciences was founded in 1985, to study contemporary social, political and economic issues and problems in an inter-disciplinary perspective and to make available its findings and recommendations to government bodies, social scientists, policy makers, people's and workers' organisations, so as to widen their options for action. The evolution of an informed and action-oriented public opinion is the primary aim of the Institute.

The research projects undertaken by the Institute cover a wide range of subjects in the areas of local governance, women's studies, environment and contemporary economic and political issues. The Institute also organises seminars, workshops, discussions and training programmes for the exchange of ideas and dissemination of its research findings.

The major research thrust of the Institute is in the areas of Local Governance (Panchayati Raj), Urban Studies, Women's Studies, Economic Affairs, Human Rights and Police Reforms and International Studies. We seek to build a community of concerned scholars and activists engaged in ushering in a humane and just society.

Chairman
Prof. U.R. Anantha Murthy

Director
Dr. George Mathew

About the Editors

Mr. Buddhadeb Ghosh is Senior Fellow, the Institute of Social Sciences, New Delhi. He has been involved in a large number of studies in the areas of decentralization, rural development and related matters. His publications include *State Politics and Panchayats in India* (Manohor, 2003) and researched papers.

Ms. Bidyut Mohanty, Ph. D. (Delhi), Head, Department of Women's Studies, Institute of Social Sciences(ISS), New Delhi is also a Visiting Professor in the Global and International Studies, University of California, Santa Barbara. She combines grassroots activism with participatory research. Her publications include several research papers and edited books, including *Urbanization in Developing Countries: Access to Basic Services and Community Participation* (1993), *Concept* and *Women and Political Empowerment (Annual volumes from 1995 till 2006)* are prominent.

Mr. Nitya Jacob is a development communications professional. His area of specialization is integrated water resources management including watershed treatment, participatory groundwater management and drinking water provision and quality. Currently, Mr. Jacob is heading the Water Community of United Nations Solution Exchange, where he contributes to and moderates debates on water issues. His recent publication: *Jalyatra: Exploring India's Traditional Water Management Systems.* (Penguin, 2008).

Local Governance

Search for New Path

Edited by

Buddhadeb Ghosh
Bidyut Mohanty
Nitya Jacob

Published for

Institute of Social Sciences

by

CONCEPT PUBLISHING COMPANY, Pvt. Ltd.,
NEW DELHI-110059

ISBN-13: 978-81-8069-717-3

First Published 2011

Published and Printed by

Concept Publishing Company Pvt. Ltd.
Regd. Office:
A/15-16, Commercial Block, Mohan Garden
New Delhi-110059 (India)
Phones : 25351460, 25351794, *Fax* : 091-11-25357109
Email : publishing@conceptpub.com,
Website: www.conceptpub.com

Editorial Office:
H-13, Bali Nagar, New Delhi-110 015, India.

Cataloging in Publication Data--*Courtesy*: D.K. Agencies (P) Ltd. <docinfo@dkagencies.com>

Local governance : search for new path / edited by Buddhadeb Ghosh, Bidyut Mohanty, Nitya Jacob.
p. cm.
Includes index.
ISBN 9788180697173

1. Local government--India. 2. Local government--India--Case studies. I. Ghosh, Buddhadeb. II. Mohanty, Bidyut. III. Jacob, Nitya. IV. Institute of Social Sciences (New Delhi, India)

DDC 320.80954 22

"The central question in the study of community governance is how a group of principals who are in an interdependent situation can organize and govern themselves to obtain continuing joint benefits when all face temptations to free-ride, shirk, or otherwise act opportunistically."

Elinor Ostrom, Nobel Laureate

Plan-India

Plan in India is part of Plan International, one of the world's largest community development organisations. Plan's vision is of a world in which all children realise their full potential in societies which respect people's rights and dignity. Plan is independent, with no religious, political or governmental affiliations.

For over 30 years, Plan and our partners have helped communities throughout India to help themselves, so that children have access to their rights including the right to protection, basic education, proper healthcare, a healthy environment, livelihood opportunities and participation in decisions which affect their lives. We encourage children to express their views and be actively involved in improving their communities. Plan currently works in eleven States in India and has impacted the lives of over a million children.

Plan's work focuses on improving opportunities for vulnerable children and their communities in India, including children living on the streets and those living in urban homeless families; those with disabilities or affected by HIV; those who are exploited and trafficked; the children of sex workers; and child labourers. Plan also works to help girls overcome the disadvantage and discrimination they face in everyday life within most communities.

Foreword

For the millions of poor and marginalized people of this country, governance has relevance mostly in so far as it relates to the local space of the villages where they live and from where they earn their livelihood. To them good governance means good local governance. Is it responsive to the local needs? Is it transparent and accountable? Are the services that the state is expected to provide to the poor adequate? Do they have the right to participate in the process of making decisions that affect their lives? All these questions are now highly relevant not only for making democracy work for the common people, but also for achieving the goal of eradication of poverty from our hundreds and thousands of villages.

In the above context, the question as to how the local space should be governed assumes importance. At present, apart from the constitutionally mandated panchayats and municipalities, several actors are at work in rural and urban governance and development: the Union Government with a host of centrally sponsored schemes, line departments of State governments, Non Governmental Organizations (NGOs) and Community Based Organizations (CBOs). The NGOs and CBOs often take upon themselves the task of addressing various developmental and welfare functions. Traditionally, the government and NGOs/CBOs had looked at each other with suspicion, resulting not only in lack of coordination between them, but, quite often, in mutual antagonism. NGOs/CBOs think the government is ham-handed, corrupt and ignores people at the grass roots. The government feels NGOs/CBOs interfere in their functions and is an inconvenient fact of life.

Such a situation is not conducive to good local governance. An integration of activities of all the actors is necessary for providing people-friendly governance at the local level and to accelerate, in the process, the pace of inclusive development. As the representative government for the local area, panchayats can play a key role in this, for the Constitution has mandated these bodies to prepare plans for economic development and social justice and to implement such schemes as are entrusted to them.

In this context the Institute of Social Sciences had undertaken a study of local governance practices in eight States — Andhra Pradesh, Bihar, Karnataka, Tamil Nadu, Orissa, Uttarakhand, Uttar Pradesh, Rajasthan, and two urban areas — Ranga Reddy District (Andhra Pradesh) and New Delhi. This publication contains the case studies prepared by the project and provides some valuable insights on the issues confronting good local governance, specially the linkage between local governments and the NGOs/CBOs.

We are grateful to Plan International—an international NGO—for sponsoring this project. Our thanks are also due to the Directors and Project Coordinators of the Plan partners for providing the logistics and support for conducting the research in the study areas.

George Mathew
Director
Institute of Social Sciences

Acknowledgements

This report is the cumulative effort of several researchers, agencies, activists and resource persons who contributed through their ideas, thoughts and support. It is the product of a project titled "Documentation of Governance in Plan Communities" commissioned by the Plan International (now Plan-India) during the period of two years between 2005 and 2007.

Our special thanks to Mr. Bruno Oudmayer, the then Director, Plan International for sponsoring this project. Ms. Nalini Abraham, Advisor, Health, Plan International, initiated this project and consistently extended all help and support to make it a pioneering study. Thanks are also due to Ms. Verity Corbett, Programme Support Manager, Plan International, for taking a keen interest in the research work and helping us to complete it on time.

The study was made possible due to the sincere cooperation of the following Plan partners: Dr Ranjana Kaul, Executive Director, Community Aid and Sponsorship Programme (CASP), New Delhi; Mr Sundar Mishra, Programme Director, and Dr. Jagadanand, Founder Director, Centre for Youth and Social Development (CYSD), Orissa; Mr. Gopal Thapliyal, Project Manager, PU, Sri Bhuvneswari Mahila Ashram (SBMA), Uttarkashi; Ms Neelima Khetan, Chief Executive, Seva Mandir, Rajasthan; Mr. Bisvash Chatterjee, Director, Gram Niyojan Kendra, Uttar Pradesh; Mr. Hari Subramanyam, Programme Point Person, Arthik Samata Mandal (ASM), Andhra Pradesh; Mr. P.K. Sharma, Centre for Documentation, Information, Research, Education, Communication and Training (Center DIRECT), Bihar; and Mr. William D'Souza, Executive Director, Mysore Resettlement and Development Agency (MYRADA). The research faculty of ISS extended their full support throughout the project.

Contents

The Contributors

Arvind Kumar Pandey, Research Officer, Institute of Social Sciences, 8, Nelson Mandela Road, New Delhi – 110 070.

B.S. Bhargava, Senior Fellow, Institute of Social Sciences, Southern Regional Centre, No.9, 8th Main Road, 8th Cross, Malleswaram, Bangalore– 560 003.

Bidyut Mohanty, Head, Women's Studies, Institute of Social Sciences, 8, Nelson Mandela Road, New Delhi – 110 070.

Buddhadeb Ghosh, Senior Fellow, Institute of Social Sciences, CF-149, Sector 1, Salt Lake City, Kolkata – 700 064.

Jitendra Kumar, Research Scholar, Department of Economics, Ch. Charan Singh University, Meerut, Uttar Pradesh – 250 005.

K. K. Patnaik, Regional Coordinator, Institute of Social Sciences, Plot No. 75/A, B.J.B. Nagar, Opposite B.J.B. English Medium School, Bhubaneshwar – 751 014.

K. Subha, Regional Coordinator, Institute of Social Sciences, Southern Regional Centre, No. 9, 8th Main Road, 8th Cross, Malleswaram, Bangalore – 560 003.

Madhulika Mitra, Research Associate, Institute of Social Sciences, CF-149, Sector 1, Salt Lake City, Kolkata – 700 064.

Manju Panwar, Assistant Professor, Department of Social Work, BPS Women University, Khanpur Kalan, Sonipat, Haryana – 131 305.

Nitya Jacob, Development Communication Specialist, New Delhi.

P. K. Das, Professor (Retd.), NCERT, New Delhi.

Pamela Singla, Senior Lecturer, Department of Social Work, University of Delhi.

Pramod Kumar Ray, Senior Research Investigator, ICMR Project on Gender Issues in Unorganized Sector, affiliated to Utkal University, Bhubaneshwar.

Puspa Asthana, Independent Researcher, Bhubaneshwar.

Sucharita Dutta, Research Assistant, Institute of Social Sciences, CF-149, Sector 1, Salt Lake City, Kolkata – 700 064.

List of Abbreviations

ABS	Antyodaya Bal Sangham
ACMRC	Akshaya Community Managed Resource Centre
ADO	Assistant Development Officer
AGS	Antyodaya Gram Sabham
ANMs	Auxiliary Nurse Midwives
APSDF	Action Programme for Slum Dwellers Federation
APUSP	Andhra Pradesh Urban Service for Poor
ASHA	Accredited Social Health Activist
ASM	Arthik Samata Mandal
AWMACTS	Antyodaya Women's Mutually Aided Co-operative Thrift Society
AWWs	Anganwadi Workers
BBM	Babu Bahini Manch
BDO	Block Development Officer
BLTF	Block Level Task Force
BP	Bal Panchayat
BPL	Below Poverty Level
BSY	Balika Samriddhi Yojana
CASP	Community Aid and Sponsorship Programme
CBOs	Community Based Organisations
CCF	Children's Clubs Federation
CEPRA	Centre for Policy Research and Advocacy
CHFS	Community Health Financing Scheme
CHSD	Centre for Human and Sustainable Development
CIDOR	Centre of Institutional Development and Organizational Reforms
CMEY	Chief Minister's Empowerment Yojana
CMGs	Credit Management Groups

CMRCs	Community Managed Resource Centres
CSOs	Civil Society Organisations
CYSD	Centre for Youth and Social Development
Centre DIRECT	Centre for Documentation , Information, Research, Education, Communication and Training
DLTF	District Level Task Force
DPC	District Planning Committee
DRDC	District Rural Development Cell
DWCUA	Development of Women and Child in Urban Areas
DSP	Deputy Superintendent of Police
ECCD	Early Childhood Care and Development
FGDs	Focus Group Discussions
GNK	Gram Niyojan Kendra
GPs	Gram Panchayats
GSs	Gram Sabhas
GVC	Gram Vikas Committee
IAY	Indira Awaas Yojana
ICDS	Integrated Child Development Services
IEC	Information, Education and Communication
IFA	Iron and Folic Acid
ILCS	Integrated Low Cost Sanitation Scheme
INHP	Integrated Nutrition and Health Programme
JIVIKA	Jeetha Vimukthi Karmikaru
JRY	Jawahar Rozgar Yojana
KSS	Kisan Sewa Samiti
LGIs	Local Government Institutions
MCD	Municipal Corporation of Delhi
MGMUS	Maa Gauri Mahila Unnayan Sangha
MMD	Mahila Mangal Dal
MYRADA	Mysore Resettlement and Development Agency
NABARD	National Bank for Agriculture and Rural Development
NDMC	New Delhi Municipal Committee
NFE	Non Formal Education
NGOs	Non Governmental Organisations
NKS	Nanda Kishori Samooh
NREGS	National Rural Employment Guarantee Scheme

NRY	Nehru Rozgar Yojana
NSAP	National Social Assistance Programme
NSDP	National Slum Development Programme
PDS	Public Distribution System
PESAA	Panchayat Extension to the Scheduled Areas Act
PHC	Primary Health Centre
PHSF	Public Health Safety Fund
PMIUPEP	Prime Minister's Integrated Urban Poverty Eradication Programme
PMRY	Prime Minister's Rozgar Yojana
PI	Plan International
PIOs	Public Information Officers
PRA	Participatory Rapid Appraisal
PRFs	Panchayati Raj Functionaries
PRIs	Panchayati Raj Institutions
PS	Panchayat Samiti
PSG	Panchayat Support Group
PTA	Parent-Teacher Association
PU	Panchayat Union
PWD	Public Works Department
RC	Resource Centre
RCMC	Resource Centre Management Committee
RMS	Rayat Mitra Sangham
RTI	Right to Information Act
SAGs	Self-help Affinity Groups
SBMA	Sri Bhuvaneshwari Mahila Ashram
SBSSS	Sami Brikshya Samanuya Sanchaya Samiti
SDM	Sub-Divisional District Magistrate
SDMC	School Development and Management Committee
SGI	Support to Gender Issue Project
SGRY	Sampoorna Grameen Rozgar Yojana
SGSY	Swarnajayanti Gram Swarozgar Yojana
SHGs	Self–Help Groups
SJSRY	Swarna Jayanti Shahari Rozgar Yojana
SM	Seva Mandir
SPARC	Society for Promotion of Area Resource Centres
SPREAD	Shanti Patient Related Education and Direction
SSA	Sarva Shiksha Abhiyan
SVYM	Swami Vivekananda Youth Movement

TDP	Telugu Desam Party
TOT	Training of Trainers
TSC	Total Sanitation Campaign
TT	Tetanus Toxid
UBSP	Urban Basic Services for the Poor
ULGIs	Urban Local Government Institutions
USEP	Urban Self Employment Programmes
UWEP	Urban Wage Employment Programme
VAMBAY	Valmiki Ambedkar Yojana.
VDC	Village Development Committee
VEC	Village Education Committee
VGDS	Voluntary Garbage Disposal Scheme
VPP	Village Planning Process
YV	Youth Volunteers

Part - I

National Report

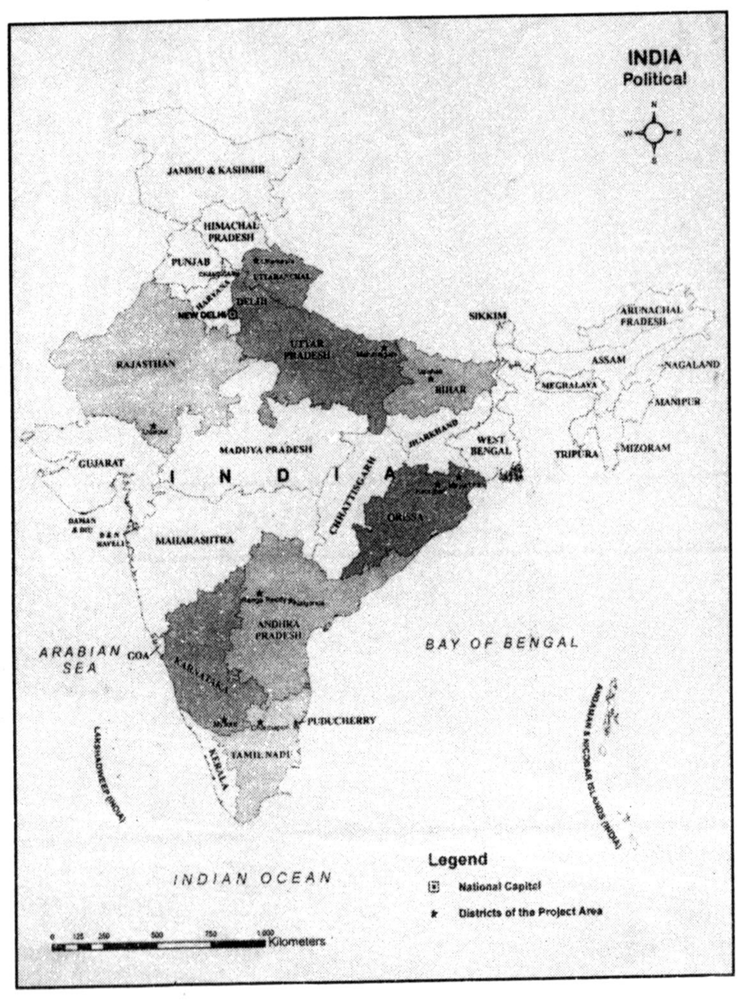
INDIA
Political
JAMMU & KASHMIR
HIMACHAL PRADESH
PUNJAB
UTTARANCHAL
HARYANA
DELHI
NEW DELHI
RAJASTHAN
UTTAR PRADESH
SIKKIM
ARUNACHAL PRADESH
ASSAM
NAGALAND
MEGHALAYA
MANIPUR
BIHAR
JHARKHAND
WEST BENGAL
TRIPURA
MIZORAM
MADHYA PRADESH
GUJARAT
I N D I A
CHHATTISGARH
ORISSA
DAMAN & DIU
D & N HAVELI
MAHARASHTRA
ANDHRA PRADESH
ARABIAN SEA
GOA
KARNATAKA
BAY OF BENGAL
PUDUCHERRY
TAMIL NADU
KERALA
LAKSHADWEEP (INDIA)
ANDAMAN & NICOBAR ISLANDS (INDIA)
INDIAN OCEAN
Legend
National Capital
Districts of the Project Area
Kilometers

1

Introduction

Context of the Study

The focus of this study is on civil society institutions (CSOs) and the role they and the local government institutions (LGI) play in local governance. The activities of the LGIs and several non governmental organizations (NGOs) and community-based organizations (CBOs) supported by Plan International India (henceforth PI or Plan)—an international NGO—provide the context in which this study has been conducted. Fieldwork for this study was conducted in 2005-2007.

PI supports about 21 integrated child-centred community development projects in the country. It is working in partnership with about 30 NGOs across 11 States. Plan partners in different States promote and support CBOs, such as self-help groups (SHGs), women's groups, youth clubs, farmer's clubs etc. These CBOs are actively engaged in managing programmes under the leadership and guidance provided by the respective partner NGOs. Thus, what Plan partners are trying to do is to promote and strengthen local level institutions of people and foster, through them, a process of change in favour of the marginalized sections of society.

Scenario of Local Governance

Development is a major function of the Indian State. Accordingly, there are various departments of the government which operate in the local areas for providing many kinds of services and public goods with the objective of bringing about socio-economic development of the common people. The traditional institutions are the large number of field offices of the line departments of the State government. They were and still remain the major service providers for the local areas in the fields of education, primary health care, creation of livelihood opportunities etc.

The new-comers in the field of local governance are the LGIs. The 73rd and the 74th Constitutional Amendments, which became operational in 1993, recognize the panchayats and municipalities as governments of the local areas and envisage that they would shoulder the responsibility of undertaking various activities for social and economic development of people. Accessibility to the State institutions has always remained a problem for the poor and the disadvantaged sections of citizens, since their social interactions remain confined to the local communities only. A bureaucratic institution of the State often located at a distance from the habitation-based small communities is beyond their reach. Through the institutionalization of panchayats, the State is being brought closer to the local communities, creating enabling conditions for their participation in the decision making process.

Of late civil society institutions—NGOs and CBOs—have also been playing an important role in development, especially in social sector development, at the local level. There are similarities and convergence of goals between the activities undertaken by them and those organized by the LGIs and various field agencies of the line departments. It is, therefore, expected that the NGOs and CBOs working in various fields of socio-economic development of people should come closer to the LGIs and those institutions of the State government which operate in the local area for providing various services. Unfortunately, however, the linkage between all these institutions remains very weak.

Community Governance

As the discussion above shows, governance at the local level is now undergoing a change. Multiple actors are involved in the field of local governance, which previously was considered to be the exclusive domain of the bureaucracy of the State government. This does not mean that one set of organizations is dispensable, since its activities overlap with others. For, it is being increasingly recognized that local governance is not merely the business of a government operating from a level far away from that of a small community. NGOs, CBOs and LGIs have a role to play in matters that were previously considered the domain of the higher levels of the government. Institutionalization of LGIs will bring the government closer to the people, making them more responsive, transparent and accountable. Increasing engagement of CSOs, particularly the CBOs, in development would go a long way in filling a void in local governance by strengthening what is often referred to as 'community governance'.

The basic idea of the concept of 'community governance' is that in many societies the communities are often found to share a part of the governance functions in situations where both the State and the market fail. In Indian villages there was a strong tradition of community governance. That tradition has not been completely lost. Instances of village communities addressing common social or economic problems in innovative ways without any intervention of the State agencies are not rare to find. If that is the case, then it stands to reason that this resource of the community should be utilized appropriately to create a synergy which may be employed for development and welfare of common people. In such a situation, the governance functions discharged by the communities would complement those being addressed by the formal institutions of the State. It will be worthwhile to explore the idea a little further.

Even though the word 'governance' is being used widely over the last two decades or so, it is hard to find a precise definition. It now covers not only the functions discharged by the government, but also such other functions in respect of public welfare or regulation of public behaviour as are discharged by other actors. Broadly from the perspective of development, 'governance' may be defined as a process which involves organizing and ordering of public life in a manner that expands the freedom and the range of choices of individuals in pursuing objectives that they have reasons to value. Community governance may be defined as 'the structure of small group social interactions ... that with ... [the] familiar forms of governance jointly determine economic and social outcomes' (Samuel Bowles and Herbert Gintis, *Social Capital and Community Governance,* http://www.umass.edu/preference/gintis/soccapej.pdf). This implies that the small community-based organizations may also play an important role in local development.

The role of small communities in development is an issue that has not received the attention it deserves. One reason for this is that in the past the discourse on development was too much state-centric. It was assumed that the state had the capacity to fulfil all the wants of the citizens and all the initiatives of development should come from it.

Experience has shown that such view has no practical utility, since state failures are very common, and in any case, the state's capacity to meet the needs of people is not unlimited. Even so, there is now little disagreement over the fact that the state has a great role to play, both in correcting distortions of the market and in undertaking proactive actions in various fields of development, especially in underdeveloped countries. But, since the state also has its limitations, it is not enough to rely only upon its familiar institutions to discharge the governance functions, especially those functions which are directly concerned with the specific needs of small communities. The market is an inappropriate institution for this, because it has no interest in things that do not generate profit, however, important those may be from the social perspective and it is most insensitive to the needs of the weak and deprived people.

The void, therefore, has to be filled by the communities themselves. Herein lies the significance of the NGOs and CBOs, which, working in close proximity with the formal institutions of the state, can make a positive impact on the lives of common people. Collective actions through such organizations are particularly important for the poor and the deprived people who generally find it difficult to access the formal state institutions. Introduction of local democracy makes institutions of the state more accessible to common people. Being closer to the local communities, the rural LGIs occupy a unique space in between the domain of the state and the community. But even then they cannot be substitutes of NGOs and CBOs, in solving specific problems of small communities.

Role of Communities in Good Governance

Contrary to the earlier belief that communities are relics of the past and will vanish with the process of modernization of the society, polity and economy, their potential role in ensuring good governance is now being increasingly recognized. A community is a group of individuals held together by mutual trust and concern for one's associates and willingness to follow certain common norms. They do so not because of altruism towards the community members, nor are they guided by self-interest alone. They feel rewarded by being members of the community, because they have a common collective identity, which they value and they have some common problems which can be solved if they work together without disturbing this identity.

There are various ways by which communities handle their common problems. The most valuable resource in their possession, as already noted, is mutual trust, concern for others, a sense of belonging to a group and willingness to abide by community norms. These are resources that are generally referred to as 'social capital'. By generating 'social capital', the local community based organizations can complement the efforts of the formal institutions of the state, including the LGIs, in promoting good governance. Working together with the LGIs and the delivery system of the higher levels of the government, they can make useful contribution towards socio-economic development of local people.

There is, however, a distinction between the indigenous community groups and the community-based groups formed at the initiative of an NGO (for example women's groups) or the government (for example village education committee). The spontaneity that is observed in the former groups may often be found missing in the latter groups of CBOs which tend to become excessively dependent upon their sponsors, creating problems of their sustainability. Besides, such informal or formal groups are created to pursue certain development goals. The group members often lack the capacity to conduct various activities independently to achieve such goals. How to build capacities of the groups remains a constant problem for the sponsoring agency.

Objectives of the Study

This study examines the activities of the NGOs/CBOs and the LGIs within the above conceptual framework, the central concern being the search for a path that leads to good local governance. One of the objectives of the study is to document the following:

- Community participation processes and mechanism.
- The deficiencies and shortcomings in the area of governance in the projects supported by PI (India).
- The mechanisms and strengths/weaknesses of the interface between the Plan partners and local government institutions.
- The status of the Panchayati Raj Institutions and their functioning in the State.

The other objective is to explore ways and means for mainstreaming community participation, strengthening LGIs and establishing viable linkages between the CBOs and LGIs as well as the local delivery system of the State government. For, it is believed that such networking of local institutions will promote good local governance and contribute towards the effectiveness and sustainability of the community-based organizations.

Fieldwork for this study was carried out in the rural areas of Tamil Nadu, Karnataka, Andhra Pradesh, Orissa, Bihar, Uttar Pradesh, Uttarakhand, Rajasthan and in the urban slums of Delhi and one town of Andhra Pradesh. In each of the areas, one NGO was taken up for study. For ascertaining the ground situation, the activities of the CBOs and the local panchayats were studied in one or two Blocks in each State. In each of the urban areas of Delhi and Andhra Pradesh, studies were conducted in the slum area of one ward. The results of the study on each State/city have been documented in individual reports. Part II contains these case studies. Part I contains the national report which gives a summary of the major findings of the case studies and draws certain general conclusions based on the lessons learnt from them.

Methodology

Methodologies adopted for research include the following:

- Desk study of various documents/reports;
- Questionnaire survey;
- Semi-structured interviews with the stakeholders;
- Focus group discussions;
- Participant-observation method;
- Field visits;
- Informal discussions with the stakeholders;
- Case studies.

Structure of the Report

The national report is divided into five chapters. Chapter 1 provides the background of the study and its conceptual framework. Chapter 2 contains the profiles of the various NGOs and CBOs spread over the rural areas of eight States and two cities. Chapter 3 presents the status of the Panchayati Raj Institutions of the study areas. An analysis of the activities of civil society institutions from the perspective of good local governance is provided in Chapter 4, which also suggests a framework for institutional integration at the local level. Chapter 5 contains some suggestions and recommendations.

The case studies of different study areas are provided in Chapters 6 to 15 of Part II. An introduction to the case studies is provided in Chapter VI.

2

Profile of Plan Partner NGOs

Tamil Nadu

Mysore Resettlement and Development Agency (MYRADA) is the partner of Plan International in the State of Tamil Nadu. This NGO was founded in the year 1968 in Karnataka. Initially MYRADA worked for the resettlement of Tibetan Refugees and this continued till 1978 when MYRADA changed the profile of its activities and started working for the rural poor. Because of its potential strength, demand for expansion of its activities increased and several State governments invited it to work in backward regions. Presently, this NGO has been directly managing 16 projects in 12 backward districts in the States of Tamil Nadu, Karnataka and Andhra Pradesh. The principles that guide the activities of this NGO include the following:

- Reliance on the active participation and complete involvement of its workers in project implementation.
- *Transparency in functioning:* The workers of the NGO, the people for whom the project is implemented and the agency that sponsors the project are well-versed with the objectives of the project and are intimately connected with its execution in different stages.
- *Ownership and accountability:* When the organization takes up a project for implementation, it accepts the responsibility of the entire project beginning from its initiation till its completion. In fact, this is a major factor that accounts for its credibility. MYRADA has a team of committed workers. It stresses on orienting its workers and prepares them to undertake the responsibility of

executing the field activities with devotion and professionalism. MYRADA puts premium on both and that, indeed, is its real strength.

Self-help Affinity Groups (SAGs)

In course of working for the development of the poor, MYRADA came to realize that affordable and hassle-free availability of credit was a basic need of the common people. In order to make credit available to the poor, MYRADA started working for an alternative credit system in 1984-85. People with similar socio-economic background were mobilized to form credit societies and they were known as Credit Management Groups (CMGs). These societies started functioning under the guidance of MYRADA. NABARD provided funds to promote these credit societies. Later, they came to be known as Self Help Groups (SHGs). Substantial investment was made to build the capacity of the groups and to generate self-confidence of the members. The success of many of these credit groups helped their members overcome poverty. The credit societies consisted of like-minded people who were close to each other in many respects. They came together to solve their financial problems collectively. It is the affinity between them that bound them together and motivated them to work collectively to solve their common problems. Since the affinity between each other forms the foundation on which these credit groups stand, they were renamed at a later stage as Self-Help Affinity Groups (SAGs). In order to strengthen the small groups and provide them constant support and guidance, a larger institution was necessary. Accordingly, federations of SAGs were created. The objectives of a federation include:

- Strengthening individual SAGs by providing a forum for regular interaction and networking;
- Resolving conflicts, if any, between the member SAGs;
- Disseminating information to SAGs;
- Taking up action programmes that cannot be accomplished by the individual SAGs; and
- Lobbying with the government and other institutions in support of the poor in general and the specific programmes and activities of the SAGs in particular.

Generally, each federation has 20 SAGs as its members. Each SAG is represented by 2 of its members. To be enrolled as a member of the federation, the SAG should have at least 20 members and should have functioned for at least a minimum period of six months.

Resource Centre

A unique institution conceived by MYRADA for providing service on regular basis to the SAGs and other CBOs in the locality is the Resource Centre (RC). A RC serves about 120 SAGs or other CBOs. It provides various kinds of services to the member CBOs. These are as follows:

- Providing various kinds of information to the member organizations as also to the public;
- Creating linkage between the CBOs, the government and the private sector;
- Providing services like capacity building, audit, conflict resolution etc.;
- Disseminating information on agriculture, market, financial institutions including insurance companies, employment opportunities etc.;
- Establishing linkages with the financial institutions;
- Organizing health camps, animal health camps and awareness programmes in collaboration with respective departments; and
- Helping the poor to access benefits from the various poverty alleviation programmes and various other government programmes for the elederly, women, children, street children, the physically handicapped, orphans etc.

The Managing Committee of the RC consists of representatives of the SAGs and the CBOs. However, a CBO cannot automatically join RC as a member just because it happens to exist in the area covered by it. It has to reach certain standards of performance and maturity, which is assessed by the RC's Managing Committee. Even the existing members are assessed or rated yearly to ensure that their standards have not declined to a level where they lose RC Membership. RC is supposed to be self-financing and accordingly the CBOs pay a monthly fee to retain membership. Besides, it charges money for various services rendered by it. Fee is also realized for organizing training programmes. Each RC has a separate office, a separate account and financial management system. They present their annual reports before the general body. Each RC has a full time employee, called the RC Manager. Till now the RC Manager has been a MYRADA staff with at least 10 years of experience.

Children's Club

A Children's Club is a CBO that works for ensuring the rights of children. The Club tries to create awareness about children's rights in respect of access to education, health and hygiene etc. Membership to the club is restricted to children who are above 7 and below 16 years of age. All members are required to attend weekly meetings. This benefits all the children and facilitates learning from each other. There also exists a federation of Children's Clubs. It coordinates the activities of all the Clubs. The Club identifies intelligent students and provides them the necessary support required for their studies. It has certain rules which every child is required to follow. Under these rules every child must go to school, should be disciplined, punctual and should attend all the meetings. The Club organizes annual field trips to broaden the outlook of children. The Children's Federation organizes awareness generation programmes relating to health and hygiene and protection of environment and induces children to go to school regularly.

To promote and strengthen appropriate local level institutions of the poor, particularly of women, has been a central concern of MYRADA. The emphasis placed on building institutions of the poor and strengthening them through capacity building and by establishing networks and linkages between and among the various formal or informal institutions has been a step in the right direction. For, it is not enough to foster the process of change in favour of the rural poor. It is necessary to ensure that such process is also sustained by them through building and managing innovative local level institutions rooted in values of justice, equity and mutual support. MYRADA, as noted above, has been doing a lot of things in realizing this mission.

It is, however, not yet clear whether the CBOs being promoted and nurtured by the NGO would be sustainable after the phasing out of the Project. Another area of concern is the lack of collaborative projects between the CBOs and the Panchayati Raj Institutions. There is evidence of cordial relationship between them. It was also found that the NGO had organized training programmes for PRI representatives. But, instances of sharing of activities between the two types of institutions for achieving a common goal were not found. It seems that innovative programmes should be taken up to improve the linkages between the CBOs, the SAGs, the NGO's and the institutions of panchayat.

Karnataka

In Karnataka also MYRADA is the partner of PI. Hence, this NGO's activities were studied once again in HD Kote taluk of Mysore district where it has been working for a long time. There are many NGOs active in this taluk, MYRADA being the most prominent among them. Since the main features of this NGO have been described earlier, the discussion here will be confined to an evaluation of their specific activities in the taluk.

Self Help Affinity Groups and Federations

As of March 2006, there were 2,314 SAGs in HD Kote. Among them, as many as 2,208 were women's groups, 17 were mixed groups and 89 were men's groups. Total savings of these groups exceeded Rs. 10 crore and total common fund was of the order of Rs. 21.9 crore. Loans disbursed amounted to Rs. 61.38 crore. Like Tamil Nadu, there are also federations of SAGs. At present 23 federations are working in HD Kote and the striking feature is that they are all reported to be working well.

Resource Centre

As of March 2006, there were six Resource Centres in this taluk. The membership of these centres varied between 80 and 114 groups. For each Resource Centre there is a Resource Centre Management Committee (RCMC) comprising largely the members of the SAGs. The Centre is managed by a regular Manager who is a staff of MYRADA. The Manager is the Chief Executive Officer and he reports to the RCMC. He is supported by several community resource persons selected by CBOs. The RCs have several features in common but also differ in terms of management policy and functions. There is no standardized framework for all RCs. Various kinds of services provided by the Centre have already been noted. One of them deserves special mention. This relates to the institutional development of the SAGs and other CBOs. Apart from the various capacity building programmes taken up for them, the Manager of the Centre visits the SAGs/other CBOs at least twice every year, helps to keep their books of accounts properly and prepares their monthly financial statements. He also arranges for audit of the accounts of these organizations.

Children's Clubs and Federation

There are several children's clubs and their federations in HD Kote. Their functions have already been described. These clubs/federations are also serviced by the RC. Nearly 200 children were found to be attached to six Resource Centres.

MYRADA and the CBOs supported by them have been involved in various development programmes relating to health, education and livelihood opportunities. Children's clubs and women's SAGs were involved in the pulse polio programme. MYRADA provided financial and technical support in the sanitation programme of the Zilla Parishad. Through various awareness generation programmes, people have become more conscious of child rights. Members of SAGs, school development and monitoring committee and Gram Panchayat jointly discuss the problems of schools. If there is a shortage of teachers, they even employ volunteers with financial assistance from MYRADA. For increasing livelihood opportunities, various skill training programmes are organized for farmers, adolescent girls and others.

The SAGs and other CBOs supported by MYRADA are encouraged to participate in the development activities of the PRIs. The members of the CBOs are asked to attend Gram Sabha meetings. Many of them contest panchayat elections. About 40 to 60 per cent of the women members of the 4 GPs that were studied were found to be members of the SAGs. Despite all this, collaboration between the CBOs and the GP leaves much to be desired. Except in respect of a few specific schemes, there was little evidence of joint effort put in by these institutions for the pursuit of certain common development objectives. The NGO or the CBOs of HD Kote cannot be faulted on this count, as they showed much interest in working with the panchayat system. In fact the enabling condition is missing under which the GP could integrate the activities of all development agencies functioning within its area. We shall have occasion to explore this issue in Chapter 4.

The sustainability of SAGs and other CBOs promoted by MYRADA and Plan International after phasing out of the project unit is the most challenging issue. MYRADA's answer to this vexed problem appears to be the institutionalization of the Resource Centre, which is supposed to be self-financing and managed by the member CBOs. It is also supposed to be run professionally, for which an experienced person is appointed as Manager. This is a novel idea, indeed, and needs to be pursued with all seriousness. But the question remains as to whether this alone can guarantee sustainability of the grassroots institutions of poor people. The CBOs have their own weaknesses and it is not clear how many of them have acquired the capacity or the orientation to manage their own affairs independently. Development of the self-management capacity of the CBOs is crucial for their sustainability, because no support institutions can do everything for the groups.

Andhra Pradesh

Arthik Samata Mandal (ASM)—a partner NGO of Plan International—has been working on various issues relating to women, children, health, education, livelihood and sanitation in the Nalgonda region of Andhra Pradesh. Suryapet—a mandal of Nalgonda district, where this study was conducted, constitutes the area of activities of the ASM. Like other Plan partners, ASM also promotes and supports community based organizations. The CBOs formed by this NGO are Antyodaya Gram Sabham (AGS), Antyodaya Mahila Paraspara Sahayak Sangham, Bal Panchayat (Children's Club) and Rayat Mitra Sangham (Farmers' Committee). Besides, the organization has also been imparting training to the Panchayati Raj functionaries. AGS is a village based organization. Men and women of a village belonging to all castes and communities may become members of the organization on payment of an annual fee of Rupees 25. The meetings of AGS take place every month. The President and other office bearers are elected by the members. The organization works for all-round development of the village and maintains close liaison with the PRIs and government agencies. Some of the development activities undertaken by it are described below.

By involving people of the community it keeps the village clean and undertakes minor repair of the approach road to the village. It participates in immunization programmes and health awareness campaigns organized by ASM. It works with the NGO, government agencies and panchayat in providing drinking water facility to the villagers. For improving livelihood opportunities, it takes up a number of activities with the help of ASM, such as, making compost, preparing organic pesticide, providing irrigation facilities etc. It provides financial assistance to the poor and the sick in drought situations. The CBO members actively participate in resolving village conflicts and intervene in matters relating to gender justice. The organization often conducts social audit of panchayats to ensure their accountability.

For facilitating saving and micro credit activities, ASM has formed the Antyodaya Mutual Aided Cooperative Thrift Society (AMACTS). ASM has also promoted self-help groups of women at the village level and a federation of the groups at the mandal level. For each SHG at village level the members elect a first leader and a second leader. The SHGs meet every month. On the 16th of every month, leaders of each SHG attend the sectoral meeting. Each member deposits Rupees 21 per month. The leader of the group maintains proceedings and other records are maintained at the cluster office level. Each member is given a bank passbook. The group provides credit facilities to its members, interest being 1.5 per cent per month. Besides savings and micro credit activities, the SHGs are encouraged to get involved in various other social issues relating to education, health, sanitation, women's rights etc. However, it was observed that the group members were more interested in thrift and credit activities and had little motivation in getting involved in community development activities.

ASM has mobilized children through the Children's Club or Bal Panchayat. It comprises children of the village within the age group of 6 and 13, irrespective of their caste or community. Under the Children's Clubs there are various committees. These include savings committee, education committee, environment committee, health committee and communication committee. Each committee has one leader and the club as a whole has one first leader and one second leader. Development activities undertaken by the children include the following:

- Through its health committee, the club addresses various health and sanitation issues, such as creating awareness on safe drinking water, diarrhoea management, personal hygiene etc.;
- It undertakes IEC (Information, Education and Communication) programmes on health, sanitation and education. It observes national holidays by mounting special campaigns. One year, it organized a rally to generate awareness on universal enrolment of children in schools on August 15, while another year, it carried out sanitation activities on Gandhi Jayanti day;
- The Children's Club also undertakes activities to improve the condition of the village road and approach road to the school; and
- Members of Children's Club have also worked for prohibiting liquor consumption

Rayat Mitra Sangham

In order to enable the farmers to have an organization of their own to pursue activities for their benefit, ASM has promoted Rayat Mitra Sangham (RMS) or Farmers' Committee. ASM also organizes various training programmes on improved and sustainable farming practices for the members of RMS. Besides, assistance is given to them in the form of seeds, fertilizer and also credit during drought situation. The farmers are also encouraged to discuss their common problems together. However, it was observed that the farmers had not yet realized the potential of such an organization and, as such, they had not been able to reap full benefits from the programmes initiated by ASM.

Despite the fact that the CBOs mentioned above are mostly engaged in community development activities and they are also reportedly maintaining liaison with the PRIs, no evidence was found of the local GP and the CBOs having worked in partnership with each other in a common development programme. Looking at the thrust areas of ASM, it seems that there are some types of activities where joint collaborative programmes between the PRI and the CBOs can produce better outcomes. These are education, primary health care including drinking water supply and sanitation and village roads. Besides, Nalgonda being a drought-prone area, various measures to mitigate drought, both in the short run and in long run, can form a common ground for collaborative planning and implementation of development programmes.

Orissa

The Centre for Youth and Social Development (CYSD), which was established in 1982, is one of the partner NGOs of PI in Orissa. CYSD works in such thematic areas as primary education, health and sanitation, prevention of drug abuse and HIV/AIDS, women's empowerment, child rights, sustainable livelihood, disaster management and participatory governance. Its strategy of work is based on four principles which are as follows:

- Village as the unit of action;
- Designing project activities for the poor and deprived people;
- Group approach; and
- Considering people as partners of development project rather than beneficiaries.

CYSD became a partner of Plan International in 1989. In 1995, it started working in Saharpada Block of Keonjhar district. Presently operational area of the project extends up to the Thakurmunda Block of Mayurbhanj district in Orissa, covering 17 village panchayats, 81 villages, 8,350 households and a population of 44,892. Both the blocks were taken up for study. The CYSD has promoted and/or supported various kinds of CBOs in Thakurmunda block. There are 411 SHGs with a total membership of over 4,700. Besides, there are 57 youth clubs, 80 village level committees and 5 joint forest management committees involving over 4,000 persons. Besides, CYSD has also promoted several farmer's groups and children's groups in the area. For strengthening SHGs and for ensuring their sustainability, CYSD has made serious efforts to set up federations of SHGs, some of which are already functioning well.

The development activities undertaken by the CBOs include the following:

- *Health*: Universalizing immunization of children, popularizing breast feeding, nutrition of children, diarrhoea management, immunization and nutrition of pregnant mothers and their pre-natal and post-natal check up, personal hygiene, smokeless *chulha* and health check up in schools.
- *Education*: Universal enrolment of children, eliminating dropouts from schools, alternative and non-formal schools, library and information centre.
- *Livelihood and Food Security*: Creating irrigation facilities, social/farm forestry, developing nurseries, kitchen gardening, skill training for farm and non-farm economic activities, extending micro-credit facilities and encouraging savings, establishing grain gola, dissemination of information on various development activities etc.
- *Empowerment of Women and Children*: Encouraging women's participation in SHGs and other CBOs, generating gender sensitivity among people, enforcing child rights, birth registration of children etc.

As the above account shows, CYSD's activities are quite significant for poverty alleviation. However, as in other areas, two nagging problems remain. One is the question of sustainability of the CBOs after the support of the NGO is withdrawn. Setting up and strengthening of federations is a step in the right direction. But it is not yet clear whether this is enough. It seems that sustained efforts are necessary for the development of self-management capacity of the groups and reduction of their dependence on the CYSD. The second problem lies in the absence of collaboration between the NGO and the CBOs on the one hand and the panchayat and the government service providers on the other. Even though all are supposedly working to achieve certain common developmental goals, they are working practically in isolation from each other.

Bihar

The NGO studied in Bihar was Centre for Documentation, Information, Research, Education, Communication and Training or Centre DIRECT located in Patna. This organization is not a partner of Plan International. The activities of this NGO are spread over 500 villages in 14 Blocks of Muzaffarpur, Bhojpur, Patna, Vaishali and Samastipur. The major activities of Center DIRECT include promotion and dissemination of useful knowledge in the areas of health, water and sanitation, non-formal and adult education, and woman and child development. The main focus, however, is on upliftment of rural women and children belonging to the economically and socially deprived groups. Center DIRECT has been working in Bihar for the last 14 years. It is closely associated with another NGO called ADITI of which it is one of the decentralized units. They have been working together towards empowerment of women and for capacity building of the Panchayati Raj Institutions.

Self-Help Groups

The Centre is doing substantial work in promoting the SHG movement in several districts of Bihar. In the Sariya Block of Muzaffarpur district and Barh and Athmalgola Blocks of Patna district, they are engaged in developing groups under Swarnajayanti Gram Swarozgar Yojana (SGSY). In these Blocks, 375 groups have been formed with membership of 4,190 persons. With the support of Women Development Corporation of Bihar, they are developing the SHG movement for poor women under Swayamsidha project in Mahua and Patepur Blocks of Vaishali district. In Mahua, 100 groups have been formed and in Patepur 105, with an average group size of 15 members. All the members belong to the families who are below the poverty line. In Shahpur and Barhara Blocks of Bhojpur district, SHGs are promoted under the umbrella of Swawlamban project sponsored by the Women Development Corporation of Bihar. 106 groups are functioning in 23 villages of these two blocks, average number of members per group being 12. The SHG related activities are also taken up under 'Deep Project' for scheduled caste women living below the poverty line. 85 SHGs for SC women have been formed in Samastipur district under this project and they are being trained and nurtured by the NGO. Thus, in all, the Centre has promoted 771 groups.

Major findings of the study on the functioning of SHGs in Mahua Block were as follows:

- *Groups formed*: 100 in 24 villages spread over 7 gram panchayats;
- *Number of members*: 1,553, that is, 15 per group on an average;
- *Amount of group savings*: Rs. 10.50 lakh or Rs. 10,500 per group on an average;
- *Inter-lending*: Rs. 14.90 lakh for consumption purpose and Rs. 8.58 lakh for productive enterprise;
- Number of members engaged in individual enterprises: 1,175;
- Number of clusters formed: 8 covering all the 100 groups;
- Number of SHGs conducting fortnightly meetings: 100; and
- Number of clusters conducting monthly meetings: 8. (The general rule is that individual groups should meet every fortnight and each cluster at least once a month. This appears to be a good practice.)

Only 10 out of 100 have been graded under SGSY, National Bank for Agriculture and Rural Development (NABARD) etc. This means that linkage between the NGO-sponsored SHG activities and those under the government or bank sponsored schemes still remains weak. This is, however, a universal problem calling for integration between the NGOs/CBOs and other development agencies.

Representatives of all the 100 groups received various types of training. Training has also been given on the methodology of managing clusters. Exposure visits also have been arranged for representatives of 60 groups.

All the groups report that they have no contact with the local GP or any government offices. This is not surprising, given the fact that the group members' exposure to public sphere outside the domain of their private lives has been almost non-existent. The BPL women who have formed the groups are familiar with the latter, but not with the former. Traditionally women are discouraged from taking part in public life, which is an exclusive domain for men. Motivating women and empowering them to participate in public life is one of the major tasks to which the SHG-activists have to pay greater attention.

The survey shows that there is no attempt on the part of the local panchayats to be acquainted with the problems of the SHGs or to involve them in development activities. This means that there is lack of awareness among the panchayat leaders about the need for supporting the CBOs for local development.

Lack of awareness and experience among people about associational activities is the major hindrance to the development of community based organizations and addressing public problems at the community level through such organizations.

Other Programmes

Apart from organizing SHGs, Centre DIRECT implements various other programmes for the development of women and children and sensitization of communities on gender issues. By far, most of the innovative programmes now being implemented by it are UNICEF-sponsored projects called Village Planning Process (VPP). Its uniqueness consists in the platform it provides for convergence of the activities of CBOs and NGOs with the government service providers and the village panchayats in pursuing a common programme for the development of women, children and other disadvantaged groups.

There are two major stages in this programme. The first stage consists of preparation of a comprehensive plan in a participatory manner after taking stock of the existing situation for which a survey of each household of a village is done. The plan is made for every village within a GP. In the second stage, implementation of the plan is monitored at regular intervals to check progress and to make mid-term corrections. All agencies involved in local governance, namely the panchayat, government service providers like anganwadi centres, health centres, schools and NGOs/CBOs are made partners of the planning, implementation and monitoring processes. The NGOs play a proactive role in the planning stage and a supporting role during the follow-up stage. There is a conscious attempt to institutionalize the process of preparing plans and their implementation and integrating the activities of all the actors of local governance under the leadership of the Gram Panchayat.

The development strategy adopted in the VPP is very simple and practical. It is simple because it aims at optimizing benefits from the delivery system that is already available in the villages. In order to achieve this, it seeks to create demand for the services by raising awareness of the community, strengthen the supply mechanism principally by enhancing the accountability of the service providers and ensure convergence of the development activities within the village by bringing all the service providers to a common platform. It is also practical because the activities involved in the project are not complicated and can well be accomplished on a continuous basis under the leadership of the local Gram Panchayat with support from the field offices of the line departments of the State government engaged in various development and welfare activities.

At the time of the study, this programme was in operation for barely a year or so and, accordingly, its impact could not be evaluated. But it held the promise for addressing the long standing problem of lack of convergence of development interventions at the local level. Considering this, we have explored this model further in Chapter 4 and argued in favour of the adoption of the basic principles of the model in other areas of the country.

Uttarakhand

Sri Bhuvneswari Mahila Ashram (SBMA) has been working on various social and economic issues in collaboration with Plan International in the State of Uttarakhand. The SBMA has been motivating people to form organizations within the community. It has been active since the last thirty years and has been working towards improving the status of the community as a whole and women in particular, laying stress on the deprived and underprivileged sections of the society. It works through community based organizations towards improving health status of women, children and infants, organizes awareness programmes and motivates parents to send their children to schools and organizes training programmes to improve the livelihood opportunities of people through skill formation. Various CBOs have been promoted by the SBMA, such as, Mahila Mangal Dal (MMD), Nanda Kishori Samooh (NKS), Bal Panchayat (BP) and the Kisan Seva Samiti (KSS).

Mahila Mangal Dal (MMD)

The primary objective of MMD is to empower women and undertake development activities relating to education, health and sanitation. It also organizes skill formation training to enable its members to be productively employed. The MMD organizes regular meetings in order to make members aware of the various development schemes.

SBMA has succeeded in motivating members of the MMD to participate in the Gram Panchayat meetings. Members of MMDs have been motivated to conserve forests and prepare vermi composts for increasing the yield of crops. MMD provides financial assistance to the poor and the sick, organizes immunization camps, conducts birth registration, protests against consumption of alcohol etc.

Nand Kishori Samooh (NKS)

NKS is an organization of adolescent girls. Its objectives are to educate members to adopt better health practices, to make them aware of social issues and to build among them confidence so that they can effectively participate in decision-making processes. Skill development programmes are also taken up to enable the members to participate in economic activities. There are 140 groups with 6,000 members.

Bal Panchayats

The activities of the Bal Panchayats include preventing animals from entering the fields, educating people against consumption of liquor, running libraries and campaigning for gender equality.

Kisan Seva Samiti

It organizes programmes to educate farmers to use better techniques of farming and provides improved seeds and fertilizers for increasing the yield. Problems faced by farmers are discussed in the meetings. KSSs have formed a federation at the district level. There are 15 clusters of KSS. Each cluster has 20 to 30 members. Each cluster nominates 2 members to represent the cluster in the federation. In SBMA area there are 30 federations of KSS. The KSS has been facing problems of finance and proper orientation because of which they have not yet had much success in fulfilling their objectives.

Balwadi

Balwadi looks after the interest of pre-school going children. Expenditure of Balwadi is borne by SBMA. All learning materials are provided by SBMA.

SBMA attaches a lot of importance to capacity building of the members of the CBOs. It was observed that except Kisan Seva Samiti, all other types of CBOs were functioning well. Their members are motivated, confident and have a keen interest in carrying out their activities. The village communities also find these institutions very useful. It seems that they have acquired some capacity to manage their own affairs. However, they still get support and guidance from SBMA. It is not yet clear whether they would be able to sustain themselves once the external support of the NGO is withdrawn.

The linkages between the CBOs and the local GP was not found to be strong. GPs have not made serious efforts to forge such linkage. But an exception was noted in the case of Basunga GP, which collaborated with the MMD in implementing the sanitation programme. MMD with support from SBMA mobilized the village community to create demands for sanitary toilets. While implementing Total Sanitation Programme, the GP found the contribution of the CBO very useful. In fact, it is because of the collaborative planning, implementation and monitoring of the sanitation programme that the GP became fully sanitized and got the Nirmal Gram Puraskar from the Government of India.

Rajasthan

The partner organization of Plan International in Rajasthan is Seva Mandir (SM). Based at Udaipur, the organization is currently working in 472 villages in the districts of Udaipur and Rajsamand. The thrust areas of Seva Mandir include development of natural and water resources, education, health, women and child development and institution building. Seva Mandir believes that the responsibility for socio-economic development of people cannot be left to the government alone. People and their organizations have an important role to play in development.

The programmes of SM are based on the following principles:

- Village is the focus;
- People's participation;
- Assigning responsibility to people; and
- People are considered as partners and not merely passive beneficiaries of development programmes.

Some of the ongoing programmes of SM in the villages are as follows :

- Natural Resource Development Programme;
- Sadhna or livelihood opportunities for tribal women;
- Education Programme;
- Health Programme;
- Women's Empowerment Programme;
- Child Development Programme; and
- Community managed School.

Gram Vikas Committees

Community Based Organizations promoted by SM are known as Gram Vikas Committees (GVC). For one village, there is one GVC. The members of GVC are elected from the 'Samuh' wherein the household is the unit. To become a member of the Samuh, a family has to contribute Rupees 5 as lifetime membership fee. GVC looks after the various development issues of the village, such as, health, education, mobilization of credit, creation of income generating opportunities, forest management etc. SHGs have also been formed in villages. GVC provides support to them.

There is little interaction between the GVC, the SHGs and the Gram Panchayats. In fact, wherever GVCs are strong, GPs are seen in poor light. The panchayats are considered to be inefficient and corrupt. This kind of relationship between the CBOs and the GP is detrimental to development. However, it was observed that wherever GVCs were functioning well, people took more interest in attending Gram Sabha meetings and raised issues of public interest. Needless to say such activism on the part of the villagers would make GPs more accountable.

Development of Gram Vikas Committees is a significant achievement. But these Committees obviously cannot be substitutes of the panchayats which are institutions of government of the local areas. For achieving better outcomes, collaboration between strong panchayats and strong community based organizations is necessary. That is missing in the study areas, as both the institutions want to work independently.

Uttar Pradesh

The NGO studied in Uttar Pradesh is Gram Niyojan Kendra (GNK). GNK started with a handful of committed social workers in 1977. It worked for the welfare of the community in general and for preventing children and women from succumbing to prostitution, improving the level of literacy, improving health conditions, organizing income generation programmes, etc., in particular. GNK has been working in an area which is one of the most backward regions of the country. Strong caste bias, gender violence, exploitation and harassment of women within and outside the family are the major social evils prevailing in these villages. Thus the problems of the GNK are manifold and they have to work in adverse situations.

There are three types of community based organizations—SHGs, Babu Bahini Manch and Village Development Committees.

SHG

GNK has taken the initiative for formation of SHGs in the villages. As the case study of one such SHG shows, experience is mixed. On the positive side, women have found an opportunity to save and to access hassle-free and cheap credit. 'We are now free from the shackles of the money lenders', exclaimed a member of a SHG. On the social front also women are now more empowered. On the negative side it is found that the SHGs are too dependent on external support. They have not yet acquired self-management capacity, which is necessary for sustainability. Besides, the functioning of the groups is often hampered by the absence of mutual trust and affinity among members.

Babu Bahini Manch (BBM)

Babu Bahini Manch is an organization of children within the age group of 10 to 14 years. Both girls and boys are members of BBM—*Babu* refers to boys while *Bahini* refers to girls. BBM members elect their leaders. The leaders meet every month to discuss problems relating to education, health, immunization, school dropouts, child labour, safe drinking water and problems of early marriage. They are encouraged to interact with government officials and panchayat leaders.

Village Development Committee (VDC)

Its main objective is to work for all round development of the village in cooperation with the CBOs and the GNK. It monitors the attendance of teachers in schools and the Auxiliary Nurse Midwife (ANMs) of the health sub-centre, ensures that birth certificates are issued to children, motivates people to adopt better health practices, campaigns against child marriage, low sex-ratio and low educational level of girls and encourages people, particularly women, to participate in Gram Sabha meetings. The VDC is supposed to interact with government departments and others for effective implementation of different development projects undertaken in villages. The case study shows that the VDC is not functioning well. It is too dependent on GNK volunteers. Members do not take interest even in attending meetings. There is no linkage with the Gram Panchayat. The GP President was found unaware even of the existence of VDC.

New Delhi

The Community Aid and Sponsorship Programme (CASP) was set-up in 1976. CASP and Plan started working together in 1986 in Delhi for the children of low-income groups, socially and physically disadvantaged groups and children in distress. Their area of operation constitutes Sangam Vihar, Badarpur and Madanpur Khadar. Sangam Vihar is a resettlement colony spread over approximately 20 square km of unauthorized land with a population of about 3 lakh, of which nearly 20 per cent belongs to scheduled castes. Most of the inhabitants are self-employed. Basic amenities of life are not available to the inhabitants in this colony. Badarpur comprises nine bastis. Most of the inhabitants are daily wage earners. CASP-Plan strives to create awareness relating to health, nutrition of infants and children, immunization, universal enrolment of children etc. Inhabitants are also encouraged to develop saving habits and made sensitive to gender issues through various awareness programmes.

Bal Panchayat

It is an organization for children. It undertakes various activities to make children aware of their rights and also organizes programmes to create awareness about nutrition, health and other development issues. The major objective is to increase the level of confidence of children and to help develop a balanced personality. It also acts as a platform from which children address issues that concern them.

Nav Jagriti Abhibhawak Sangathan

The main objective of this group is to improve the quality of lives of children, their families and communities through interventions in the areas of health, education, income generation and community development. Community based clinical services have been an integral part of its comprehensive reproductive and sexual health programmes. The programmes follow the bottom-up approach that is based on the perceived needs of the community. The organization is involved in micro-credit activities also. It is working in Badarpur.

Nav-Prabhat Abhibhawak Sangathan

Its main objective is capacity building of community members. It also tries to link the community with other NGOs and government agencies, organizes programmes to adopt better healthcare and motivates members to increase their level of literacy.

Nav Yuvak Sangathan

This is located in Badarpur. It was formed in 2005. Members are drawn from both BPL and Non-BPL families. The group is involved in micro-credit activities extending credit facilities to the needy members on a simple interest rate of 2 per cent per month.

Saheli

With the help of CASP-Plan this group was formed in 2006. It consists of women from Badarpur area. It provides micro-credit facilities to its members.

Nai Disha

It was formed in 2005. It is located in Sangam Vihar. It is also involved in activities relating to micro-credit.

Through the above activities, significant work is being done to raise the level of awareness of the communities at the grassroots level on various development issues to provide services to create economic and social opportunities and to mobilize common people to create their own institutions. Such community driven activities are, however, not supplemented by the services of the Municipal Corporation of Delhi. The linkage between the CBOs and the urban local body is very weak. The slum dwellers do not receive satisfactory municipal services in respect of garbage clearance, water supply, health care and educational facilities.

Urban Andhra Pradesh

Action Programme for Slum Dwellers Federation (APSDF)—an NGO based at Hyderabad—has been working in the slums of various towns and cities of Andhra Pradesh. Its aim is to improve the quality of life of slum dwellers with a focus on women and children. While it works for integrated development of slums, the emphasis is on health and sanitation, nutrition, childhood development, formal and non-formal education, environmental improvement, housing and creation of livelihood opportunities. In order to encourage community initiatives in the development process, it has promoted CBOs of women known as Mahila Milan Sangam. About 90 such groups comprising 1,800 women have been formed in different towns and cities. There is a federal body of all such groups known as Andhra Pradesh Mahila Milan. In the Moulali slum of Kapra municipality of Ranga Reddy district where the present study was undertaken, six such CBOs were found to be working. A brief account of the activities of one such group is given below:

Ujeeva Mahila Milan

This group undertakes following activities:

- One of the important activities of the group is saving and micro credit. The group collects rupees 3 from each member everyday. It provides credit facilities to its members, both for household consumption and for productive purposes at a moderate rate of interest. The group has undertaken several economic activities.

- The group also gets involved in other development activities like slum sanitation, health, education, environment etc. As the case study done in Rajeeva Nagar *basti* of Kapra municipality shows the group's contribution in slum improvement has been considerable. At its initiative, a 50 metres long approach road to the slum area was constructed. A part of the total expenditure amounting to rupees 20,000 was met by the group. Some funds were made available by APSDF. Besides, the community members contributed voluntary labour. Thus a vital need of the slum dwellers could be met without any assistance from either the State government or the municipality. Another instance of success of the group was in raising awareness of parents about the education of their children. Thanks to the door-to-door campaign by the group members, at least 20 slum children, who had earlier dropped out of school had again been enrolled. The group's activity in raising awareness of the community about HIV/AIDS has also been quite significant.

It is unfortunate that the local municipality does not make use of such community initiatives for improvement of slums. Even though the local Councillor has been helpful, the municipality does not involve the CBOs in the decision making process. In fact the linkage between the CBO and the municipality is very weak because of which even genuine demands of these grassroots organizations are not sympathetically considered by the municipality.

3

An Evaluation of the Panchayats

Tamil Nadu

The new Panchayati Raj Act of Tamil Nadu was enacted after the 73rd Amendment Act became a part of the Constitution of India. A three-tier rural local government was introduced in the State—the Panchayat at the level of a village or a cluster of villages, the panchayat unions at the Block level and District Panchayat Council at the district level. The members of all these bodies are to be directly elected by the people, as envisaged in the Constitution.

The Village Panchayat is supposed to provide basic civic services like construction, repair and maintenance of the village roads, drainage facilities, sanitation, water supply, street lights, maintenance of burial grounds/crematorium, public toilets, etc. The responsibilities of the Panchayat Union include construction, repair and maintenance of roads, establishment and maintenance of dispensaries and elementary schools, prevention and remedial measures for epidemics, conducting fairs and festivals, establishing and maintaining panchayat markets, promoting cottage industries, etc. The functions of the panchayat system, however, do not remain confined only to providing civic services. It is also involved in the execution of various poverty alleviation programmes such as employment generation schemes, noon-meal schemes in schools etc.

As per the Panchayat Act of Tamil Nadu, the Gram Sabha has to meet thrice a year. The President of the Gram Panchayat presides over the meetings of the Gram Sabha. The Gram Sabha approves budget proposals and annual plan of the Village Panchayat and selects the list of beneficiaries of different schemes of government. Government officials attend these meetings as observers. Recently, the government passed orders for convening the Gram Sabha meetings four times a year and the quorum of the meetings has been fixed at $1/10^{th}$ of the total registered members of the Gram Sabha.

House tax, property tax, profession tax, tolls on roads and tax on advertisement are the sources of income of panchayats. Besides, the government provides them grants-in-aid. However, the Panchayati Raj Institutions of the State are not financially strong.

Establishment of PRIs has facilitated the common man's participation in the decision-making process. Because of reservation of seats for the weaker and marginalized sections of society such as women, SCs and STs, representatives from these sections have been inducted in the PRI system. PRIs now seem to be better represented by all sections of society. People can easily approach elected representatives and because of their close proximity to the electorate, they are relatively more transparent and accountable than the bureaucracy which has traditionally dominated the local governance system in the country.

In spite of the above changes, there are several obstacles that prevent PRIs from functioning effectively. Firstly, people do not seem to take much interest in the affairs of panchayats. Secondly, funds available with the local bodies are always inadequate to do justice to the responsibilities given to them. Thirdly, the local bodies have limited powers. Quite often interference from the local MLA, MP or the bureaucracy undermines the authority of the panchayat leaders and affects their autonomy.

In Tamil Nadu, traditional panchayats still function in some parts of the State. In many rural areas such panchayats have been operating alongside the statutory panchayats. As a result, confusion in their functioning prevails. In such cases, there is a feeling that formation of formal panchayats is an imposition on them. However, there are villages where the synergy between the traditional panchayat and the formal statutory panchayat has enabled the latter to function more effectively.

Panchayats in the Study Area

Two GPs were selected for case studies in the Dharmapuri district: (i) Kundamaranapalli Gram Panchayat, and (ii) Mallasandra Gram Panchayat.

Kundamaranapalli GP

This GP comprises 8 villages with a population of 4,842. There are 6 schools in the panchayat (4 primary schools, 2 high schools) and 2 balwadis. The villages now have concrete roads. There are 4 bore-wells. Pipelines have also been laid in the village. Initially, this GP laid emphasis on street lights and execution of sanitation works in the villages. Later the priority shifted to rainwater harvesting. Even though GP's development functions cover various subjects, implementation of poverty alleviation schemes has become its major activity.

It was encouraging to observe that there is interaction between the GP, SAGs and also the government departments. The major source of finance of the GP is grants received from the government. Revenue collected from taxes is very limited. Thus the GP faces financial constraints in discharging its various responsibilities.

Mallasandra GP

There are eight villages in this GP. Though the GP collects house and profession tax, the generation of resources is not substantial. It is mainly dependent on funds allotted for the implementation of various poverty alleviation schemes. The GP has good linkages with the local MLA and MP. It has been able to get grants for construction of houses for SCs and STs, road construction, drilling bore-wells and construction of a school building. The GP has a good linkage with the CBOs/SHGs, government departments and officials.

Karnataka

In Karnataka, the three-tier system of Panchayati Raj consists of the Gram Panchayat at the village level, the Taluk Panchayat at the middle level and the Zilla Parishad at the district level. Their functions have been indicated in three schedules, which contain all the 29 subjects of the Eleventh Schedule of the Constitution. Funds and functionaries have also been transferred, but complete devolution of local level functions of different subjects is yet to take place.

The panchayat has the responsibility to provide drinking water to the inhabitants, ensure sanitation and drainage and construct and maintain community latrines. Its other civic responsibilities are construction and maintenance of roads, removal of encroachments on public places, providing street lights and management of solid waste. The panchayat enjoys financial powers to levy and collect taxes, tolls and fees. It has to register births and deaths and maintain records relating to population census, cattle census, census of unemployed youth and the list of people living below poverty line. It also has the responsibility to maintain all public assets.

Apart from the tax on land and buildings, the panchayat can levy fees on registration of vehicles other than motor vehicles, fees on hoardings and pilgrim fees on persons attending *jatras* and festivals where arrangements are made for water supply and sanitation. It can also levy taxes on the commodities sold in the market including cattle. It gets grants from the government.

The panchayat has to hold Ward-level meetings to get approval for its budget, projects to be executed in the Ward and the beneficiaries for individual beneficiary-oriented development schemes. In order to make the panchayat election process fair and transparent, the government of Karnataka made it mandatory for all candidates contesting the election to declare their assets and abide by the conditions imposed by the State Election Commission on expenditure. The PRIs have been brought under the purview of the Lokayukta.

Panchayats in the Study Area

There are four GPs in the study area. A short account of the functioning of CBOs in these areas is given below:

Annur GP

This GP covers 12 villages with a total population of 6,000. MYRADA Plan succeeded in forming 42 SAGs and 3 federations in this area. The GP has 6 lower primary schools, 5 higher primary schools, 1 high school and 9 Anganwadi centres.

Bidarhalli GP

The total population of this GP is 8,385 including 1,714 BPL families. There are 5 primary schools, 4 higher primary schools,

1 high school and 7 Anganwadi Centres. Most of the people are self-employed, engaged either in agriculture or small business. 49 SAGs have been formed within the area of this GP. There exists a cordial relationship between the GP and the SAGs. Out of the 20 GP members, 8 are women and 6 of them are members of the SAGs.

Hebbal Kuppe GP

Hebbal Kuppe GP comprises 4 villages. There are 3 lower primary schools, 2 higher primary schools and 1 high school in this GP. There are 4 Anganwadi Centres and one private high school. Total population of the GP is 6,187. Out of 17 elected members of the GP, 7 are females of which 3 belong to SAGs. The GP undertakes activities related to health and hygiene and implements various poverty alleviation programmes. There is close interaction among members of GP and the CBOs.

B. Matager GP

This is a comparatively big panchayat comprising 22 villages with a population of nearly 10,000. There are 22 elected members, including 8 women members. Of these 5 are from SAGs. There are 15 primary schools, 1 high school and 10 Anganwadi centres in this GP.

MYRADA Plan makes systematic efforts to motivate the CBO members and through them other villagers to attend the Gram Sabha meetings and to take active part in the deliberations of such meetings. It also organizes capacity building programmes for the elected members of GPs. At the same time, the CBOs are made aware of the role of the GP in local development. As a result, the understanding between the GP and the CBOs has increased.

Andhra Pradesh

Gram Panchayats undertake various developmental works in the villages. Obligatory functions of the GP include health, education, construction of roads and buildings, village sanitation, immunization programmes etc. To undertake these activities a GP receives funds from the government as well as under schemes like JRY, SGRY, etc. The GPs collect taxes, tolls and fee. They also receive a part of certain assigned taxes collected by the State. Income from own sources forms only a very small portion of the total revenue of a GP. The resources available with the panchayat are highly inadequate to carry out developmental activities on any significant scale. The GPs are, however, involved in the execution of various government programmes, such as, Sarva Shiksha Abhiyan and programmes relating to public health and social welfare. Attendance in Gram Sabha meetings is not very encouraging.

In the study areas, there are CBOs such as Antyodaya Gram Sabha, Antyodaya Women's Mutual Cooperative Credit Society, Antyodaya Bal Sangham, Rayat Mitra Sangham, Youth Clubs, the School Health Committee and the Village Education Committee. GPs do not seem to be aware of the need to involve CBOs or the ASM in their programmes.

Panchayats in the Study Area

Balemla GP

Two GPs—Balemla and Imampet—were selected from the study area. Balemla is spread over 12 sq. km covering four villages and two hamlets. There are 12 wards and the total population is 2,373 with 21 per cent SC and 28 per cent ST population. There are about 575 BPL persons. There is no hospital in this GP. It faces the problem of potable water. Five villages have all-weather roads and many houses still remain to be electrified. The main occupation of the village is agriculture. The GP has 12 members of which 4 are women. The Gram Sabha meets thrice a year. Several CBOs/SHGs have been formed at ASM's initiative. They have a cordial relationship with the GP and government departments and their members take an active part in Gram Sabha meetings. The GP is expected to provide various civic services, such as construction and maintenance of roads, street lights, water supply, sanitation, etc. It is also involved in executing some social welfare schemes of the government such as financial assistance to disadvantaged groups, old age pension, Annapurna and Antyodaya schemes, etc.

Imampet GP

This GP covers 10 sq. km and has one village and three hamlets with a population of 1,964 out of which SCs constitute 31 per cent and STs, 17 per cent. There is one primary school but no high school. The main economic activities of the people are agriculture and sheep-rearing. Houses are yet to be electrified. Only 85 households have toilets and only one-fourth of the total population has access to drinking water. The GP provides potable water, organizes health programmes, looks after village sanitation and provides financial assistance to the disabled and disadvantaged groups and old age pension. It is involved in the construction and maintenance of infrastructure like village roads, small irrigation projects, etc. ASM Plan supports Balwadis and the GP supervises their functioning. The major source of income for the GP is government grants. Its own resources are limited mainly to revenue from house tax, which is insignificant. The GP seems to maintain good relations with the CBOs.

Orissa

Immediately after independence, Orissa was one of the pioneering States to introduce village panchayats. It enacted a new legislation in 1964 to set up a three-tier panchayat system following the report of the Balwant Rai Mehta Committee. But, the Panchayati Raj Institutions did not receive the kind of support they needed from the State government. In 1968, the Zilla Parishads were abolished and thereafter, with irregular elections, the other two tiers began to languish. In the early 1990s, the three-tier Panchayati Raj system was revived in the State with reservation of seats for women and the weaker sections. The post Seventy-third Constitutional Amendment witnessed conformity legislation, but adequate devolution of power and authority in terms of functions, functionaries and finance still remains an area of concern. Involvement of elected representatives and the community in grassroots planning is, by and large, absent, except sporadic intervention mostly by NGOs and CBOs. The State seems to be lagging far behind many other States of the country in terms of decentralization of governance.

At the village level, the Gram Panchayat, as usual, has been given various responsibilities in respect of construction and maintenance of roads, construction of small/minor irrigation projects, providing primary health care facilities, supervising primary and non-formal education, implementation of poverty alleviation programmes, management of programmes relating to old age pension and financial assistance to the disadvantaged groups. But the institution is financially weak. It has limited fiscal powers to raise revenue from tax and non-tax sources and from the assets it owns. Own Source Revenue generated by the GPs is insufficient for taking up meaningful development works. Grants from the State and Central governments for executing poverty alleviation schemes constitute the major part of the revenue of the panchayat. Apart from finances, panchayat's effectiveness is hampered by some other factors. Firstly, little has been done to build capacity of the elected representatives. They often lack appropriate orientation, knowledge and skill to discharge their responsibilities. Secondly, in some places inter-caste rivalry and factionalism hamper their effectiveness. Thirdly, there is poor coordination between CBOs and the GP.

Digposi and Gorasia GP

The panchayats selected for the study area are Digposi and Gorasia located in the tribal areas of Keonjhar and Mayurbhanj districts, respectively. Since the population density is very low, these two panchayats comprise a number of hamlet villages. Nearly 80 per cent people of these areas live below the poverty line. Development works undertaken by the GP include construction works, such as, roads, irrigation projects, drinking water facilities and health care facilities. These are undertaken from the funds made available to them under the various poverty alleviation schemes. Their own sources of income are negligible and funds from the State and Central governments are their main sources of finance. The ward level assembly (*Palli Sabha*) and Gram Sabha have the power to identify the projects to be taken up by the GP, but these assemblies are yet to become strong and vibrant. The attendance in *Palli* and *Gram Sabha* meetings is low.

Most of the CBOs in the areas covered by the above GPs are sponsored by CYSD. With the joint intervention of CYSD and Plan, these CBOs are being motivated to take active part in the development activities of panchayats. CYSD Plan has organized several programmes to enhance the awareness level of all villagers but such efforts have not yet yielded results. Caste rivalry and factionalism in implementation of schemes together with the lack of support of the bureaucracy have resulted in a low level of performance by GPs.

Bihar

Bihar's record of Panchayati Raj is dismal, even though it was one of the few States which passed a law on village panchayats immediately after independence. The institution of GP and its judicial arm, Gram Kuchehries, started functioning in 1948 under the Bihar Panchayati Raj Act of 1947. Elections to these bodies were held regularly till the mid-1960s. Thereafter, elections to the village panchayats became irregular. A new law passed in 1961 to set up a three-tier panchayat system was not implemented properly.

Between 1964 and 2000, panchayat elections were held only twice—once in 1971 and then in 1978. Bihar is one of the few States in India, which made inordinate delay in setting up the new system of Panchayati Raj in terms of the 73rd Constitutional Amendments. First election to the new three-tier system of Panchayati Raj was held in 2001 and the second in 2006. Panchayats in Bihar, like other States, consist of Gram Panchayats at the lowest level, Panchayat Samitis at the Block level and Zilla Parishad at the district level. In Gram Panchayats, there is one elected member for every 500 voters. The most remarkable aspect of the composition of the present-day panchayats of Bihar is that reservation for women has been raised to 50 per cent in all three tiers by amending the Panchayat Act before the 2006 State assembly elections. This makes Bihar's panchayats most gender-inclusive in the country. Later, some other States emulated the example of Bihar.

During the first term of the new generation of panchayats, the State government had done little to develop them as real institutions of self-government. Insufficient devolution of functions, finances and functionaries have crippled the PRIs. No serious attempts have been made to build the capacities of the elected representatives. The present State government of Bihar has expressed its intention to empower the PRIs and build their capacities, but the new policy is yet to make any impact.

The Act provides for devolution of 31 functions to the panchayats, but this has not happened. The panchayat is involved in some agency functions of the State government concerning the selection of beneficiaries for social assistance schemes, such as widow or old age pension, Annapurna or Antyodaya schemes, some activities in the management of ICDS centres, sub-centres and primary schools. One of the important functions in which the Gram

Panchayat is involved in construction and maintenance of roads. It is surprising that the Gram Panchayats have not been involved in drinking water supply and sanitation which are of immediate importance for the villages. However, this does not prevent the panchayat from taking up work in these sectors from the schematic and the Central Finance Commission funds.

The GPs do not have adequate staff. GP's staff consists of only one person, namely the Secretary. Even he is not available on a full-time basis, as he serves more than one Gram Panchayat. Panchayats also suffer from lack of financial resources. The GP has the power to levy holding tax and profession tax and realize certain kinds of fees, user charges, etc., but these powers are not properly utilized to generate resources. Accordingly, the GPs remain largely grant-dependent. As of now the GPs are getting Block grants sanctioned in terms of the recommendations of Central Finance Commissions. They also get funds under the National Rural Employment Guarantee Scheme.

In the study area of Mahua and Mahnar blocks of Vaishali district, it was found that attendance in Gram Sabha meetings is very low, ranging from 2 to 7 per cent. There has not been any appreciable rise in this over the last three years. One good feature that was noticed was a lack of gender bias in the attendance of Gram Sabha meetings in the Gram Panchayats.

In most parts of the study area, there are SHGs while Mahila Samitis and Youth Clubs exist in some GPs. There is not much interaction between the CBOs/NGOs and the GP. Quite often, CBOs work independently without any support from the GPs. The GPs have not been given any role in developing SHGs.

An innovative project has been launched by the NGO under study (Centre DIRECT) with UNICEF support in the Mahnar Block under which village/GP level participatory planning processes have been initiated. This project shows that it is possible to bring the NGO/CBOs, the GPs and government service providers together for a common development programme thereby enhancing effectiveness of different actors involved in local governance, including the GP.

Uttar Pradesh

After enactment of the 73rd Amendment, three-tier PRIs have been established on a sound footing in Uttar Pradesh. The GP implements various poverty alleviation programmes like Indira Awas Yojana, SGRY, etc. Various works related to housing, sanitation, improvement of school buildings, village roads and small irrigation projects are taken up under these programmes. The Gram Sachiv looks after the administrative works of the GP and members are heavily dependent on him, as they have very little understanding about implementing government schemes. The GP has the power to levy house tax and various fees and tolls, but in most cases these fiscal powers are not properly used. Accordingly, their own source revenue is negligible. Schematic funds received from the Government remain the main source of revenue of panchayats.

Panchayats in the Study Area

The two panchayats chosen for case studies are Trilokpuri and Mauva Panchayats of Natwana Block.

Trilokpuri GP

This GP has a population of 2,216. A woman is the president of this GP. She had difficulty in discharging her functions independently. Her husband often acts on her behalf, especially while interacting with others. For running administration of the GP, both are dependent on the Gram Sachiv.

The GP collects a paltry sum from house taxes. The major sources of panchayat finance are schematic funds from the government. Development programmes of the GP are supposed to be discussed in Gram Sabha meetings but considering the level of awareness of the villagers and lacklustre functioning of the GP, it seems doubtful whether any lively discussion takes place in these meetings. There is little interaction between the GP and the CBOs. The fault seems to lie on both sides.

Muava GP

This Gram Panchayat has a population of 1,921. Its major activity is implementation of poverty alleviation schemes like SGRY, SGSY and IAY. The panchayat generates very little revenue from its own sources. House Tax collected by it does not exceed Rs. 1,800 a year. No non-tax revenue was collected in the last three years. For finances, the GP is dependent on the schematic funds of the government. GNK, the NGO under study, has promoted a number of CBOs, but these are still at a nascent stage and their members do not take active interest in the functioning of GP. The panchayat also takes little interest in the activities of CBOs. GNK tries to motivate CBO members to attend Gram Sabha meetings, but this has not yielded results. Women are reluctant to attend Gram Sabha meetings.

Uttarakhand

Panchayats in the Study Area

Two Gram Panchayats were studied in Uttarakhand: Basunga and Ganeshpur.

Basunga GP

Main activities of Basunga GP are implementation of poverty alleviation schemes like SGRY, IAY, etc. It generates little resources of its own. It collects Rs. 1,100 per year from house tax. Its own revenue constitutes less than 0.55 per cent of its total receipts. This means that the GP is dependent on funds received from the government.

There are several CBOs functioning in the GP, such as Mahila Mangal Dal, Nanda Kishori Sangh, Bal Panchayat, Village Education Committee, etc. The GP has played a significant role in undertaking the total sanitation programme with the help of Mahila Mangal Dal. This is a shining example of the synergy that can be created by combining the efforts of the GP and the CBO.

The GP extends education facilities through the Village Education Committee. This is yet another example of collaboration between the GP and the CBO. It has organized health camps with the help of the Health Department. The Basunga GP has succeeded in building a link road with funds from the State and Central Governments. It has utilized various schematic funds to construct roads, a panchayat building and houses for those who are below the poverty line. The interaction between the panchayats and CBOs is quite close and this has helped it bag the Nirmal Gram Puraskar. The CBOs also mobilize their members to attend Gram Sabha meetings and to take active interest in the Panchayat's development work. This is one reason why Gram Sabha meetings are well attended. Because of the involvement of the villagers in public affairs, this panchayat appears to be more transparent and accountable to the local people.

Ganeshpur GP

This is located in Bathwari Block. Total population in this GP is 900. It has adequate facilities for education, sanitation, electricity and roads. The main occupation of the inhabitants is agriculture and animal husbandry. SBMA Plan has promoted many CBOs such as Mahila Mangal Dal, Nanda Kishori Samooh, and Bal Panchayat. With funds from the State government, the GP has completed the drinking water project in its villages. It organizes health camps and immunization camps with the cooperation of the CBOs. The GP executes schemes under SGRY, IAY and SGSY. Several schemes were implemented with the funds received from the Eleventh Finance Commission Awards. As in other places, resource mobilization of the GP is very poor. It collects a paltry sum of Rs. 1,700 as house tax and has no non-tax revenue. Its finances are dependent mainly upon the government's poverty alleviation schemes. As already noted, the SBMA and Plan have succeeded in organizing the CBOs/SHGs in the villages. The GP has taken initiatives in developing close linkages with the CBOs and the government agencies. It is reported that the members of CBOs/SHGs and other villagers attend the Gram Sabha meetings and participate in the discussions on different developmental activities of the GP.

Rajasthan

In Rajasthan, one GP was studied, namely Madla GP, located in the tribal zone of Udaipur. The GP comprises a cluster of villages as population density is low. The main occupation of people in these villages is agriculture. The GP provides drinking water, supervises primary education, organizes health camps for immunization and other health programmes, registers births and deaths and implements different poverty alleviation programmes, such as, employment generation schemes, Annapurna and Antyodaya schemes etc. The schemes taken up by the GP for execution are finalized after discussion in Gram Sabha. This GP generates no resource from its own sources and the entire fund for development comes from the government. The major share of funding is borne by the various poverty alleviation schemes like SGRY or NREGS.

Seva Mandir and Plan have organized a number of CBOs and SHGs in the villages. These include the Mahila Samiti, SHGs and Joint Forest Management Committees. No linkage has been established between the CBOs/SHGs and the GP. There are factions and groups in the village and the electoral rivalry between them adversely affects the functioning of the panchayat. The Gram Sabha meetings are not held regularly and even when they take place, very few persons close to the Sarpanch and Secretary attend it. It seems that the leadership of the panchayat is dominated by the elite of the village and the participation of the marginalized groups is low.

General Observations

A common feature of the GPs, as revealed from the case studies, is that they discharge principally agency functions. Almost all of them are involved in executing various poverty alleviation schemes of the Central Government. The National Social Assistance Programme (NSAP) through which financial assistance is given to old people and pregnant women is also executed through them. In some States, they are involved in other development programmes like Sarva Shiksha Abhiyan, Total Sanitation Programme and National Rural Health Mission.

The public goods being provided by the panchayats like village roads, water supply, improvement of school buildings and small irrigation projects are generally funded from wage employment schemes like SGRY or NREGS. In recent times, funds from the Central Finance Commission Awards for local governments have been made available to the panchayats. For executing any development works, panchayats are dependent almost entirely on the schematic funds of the Central or State Government.

Generally, the GPs are given powers to raise resources from house tax, profession tax, fees, tolls and user charges. In most of the cases studied by us, it was found that these fiscal powers were not being utilized properly, as a result of which GPs have been unable to mobilize enough local resources for development. They collect a pittance from the tax and non-tax sources in most of the States. In some States, certain State government taxes (like land revenue) are shared with the local bodies. But collections from such sources remain poor and, as such, the local bodies do not benefit much from sharing of State taxes. Panchayats of Karnataka were found to be comparatively in a better position, but in other States, panchayats were very poor performers in respect of revenue generation. In Rajasthan, it was found that the GP under study was not collecting even a single rupee from its own sources.

Being entirely grant dependent, panchayats have very little financial autonomy in pursuing their own development programmes. Such a situation is not healthy for the growth of autonomous local governments. Panchayats were not created as yet another implementing agency of the State government. In effect, however, they have become so and in the process the potentiality of this institution to become responsive to local needs has remained underutilized. To realize this potentiality, the mindset that treats panchayat as nothing more than the implementing agency of the State government has to change. They should be given exclusive and autonomous functional jurisdiction in respect of providing some essential services and public goods for the local area and functional devolution has to be accompanied by appropriate fiscal and administrative devolution, so that they can do justice to the responsibilities given to them.

Even though there is a constitutional mandate that panchayats should prepare plans for economic development and social justice, there is no evidence of panchayats preparing such area based development plans for different sectors in any State. It is true that panchayats have little access to untied funds without which it is difficult to undertake a planning exercise. But even within the limitations that accompany tied funds, panchayats could take up such an exercise in order to ensure convergence of their schemes with those of the State government's local level development agencies and the local CBOs and NGOs. Such convergence of the efforts of different agencies could result in better social and economic outcomes. However, they seem to be unaware as how to proceed in this direction.

In many States, there is no coordination or interaction between the panchayat and the local CBOs/NGOs. In at least one State, it was noticed that there is mistrust between the panchayat and the

NGO/CBO. Some NGOs have taken positive steps in working closely with the panchayats. However, in the absence of a common programme in which all these institutions could participate, examples of collaboration are rare to find.

A very promising example of such collaboration in a common programme was found in Uttarakhand where the GP achieved significant success in the Total Sanitation Campaign in which the local CBO of women participated whole heartedly. Another promising example was found in the Mahnar Block in Vaishali district of Bihar. Here the local NGO provided technical support for initiating a process of village and GP level planning. Through this process, it has been possible to bring the GP, CBOs and the government service providers (school teachers, anganwadi workers, health workers or ASHA) to work together for implementing the plans prepared for every village through a participatory process. These examples show that even within limitations, the GPs have the capacity to take various innovative steps in integrating services at the local level thereby improving the quality of local governance.

Quite often the Gram Sabha is referred to in somewhat romantic terms. It is assumed that this forum of direct democracy would function ideally immediately after it is set up. In reality this does not happen. In our case studies, examples of effective Gram Sabhas were rare to find. The reasons vary from place to place. In some places, the Panchayat Presidents are reluctant to convene the Gram Sabha. In others, attendance in Gram Sabha meetings is generally very poor or local elites dominate the discussions in the meetings. Participation of women is problematic in many places.

These examples need not be seen in negative light alone. There are several reasons why Gram Sabhas are not functioning as they should. One may leave aside the administrative problem of failure to convene the Sabha regularly by the GP. These are lapses which can be corrected by taking administrative actions.

There are more serious reasons. First, it is possible that the villagers do not consider the GP an important institution that can respond effectively to their problems. People have to believe that the GP has enough power and resources to respond to their urgent needs. Here the problem lies with the kind of agenda that is placed before the Sabha for discussion. If the Sabha is called for selection of one or two beneficiaries of old age pension or Indira Awas Yojana, villagers may not be interested. If on the other hand, urgent problems of the village are discussed for finding a solution that can be quickly implemented, the villagers might be motivated to attend the Gram Sabha. Unless the GP has the autonomy to take final decisions concerning local problems, the Gram Sabha may not be considered important by villagers.

Secondly, and this is important for the NGOs working for rural development, the social life of the villages is often ridden with factionalism of various kinds. There is a need for building communities and enhancing the capacity of the communities to solve public problems collectively. In other words, there is need to expand the scope of community governance. Gram Sabha will be vibrant if the community governance system of the village is strengthened. These are the issues to which the NGOs and the CBOs have to give more attention.

In some States, the effectiveness of panchayats has been affected adversely, due to interference of the MLAs and MPs. Similarly, in some places bureaucracy shows reluctance to provide support to the panchayats. Respective State governments need to give attention to such problems, so that the relationship between PRIs, MLAs/ MPs and the State administration remains cordial and mutually supportive. This will facilitate the functioning of the panchayats.

Case studies of selected panchayats show that some of them have been functioning effectively, while some remain extremely weak. One reason for such varied performances is the capacity of panchayat representatives. This underscores the importance of capacity building of panchayat members. Special attention has to be given to those panchayat representatives who come from the disadvantaged groups, because for most of them assuming a public office is a completely new experience. This is a field in which NGOs can contribute much.

4

Institutional Integration for Better Governance

In large countries, as in India, the poor live in hundreds of thousands of villages or urban slums. To be responsive to their needs and for benefits of the pro-poor programmes to reach the deprived people become challenging tasks in governance. The extent to which this challenge can be met depends upon how good the system of local governance is in terms of responsiveness and accountability to and participation of the poor as also efficiency of the State institutions in delivering services. Seen from the perspective of the poor and the deprived, what matters most is good local governance.

The functions involved in the institutional structure of local governance may be discharged not only by the institutions of the State which include the local government institutions and the local development agencies of the State government, but also by community based groups. By discharging developmental functions, such groups shoulder a part of the governance functions themselves and, this is termed as community governance.

Viable community governance may strengthen the demand side of the interventions for development, because it may create awareness among the deprived people and propel their self-help efforts through their own institutions. But this has to be matched with the supply side which means that the institutions of the State should not only be efficient in providing public goods and services at the local level, but also be responsive, participative and accountable to local people. The outcome of development interventions can be positive for the deprived people if there is a match between the functions discharged by the institutions of the State (including local government institutions) and CBOs discharging various development functions for their members.

Role of the Plan Partner NGOs and CBOs in Community Governance

A brief account of the role being played by Plan's partner NGOs and CBOs in community governance for development has been provided in Chapter 2. Table 4.1 gives a synoptic view of the development objectives and issues being pursued by the NGOs and the profiles of the CBOs that are being promoted and/or nurtured by them.

Community-Driven Activities: Analytical Observations

An analysis of the functioning of the above mentioned NGOs and the CBOs reveals certain facts, which have a bearing upon good local governance.

All activities are being organized at the grassroots level. This is important because for the poor and other disadvantaged groups the development interventions can be meaningful, only if they reach this level. It is easier said than done. The experience of the Indian State indicates that to reach the grassroots with a set of development agenda for the poor is extremely challenging. The bureaucracy has repeatedly failed to accomplish this task. This underlines the importance of the need for integration of State-sponsored development interventions with community-driven initiatives.

There is a commonality between the development issues being handled by the different NGOs. The thrust is on the development of women and children—their all-round development, with a focus on their health, education and social empowerment. Since in most places, social deprivations are accompanied by economic deprivations, creation of livelihood opportunities finds priority in the development objectives of some NGOs. All such activities converge with the poverty alleviation agenda of the State and hence, there is scope for integrating these activities with those of the different State agencies.

The most significant feature of the activities of PI's partners is that the entire development programme is being executed through a variety of CBOs. A profile of these CBOs may be seen in the last column of Table 4.1. Women, children and the youth of poor households are being mobilized through these CBOs to initiate self-help efforts for their own development. The significance of this

Table 4.1: Development Objectives and Areas of Activities of the NGOs and the Profiles of CBOs

State	*NGO*	*Development Objectives*	*Activities*	*Target Groups*	*CBO Promoted*
Uttarakhand	Shri Bhuvne-swari Mahila Ashram	Development of women and children	Health and sanitation, education, livelihood opportunities	Women and children	One each for women, girls, children and farmers
Rajasthan	Seva Mandir	All-round development of villages	Development of women and children, health, education, livelihoods	All villagers with a focus on women and children	Village CBO, Gram Vikas Committee, SHGs
Uttar Pradesh	Gram Niyojan Kendra	Community development, education, health, livelihood, gender justice/ addressing issues like violence against women	Education, health, improving service delivery at the village level, advocacy for gender justice	Focus on the deprived women	VDC for the entire village, SHGs of women and Youth Clubs
Orissa	Centre for Youth and Social Development	Primary education, livelihoods, disaster management, women's empowerment, health, sanitation preventing drug abuse and advocating child rights	Micro-credit, health services, education of children and improving livelihood opportunities, child rights	Women, children and youth	SHGs and their federations, committees for children, youth, farmers and JFM

Table 4.1: *Contd.*

State	*NGO*	*Development Objectives*	*Activities*	*Target Groups*	*CBO Promoted*
Bihar	Centre DIRECT	Empowerment and development of women and adolescent girls and capacity building of Panchayati Raj institutions	Micro-credit through SHGs of women, capacity building of women and adolescent girls and PRI representatives	Women	SHGs and clusters of SHGs for women, organization of youth volunteers
Andhra Pradesh	Arthik Samta Mandal	Improving health and educational status of people, improving livelihood opportunities	Development of women and children, health education and livelihood of people	Focus on women and children	Village based organization—Organizations for women, children, youth and farmers
Karnataka/ Tamil Nadu	Mysore Resettlement and Development Agency	Build poor people's institutions for development, realize full potential of women and children	Training SAGs, empowerment of women and girls, watershed and habitat, education and health	Women and children	Self affinity groups (SAG), Federations of SAGs, Resources Centre, Children's club etc.
Delhi	Community Aid and Sponsorship Programme	Improve the quality of life of the poor communities in slum areas	Literacy, elementary education, health, thrift and credit, gender justice and delivery of services	Women and children	Groups of children, women's groups, Savings and credit groups etc.
Urban Andhra Pradesh	Action Programme for Slum Dwellers Federation	Improve the quality of life of the poor communities in slums of the city	Slum development, housing facilities, health, sanitation nutrition, childhood development, education	Entire slum community with focus on women and children	Women's groups

strategy has to be judged from different angles. The involvement of women or adolescent girls in associational activities initiates the process of awareness generation, self-confidence building and social empowerment among these disadvantaged groups. At another level, it strengthens the role of community governance and by doing so complements the efforts of the State in eliminating social and economic deprivations of common people. Lastly, the CBOs being nurtured by Plan partners are preparing ground for participation of women and the youth in public activities. This is a new phenomenon in the public life of villages, for traditionally they have remained outside the community-level decision-making process, their roles being confined within the narrow precincts of households only. Participation of women in the local level public sphere will, no doubt, add a new dimension to the nature of community governance.

The role of CBOs in improving governance for local development is now being recognized in the development policies of the State also. This is evident in the encouragement and support being given to the promotion of various kinds of CBOs under different development programmes, such as SHGs of women, parent-teacher committees for managing schools, health committees, joint forest management committees etc. Developing self-management capacity of CBOs is one of the most challenging tasks. This requires creating awareness among community members, developing leadership skills particularly of women and imparting appropriate knowledge and skill to the members of the CBOs. The interventions being made by the NGOs in this field is very significant, because no other institution is available to take up this task. By rendering service in this field in remote habitations of villages or slums, they are filling a vital institutional gap.

The present study shows that almost everywhere sustainability of CBOs in the event of withdrawal of the supporting NGO from the scene has remained a problem. CBOs are almost entirely dependent on NGOs in most of the States. Even in States where the supporting NGOs are trying to take positive steps towards sustainability of these grassroots organizations of common people, the problem does not seem to have been overcome. In this background, development of the self-management capacity of the CBOs, particularly of the numerous SHGs, becomes the most crucial task in strengthening community governance and generation of social capital. Instead of investing NGO resources on the supply side, as some NGOs tend to do to achieve quick results, it is necessary that they concentrate more intensively on generating motivation and building capacity of the CBO members, so that they can manage their own affairs.

Local Government Institutions: The Present Scenario

Traditionally, the State bureaucracy has been in charge of controlled local governance. The development functions of governance are delivered through a network of field offices and institutions of line departments such as education, health, social welfare, irrigation, agriculture etc. The Collector and his subordinate offices at the taluka, subdivision or Block levels are involved in developmental functions either directly or through different line departments. Such a structure of local governance has certain in-built deficiencies. On the one hand, it has limitations in reaching services and public goods to the grassroots. On the other hand, a bureaucratic administrative structure can function only within the parameters of its own institutional rules and, as such, finds it difficult to operate in that terrain of governance where positive outcomes of a development programme are highly dependent on community participation. Besides, a bureaucratic administration, by its very nature, is opaque, non-responsive to the local needs and, above all, not directly accountable to the people whom they are supposed to serve.

The 73rd and 74th Constitutional Amendments were an attempt to correct these anomalies and deficiencies. There were two major objectives of these amendments. Firstly, the governance system was intended to be decentralized, giving more decision-making powers and freedom to utilize resources for development at the local administrative level. Secondly, the local governance system was sought to be debureaucratized by giving powers and responsibilities to democratically elected panchayats in rural areas and municipalities in urban areas.

Article 243(d) of the Constitution, for example, defines a Panchayat as an 'institution of self-government'. Article 243G expresses the intention that while framing laws on panchayats, the State legislatures should endow these institutions 'with such power and authority as may be necessary to enable them to function as institutions of self-government'. Thus, panchayats (and municipalities) are governments at their own levels and must be allowed to function as such. This means that they should have an autonomous jurisdiction of their own. It will be a sphere of independent action and the State government is not expected to exercise any control over the LGIs in this sphere except for general guidance and support. How much autonomous jurisdiction can be carved out for panchayats (or municipalities) is a matter of judgment. But it cannot be too small to make the concept of self-governing institution at the local level meaningless. In some cases the LGIs may also act as 'agencies' of the State government, but this sphere cannot be allowed to overshadow or diminish the distinctive character of these institutions as governments at their own levels.

Unfortunately, the intentions of the Constitution have only partially been fulfilled. It is true that the amendments have brought about substantial changes on at least three fronts. First, the certainty of panchayat institutions has been ensured. Nearly all States now have a multi-tier panchayat system (three tiers in large States and two tiers in States with a population of less than 2 million). Their space in the institutional set up of local governance is guaranteed. Second, the continuity of the institutions through elections every five years is also guaranteed. Third, the weaker sections including women have entered the power structure of panchayats through reservation provisions mandated by the amendments. The emergence of these local bodies with representation from people of weaker sections is a significant event.

Despite these achievements, the grand possibility of the Constitutional Amendments replacing the bureaucratic local administration by democratic local government institutions has not materialized. Most States have shown a lack of political will to decentralize. No exclusive functional area has been carved out for panchayats by withdrawing specific activities being performed in different sectors by the State government and transferring them to these bodies. Even though the statutes permit them to take up development work in a variety of sectors, commensurate financial resources, staff and management responsibility of service providing institutions like health centres, Anganwadis or primary schools have not been transferred to them. Hence, the impressive list of various functions that every Panchayat Act provides remains ineffective. The 73rd Amendment intended an 'exclusive' functional domain backed up by resources for the panchayats, but this has not materialised.

Today the panchayats have a space in local governance, but these bodies are denied adequate functional responsibility, finances and staff. In most States, however, they are given some agency functions of the State government such as execution of employment generation schemes, selection of beneficiaries of welfare schemes, management of the scheme of mid-day meals in schools, etc. But the autonomy to devise their own development agenda and execute them is severely limited. The Constitution has given them the task to prepare development plans for their areas and implement them. But even this constitutional mandate of introducing decentralized planning has been neglected. We found no evidence of panchayat-level planning in our study areas. In the absence of exclusive functional jurisdiction for local bodies, the panchayat representatives have only a vague idea about their specific roles in local development. Since their major function has been to execute certain State government schemes, they cannot think beyond utilization of schematic funds. If the lack of functional devolution was one type of constraint, the lack of access to guaranteed flow of untied funds to the local councils is another factor that has impeded institutionalization of panchayat-level planning. But, it is necessary to point out that these constraints do not necessarily foreclose all the options available to the panchayats in providing a common framework of planned local development.

As the matter stands now, despite the existence of local governments with the mandate to prepare holistic development plans at the local levels, convergence of activities of different local actors, namely the field offices of line departments, panchayats and civil society institutions still remains a distant dream. Lack of convergence of activities of multiple actors pursuing similar development goals is a hurdle that has to be crossed in the way forward to good local governance. Such convergence would be possible only if the activities of all actors involved in local development get integrated. In the rest of this chapter, a rationale for such integration will be built up and thereafter an attempt will be made to develop a framework within which such integration can take place.

Rationale for Institutional Integration at the Local Level

Several institutions are at work for local development. Broadly they may be classified into the following groups:

- Government Service Providers run by the sectorally organized line departments of the State government (for example, schools, health centres/sub-centres, anganwadi centres etc.);
- Panchayati Raj Institutions;
- NGOs; and
- Community Based Organizations (Such as Mahila Samiti, Youth Club, SHG, Village Education Committee etc.).

All of these have a role to play in the development and welfare of common people. Their objectives are the same. They also share some of the basic principles of development, such as, focus on the poor and other socially disadvantaged groups, efficiency and responsiveness in service delivery, enhancement of local capacities etc.

Local development requires strengthening of all these institutions. But if they work in isolation from one another their effectiveness may be adversely affected on the other hand, by linking their activities within a common framework, synergy may be created to generate better outcomes from individual efforts. For, each institution has strength in certain fields, but suffers from limitations in some others. Through integration it would be possible to utilize the strengths of each institution for development and cover up limitations by the support provided by other institutions. For a clearer understanding of the point we are trying to make, it would be worthwhile to have a look at the respective strengths and weaknesses of each of the four types of institutions mentioned above. This is presented in Table 4.2.

Table 4.2 highlights the fact that all four types of institutions are relevant for local development, each has distinctive strengths that may not be found in others and again each has limitations, particularly when functioning individually and in isolation from other institutions. Integration between them may cover up such limitations and combine the strengths of different institutions to produce synergy, which may be employed to achieve better outcomes from development interventions. In Table 4.3 some illustrations are given to show how simultaneous interventions of more than one institution help produce better outcomes. Illustrations in Table 4.3 focus specifically on the development of women and children. The same framework may be extended in respect of the development interventions for other sectors.

Table 4.2: Strengths and Limitations of Local Institutions

	Local Level Service Providers Under State Government	*PRI*	*NGO*	*CBO*
Strength	Relatively more financial and human resources; Well organized delivery system; Evenly distributed coverage.	Relatively greater flexibility in taking decisions; Makes horizontal coordination possible; More responsive to local priorities and demands; More accountable to local people.	Capacity for social mobilization; More flexibility in responding to local problems; Transfers updated knowledge and skill to the community more effectively; May build community structures; promote self help efforts of the community and provide support to the community governance process.	Generates social capital; Makes marginalized groups self-reliant and thus empowered; Poverty alleviation through self-help efforts; Fills up a vital institutional gap for the poor; Strengthens local democracy by encouraging participation.

(*Contd.*)

Table 4.2: (*Contd.*)

	Local Level Service Providers Under State Government	*PRI*	*NGO*	*CBO*
Limitations	Little local discretion to respond to local needs; No popular participation in decision-making; No accountability to local people; Difficulty in coordination with other development sectors.	Suffers from the lack of adequate resources; Lack of full scale decentralization limits the capacity of the PRI to respond to local needs; Elite capture of panchayat makes the poor vulnerable; Lack of capacity makes the PRI ineffective; Without an active citizenry local government may not be efficient and responsive.	Marginal coverage; Tendency to work in isolation from the LG and other government. departments; Makes the communities dependent upon the NGO; Pumping of additional funds and materials for service; Delivery not sustainable, because flow of additional resources stops after the project period.	Problems of sustainability; Weak links with the State institutions and LG; Lack of enabling support system; Inadequate capacity for self-management; Risks of elite capture.

Table 4.3 indicates how better outcomes may result from collaborative efforts that utilize the strengths of participating institutions and at the same time insures against the risk generated from the limitations of each of such institutions. In more concrete terms, the beneficial effects of integration result from the following processes.

By facilitating more collaboration and coordination between the institutions, integrated activities ensure better outcome from different types of development interventions. For example, the case of Total Sanitation Programme of the Basunga GP in Uttarakhand where the Mahila Mangal Dal strengthened the demand by creating public awareness and the GP and the government service providers ensured service delivery. Such matching of demand and supply of the services would not have been possible if they had worked in isolation.

When CBOs/NGOs participate in a common development programme with the institutions of the State, the whole process becomes open and transparent making both the local government institutions and the government service providers more responsive and accountable. The experience of the village planning process in the Mahanar Block of Bihar is an example.

Integration can mainstream community governance and in the process may contribute towards empowerment of the marginalized groups. All this would not be possible if the institutions work in isolation from each other, as is the case in the prevailing situation.

A Framework for Integration

Integration needs a common programme in which each institution has a stake. It also needs a lead institution to run such a programme in partnership with all other institutions engaged in local development. Such a common programme may be built around the continuous process of preparation of a participatory plan of action, its implementation by different actors jointly in which one institution complements other institutions to achieve common objectives and monitoring of the implementation activities by all the actors jointly at regular interval, say every month. The local panchayat may take the lead in providing a common platform for the government service providers, NGOs, CBOs and the panchayat to function in partnership with each other to achieve the development goals through the participatory process of planning, implementation, monitoring and evaluation.

Table 4.3: Illustration of Integration of Activities of Different Institutions in Delivering Services

Subject	*Activities*	*Institutions Involved*
Health	Breast feeding, Delivery by trained midwife, Vitamin A for children, Diarrhoea management, Use of iodised salt, Growth monitoring of children, Supplementary nutrition for children, Institutional delivery, Immunization.	For providing services: Sub-centre through health workers, Anganwadi centre and PHC/BPHC. For awareness generation: CBO, NGO For monitoring, coordination and providing critical services: GP and Panchayat Samiti.
Water and Sanitation	Access to potable drinking water for each household, Sanitary toilet for each household, Personal hygiene, Waste disposal and Environmental cleanliness.	For delivery of services: Gram Panchayat/ Panchayat Samiti and Public Health Engineering (PHE) department of State government. For awareness generation, demand generation and maintenance of community assets : CBO/NGO
Child Protection	Birth registration, Preventing child marriage, Preventing exposure of children to hazardous labour.	For campaign, awareness and demand generation: CBO/NGO. For service delivery and monitoring: Gram Panchayat.
Women's Empowerment and Livelihood	Micro financial services, micro enterprise.	For formation, capacity building and nurturing of self-help groups, establishing linkage between them and financial institutions, marketing of products and similar services: NGOs. For providing support and liaison with banks and government agencies: GP and PS.

Table 4.3: (*Contd.*)

Subject	*Activities*	*Institutions Involved*
Education	Universal enrolment and preventing dropouts Ensuring attainment of minimum level of learning through various interventions, such as Monitoring teachers' attendance; Ensuring acceptable standards of teacher-child ratio; Ensuring mid-day meal etc.	For awareness generation: NGO, CBO (parent-teacher committee, managing committee of community-based schools, SHGs) and GP/Gram Sabha. For monitoring and liaison with line department: CBO (parent-teacher committee, managing committee), NGOs, GP/PS. For service delivery: Education department and/or GP/PS. Service provider: CBO or school staff. Monitoring and support: GP.

Components of the Framework of a Common Programme

Major components of the framework of a common programme may be as follows:

- Preparation of an action plan in a participatory manner for every village and then consolidation of the village plans at the GP level. This plan will consist of activities to be performed in different sectors by different types of institutions functioning within the GP area.
- Implementation of the activities assigned to each individual institution by the action plan.
- Monitoring of implementation at regular interval by the representatives of all the institutions at the GP level.

Planning Process

There shall be a plan for every village within a GP, because services have to be converged at that level. Village action plans will be consolidated at the GP level and may be treated as the plan for the GP area. The planning process will go through the following stages:

- Situation analysis of every development sector.
- Sharing of information with the concerned village communities and all development institutions.
- Problem analysis and priority ranking of problems by participatory method.
- Preparation of plans of action for individual villages and the GP which would include assignment of specific activities to each institution, namely the PRIs, government service providers in the area, NGOs and CBOs.

GP has to take the initiative in preparing the plan of action. For, as the institution of local government, a panchayat has not only the legitimacy, but also the authority to take up such a holistic planning exercise. In fact by undertaking such function, it will fulfil its constitutional mandate of preparing and implementing plans for 'economic development and social justice'.

Monitoring

- After the plan is prepared, its implementation has to be monitored at regular interval, jointly by all the institutions and representatives from the village communities.
- Such reviews should be a continuous process and should not be reduced to a few ritualistic events.
- Its purpose is to strengthen collaboration between institutions and to ensure that each is playing its assigned role. The other purpose is to solve problems being faced by one type of institution while functioning individually or to solve the interface problems. (For example, an NGO facing a problem in forming a joint forest management committee, may seek assistance of the panchayat in solving the problem. Health centre officials wanting to organize an immunization camp can seek the assistance of the NGO to organize an awareness campaign).
- CBOs and the community leaders should be involved in providing feedback on the progress made in different sectors in their respective villages.
- GP has to take the leadership role in the process.

Dividends from Institutional Integration

Developing a partnership between the panchayat, government service providers and NGOs/CBOs operating at the Gram Panchayat level is the most valuable benefit that may be derived from the kind of programme indicated above (See Figure 4.1). If successful, such a partnership may go a long way in solving the perennial problem of convergence of different development activities at the grassroots level and in the process may also ensure optimal use of resources available not only with the institutions of the State, but also with voluntary organizations and community based organizations. Since the partnership recognizes the role of each individual actor and brightens the prospect of achievement of shared goals, it would create a win-win situation for all actors involved in local governance. At the same time each actor has to organize its own activities in a planned, disciplined and transparent manner, so that it can justify its existence by making positive contribution for achieving common goals. This will provide an opportunity for capacity enhancement of all actors of local governance. Last but not the least, community involvement has a major role to play in the proposed framework of a common programme. This will provide an opportunity to the CBOs for enhancing their self-management capacity and for motivating their members to become active participants in their own development. All these taken together will improve the quality of local governance, which is so vital for the poor and other disadvantaged groups.

Figure 4.1: Institutional Integration at the Local Level

Workability of the Framework

Is this common framework for institutional integration at the local level workable? There are reasons to believe that such a model may work provided the following conditions are met.

Full support of the State government will be necessary. Without such support, it will be difficult to bring the government service providers, who continue to play a crucial role in local governance, within the framework of joint planning-implementation-monitoring/process.

The GP will have to be strengthened by providing some essential staff and untied funds, so that it can address urgent local problems. Unless the GP is able to address even minor local problems, the community will lose faith in its leadership.

Integration between the GP and the two higher tiers will have to be established, so that the problems that cannot be tackled at lower levels can be addressed by the higher level panchayats.

Intensive capacity building exercises will have to be conducted at all levels.

In the initial period, say for a period of three years, the services of competent NGOs will be necessary to institutionalize the process and build the capacity of the institutional actors.

5

Conclusion

An important characteristic of the lives of the poor and marginalized is that they are isolated, their world being limited to the local space where they live and from where they earn their livelihood. Governance is relevant to them only in so far as it has relevance in that space. Hence, interventions for poverty alleviation can be meaningful only to the extent that they can reach the local space and are responsive to local needs. Improving the quality of local governance is, therefore, a necessary condition for any pro-poor governance.

Some people define governance as the art of steering societies. Governance is not synonymous with government. There are other institutions also which are involved in governance functions, such as, exercising authority and taking decisions which have an impact upon a group of people. Villagers often come together to address some problems of their public lives involving both regulatory and welfare/developmental activities. Obviously, they address those issues which are beyond the reach of the familiar institutions of governance. Wherever such self-governed community activities are strong, severe damage caused by the failure of the government may be prevented by community-based formal or informal institutions. In doing so, they participate in governance. Three essential attributes that make such institutions function are mutual trust among the members of the community, concern for one's associates and willingness to live by the norms of the community. These are the attributes which are also referred to as social capital—a resource that is considered essential for good governance.

By generating social capital, community governance may make important contribution for producing good governance, particularly in the local space where it is most effective. In improving local governance, one cannot, therefore, deny the role of the local communities themselves and their institutions. The present study has sought to highlight this point and has argued for integration of the community-driven activities with those of the familiar institutions of government for pursuing a common development agenda.

It is the local government which, in normal circumstances, should have assumed the most important role in local governance. Being nearest to the local communities, institutions like panchayat stand between the State and the local community. From this unique position, they can play a major role in providing support to the community-led activities and in integrating such activities with those of the State. They can play this role, if the panchayats become autonomous, responsive and accountable local government. The 73rd Constitution Amendment held the promise for the emergence of such institutions of democracy. In practice, the promise was not fulfilled. This study has made a strong plea for reforming Panchayati Raj Institutions, so that they are endowed with more powers and resources.

The present study has argued for creating a situation in which, on the one hand, strong and viable institutions of people would emerge at the grassroots in the form of various kinds of CBOs to operate in that terrain of community development where the institutions of the State cannot reach, and on the other LGIs would ensure efficient delivery of local level services and promote participatory, responsive and accountable governance. What will emerge as a result is good governance at the local level, which is of crucial importance for the poor and the deprived.

This study surveys the efforts being made by Plan and its partner NGOs in different States for strengthening community governance through CBOs that are typically institutions of the poor. In most cases they are promoted by the NGOs to encourage self-help efforts of the poor for their own development. Of late, the government has also been promoting CBOs. Mostly these grassroots organizations are weak in terms of resources and capacity. They need support. Many instances of such support being provided by the NGOs have been recorded in this report. This is, no doubt, a very important service that the NGOs are rendering.

However, the nagging question of sustainability of CBOs remains. No definite evidence was available anywhere that CBOs would be able to sustain themselves after external support is withdrawn. The present study has not been able to provide any satisfactory answer to this problem. It has accordingly suggested that the energy and the resources of NGOs should be spent more on developing the self-management capacities of the CBOs rather than providing hardware support in the form of goods and other resources for local development.

Temptations to create oases of development or good practices may be natural for an NGO, but ultimately they do not make much impact upon poverty reduction as they cannot be replicated in large scale. The test of the usefulness of NGOs should rest not on the oases of development they create, but on their success in ensuring the sustainability of CBOs by developing their self-management capacities.

The other area of concern is the weak linkage between CBOs and panchayats. There is practically no realization on the part of the panchayats about the need to collaborate with CBOs and provide support to them for growth and development. Needless to say, the orientation of the panchayat leaders needs to change. NGOs also need a change in mindsets. There are some NGOs who prefer to keep a distance from the panchayats and the relationship between the CBOs supported by them and the panchayats is often marked by mistrust and aloofness.

However, all NGOs do not think in this manner. In many cases, NGOs provide various kinds of support to the Panchayati Raj system. In such cases, linkages exist between CBOs and the panchayats. Despite this, instances were rare to find where these two categories of institutions collaborated with each other to achieve a set of common development objectives. The one or two instances of such collaboration documented by the present study clearly indicate that there are many exciting areas of development in which collaboration between the CBOs and panchayats can be extremely rewarding. This is an area that deserves more attention.

This brings us to the question of institutional integration for local development. The rationale for institutional integration at the local level has been elaborated in this study. Since individual institutions have their own priorities and methodologies, they need a common framework within which they can work together to achieve certain common development goals without sacrificing their individual identities. Based on the village planning process in the

Vaishali district of Bihar, a collaborative process of planning, implementation and monitoring activities on a continuous basis at the GP level was proposed. This could be a framework that would permit all institutions working in a GP's area to collaborate without disturbing their individual programmes. We believe that such a model has immense possibilities for bringing about institutional integration at the local level.

All actors involved in local governance have to come together to set a vision for their community's future, agree upon an activity map consistent with the vision and act in collaboration with each other to realize the vision. At the micro-level of a village community, the panchayat has to provide strategic leadership in establishing this process, because this institution is recognized as local government. But it can provide such leadership only if it has autonomy in defining its own agenda and is endowed with adequate power and resources.

In other words, panchayats have to develop as institutions of self-government in the real sense of the term. Like panchayats of the present study areas, these institutions in most parts of the country remain weak. No doubt, reversal of this position is urgently called for. But even in its present form, the Panchayati Raj System can do a lot to improve local governance by integrating the activities of all actors. It is also their constitutional duty, since the Constitution envisages that PRIs should be involved in the process of preparing area plans for economic development and social justice. To enable the PRIs to play this role effectively is a task that calls for serious attention.

Summary of Lessons

The basic lessons of this study may be summarized as follows:

- Improving local governance is the most crucial task of poverty alleviation interventions.
- The Panchayati Raj Institutions should be adequately empowered in order to enable them to function as autonomous local governments, as envisaged in the Constitution.
- Familiar institutions of government are not the only ones involved in governance. NGOs and CBOs have a major role in development and poverty alleviation.

- The panchayats and the local agencies of higher levels of government must recognize the contribution of civil society institutions in local development and provide support to enable them to make meaningful contributions.
- The concern of panchayats should extend beyond the services they provide directly. They should play a role in empowering CBOs.
- NGOs and CBOs should not work in isolation. They should work on a common programme under the panchayat's leadership without sacrificing their own institutional identities.
- In the interests of the village community, all local institutions should remain transparent and accountable to the Gram Sabha.

Part - II

Case Studies

6

Introduction

Bidyut Mohanty

One of the priority areas of action research of Plan International (hereafter Plan), is to promote child centred community organizations. It works with children, their families, community organizations and also local government institutions. Plan concentrates on socio-economic issues such as health, education, habitat and livelihood involving both children and their families. One of the mottos of Plan is that if children and adults work together, a positive change can take place in society. Plan works in remote and backward areas of the country with the poor and marginalized sections of society. In 2005, the Plan-I assigned the Institute to assess the impact of Community Based Organizations (CBOs) on the service delivery at the grassroots level and its linkage with local government institutions. One of the objectives of the study was to find out whether the CBOs would be able to sustain themselves in case the parent organization withdraws from that area. The study was conducted from 2005 to 2007. This was the period when the National Rural Employment Guarantee Scheme (NREGS) was about to start. Since the role of panchayats as well as that of communities have become more important after the introduction of the NREGS, the present study has missed out a lot.

The districts in which the study was conducted included Udaipur (Rajasthan), Maharajganj (Uttar Pradesh), Uttar Kashi (Uttarakhand), Mayurbhanj and Keonjhar (Orissa), Dharmapuri (Tamil Nadu), Mysore (Karnataka), Nalgonda (Andhra Pradesh), and Vaishali (Bihar). The slum areas, which were studied, are located in New Delhi and in a small town of Ranga Reddy District in Andhra

Pradesh. We studied the practices of NGOs and CBOs supported by Plan in seven States including one slum colony of New Delhi. In Bihar and the slum settlement of Ranga Reddy District we took up other implementing agencies which are not supported by Plan in order to have a comparative perspective. As mentioned above, in all the Blocks of the studied area the percentage of SC and ST community is high.

The respective implementing agencies are Seva Mandir; Gram Niyojan Kendra (GNK), Shri Bhuvneswari Mahila Ashram (SBMA), Centre for Youth and Social Development (CYSD), MYRADA, Arthik Samata Mandal (ASM) and Centre Direct. In New Delhi, the organization which got identified was Community Aid and Sponsorship Programme (CASP). The activities of CBOs formed by the organization Action Programme for Slum Dwellers Federation (APSDF) in Ranga Reddy district, Andhra Pradesh were also studied.

Relevance of Community Governance

In simple terms, community governance refers to the social phenomenon in which the members of a community are seen to be taking some responsibility of service delivery in the local area, thereby becoming a part of the system of governance. In recent years the paradigm of people centred and people controlled development has acquired urgency. Hence, renewed efforts are needed to promote strategies for enhancing people's participation in development.

Community participation has become a necessity because neither the State machinery nor the NGO community nor even the market can deliver basic services like drinking water, medical care or sanitation in a cost effective manner and on a sustained basis to the marginalized sections of the population unless they have the support of the local people. The strength of the community in making the management of service delivery system work lies in the fact that it has a direct stake in such services. The basic conditions for the success of community-managed delivery system are mutual trust and sharing of common goals of village welfare among the members of the community-based groups that generate resources in the form of social capital. Keeping that in mind, the NGOs as well as the State machinery try to form community-based groups, such as, Self Help Groups (SHGs), children's groups or *Kishori* groups. In a single caste or community village they work well. But in multi-caste villages, NGOs try to overcome the bottlenecks of caste and class by forming federations of SHGs and children's groups. CBOs are performing very well in many places in ensuring provisioning of drinking water facilities, preparing mid-day meals, providing health care facilities under the supervision of NGO community and with support of donor agencies and are heavily dependent on the NGOs or the donors for their survival.

Recent times have seen the emergence of PRIs. These institutions have in varying degrees been equipped with necessary functions, funds and functionaries. Various welfare schemes to cater to the basic needs of the villagers are being routed through these institutions. But in many places they are unable to deliver the goods because of inadequate devolution of functions and resources. So even though these grassroots institutions have been created to provide services at the door steps of villagers, the services do not get delivered. Hence the ideal situation may be created through mutual cooperation between the two sets of institutions, namely, NGOs and CBOs on the one hand and local government institutions as well as line department executives on the other. If both CBOs and local governments can work together, it would be possible to ensure both efficiency and accountability in the delivery of services. On the same stroke, the sustainability of the CBOs also may be ensured.

Some Highlights of the Study

It may be pointed out that all implementing agencies have a long association with the people of the study area. Plan partners have worked with children, women's groups, *kishori* groups, youth and farmers' groups out of which only children and youth groups, women groups and to some extent *kishori* groups have been performing relatively well, while farmers' groups have miserably failed almost everywhere. In contrast, the non-Plan partners are working with women and children but have not tried to form children's groups, though they work with mothers' or women's groups.

Children's and Women's Groups and their Activities

The implementing agencies have given impressive names to the various CBOs. For example, in Udaipur the villagers' committee is known as Gram Vikas Committee, in Uttarakhand the women's groups are known as Mahila Mangal, whereas, MYRADA in Karnataka has termed the village-based CBO as the Village Monitoring Committee. The names of children's groups are even more interesting. For instance SBMA has named them Bal Panchayat but GNK calls them Babu Bahini. In Andhra Pradesh, they are known as Antyodaya Bal Sangam. In all these cases, however, the children's groups are doing extremely well and are very visible in the public arena. Some of the activities of children's groups are described below.

In New Delhi, for example, the youth group sponsored by CASP has registered itself with the purpose of accessing funds from other agencies under the name of Jan Jagriti Samiti and spearheads the social and economic movement among the snake charmers of the slum colony. Now the group gets funds from the Municipality to look after sanitation issues. They organize meetings of colony dwellers, propagate messages regarding sanitation and appeal to the residents of the colony to keep small baskets to store garbage for the Safai Karmacharis of the Municipality. They have also started registration of births and deaths. Similarly *kishori* groups in Orissa and Uttarakhand, discuss health related issues. In many places the children's groups bring out monthly journals to discuss the problems of children like dropouts from school, domestic violence against children, health related issues etc. They write, edit and distribute the journal. In Uttar Pradesh, Babu Bahini has done commendable work and got a pat on the back from the Government of India. They have created a strong public opinion to resist the age-old practice of trafficking of adolescent girls. One of the children's groups in Uttar Kashi on the other hand has helped protect the crop from stray cattle and have been able to set up a library with the help of the Pradhan of their panchayat. They have also raised their voice to get their demands heard. They helped the women's groups and the panchayat in effectively implementing the sanitation programme. The children even tried to shame those who defecated in the open field and thus forced the villagers to use toilets.

Women's groups have not lagged behind either. In Uttarakhand the women's groups could achieve the Nirmal Gram Puraskar with the help of children's group, SBMA and the local Gram Panchayat. In Orissa on the other hand, one of the women's SHG federation has not only started a programme on health insurance whereby poor villagers have access to health care at minimal cost, they also stand collateral for the youth group to take contract from the panchayat. Antyodaya Women Mutually Aided Cooperative Thrift Societies in Nalgonda are very active and along with Antyodaya Gram Sabham they have worked to ensure transparency and accountability of Gram Panchayats and increase attendance in Gram Sabha. They also take up other issues like sanitation, birth registration, immunization etc. Rajasthan has combined both women's and men's groups to form Gram Vikas Committees which look after development issues like health, sanitation etc. In the south, MYRADA has adopted a unique strategy to involve the women's groups, namely the formation of community resource centres which provide support to different SAGs for enabling them to function on a sustained basis. These SAGs help in disseminating information regarding the delivery of health care services as well as in reducing school dropouts.

In Bihar the SHGs have become partners in the village planning process along with government functionaries, Mukhiyas of Gram Panchayats, representatives from Centre DIRECT and UNICEF personnel. They are part of the process of identifying and prioritising the requirements of villagers and trying to deliver those services.

Linkage with Local Government

The most important point to note is that even though the new set of panchayats and municipalities have come into being, the traditional panchayats were still found to be very powerful both in Tamil Nadu and in Sapera Basti colony of New Delhi. In Tamil Nadu, for example, it was noticed that the traditional caste panchayats decide what kind of development issues should be taken up pushing the elected panchayats to the back seat. In a way it is a good sign if the traditional panchayats also take a positive role in the development issues. Similarly in the Sapera Basti slum colony, migrants from Rajasthan are still guided by caste considerations in resolving social issues. But fortunately the younger generation is trying to defy caste rules in so far as economic and political issues are concerned particularly in Delhi. However, a note of caution has to be mentioned since the stronghold of caste panchayats has a negative message for the marginalized sections of society including women and girl children.

Both in Plan and non-Plan areas, NGOs/CBOs are not structurally linked with the local government. Only in certain cases have efforts been made by NGOs/CBOs to get associated with the panchayat's development work. While NGOs like Seva Mandir have a complete aversion towards panchayats, some others like MYRADA, ASM and CYSD are trying to help panchayat representatives through capacity building and handholding support. But barring a couple of instances like New Delhi, tribal Sarpanch in Keonjhar, Orissa and Bal Panchayat and universal sanitation through SHGs in Uttar Kashi, there are hardly any instances of mutual inter-dependence between these two sets of institutions. On the other hand in many cases there seem to be a mutual suspicion between the two.

Sustainability of CBOs and Concluding Remarks

The question of sustainability of CBOs as well as service delivery through them to the marginalized groups of the society is linked with such issues as financial stability and capacities of the groups to manage their own affairs. Almost all implementing agencies have tried to provide solution to both the problems by forming federations and diversifying the activities like introduction of micro insurance health scheme or encouraging the CBOs to strengthen their own organizations and to access funds directly from the donors or the government, including the local government institutions. Convergence of State level service providers, NGO, CBOs, panchayat members and the donor agency is a novel idea.

As mentioned in Part I of this report, the study has drawn attention to two problem areas. One is the sustainability of the NGOs and the CBOs supported by them. More attention needs be paid to this issue. The other issue is that of integration of the activities of different local level institutions for creating synergy in service delivery. The State reports clearly show the need for creating a synergy between different actors of the local governance, namely NGOs, CBOs, panchayats/municipalities and the State level service providers in order to reach out to the excluded groups on a sustainable manner. Integration of the activities of different institutions would definitely make local governance more transparent, responsive, participatory and accountable. A framework for institutional integration at the local level has been suggested in Chapter 4 of Part I of this report.

7

Andhra Pradesh

Pramod Kumar Ray and *P.K. Das*

Introduction

Over the past three decades, Arthik Samata Mandal (ASM) has been working in the economically backward areas of Nalgonda district in Andhra Pradesh. From sustainable livelihoods, health and education to issues concerning the rights of women and children—ASM's developmental activities cover a wide range of issues. These are carried out in collaboration with Panchayati Raj Institutions (PRIs) and Community Based Organizations (CBOs). Some of the activities of ASM have been sponsored by Plan International. The thrust of these activities is on strengthening PRIs through participation of the community. Activities of ASM also aim at building social capital in the form of CBOs, which in turn strengthen local self-governance. Antyodaya Gram Sangam, Antyodaya Mahila Paraspara Sahayak Sangam, Bal Panchayat (Children's Club) and Rayatmitra Sangam are some such CBOs. With the help of experts ASM has also been imparting in-house training to the Panchayati Raj Functionaries (PRFs) at its Project Unit Office at Suryapet in Nalgonda district.

Objectives of the Study

The objective of the present study is to examine the processes, functions and outcomes of CBOs working with PRIs in the Suryapet Mandal of Nalgonda district and those working with Urban Local Bodies (ULBs) in the Kapra Municipality in Hyderabad.

SECTION I: RURAL

Methodology

Selection of Gram Panchayats and CBOs

The activities of Arthik Samata Mandal are spread over 4 Mandals of Nalgonda district—Suryapet, Chivmela, Atmakur and Mothey. Two Gram Panchayats, Balemla and Imampet in the Suryapet Mandal were selected for the purpose of the study. The CBOs selected were Antyodaya Gram Sangham, women's Self Help Groups (SHGs), Bal Panchayats, Rayatmitra Sangham (farmers' group) and youth clubs.

Data Collection

Interviews and focus group discussions (FGDs) with Panchayat representatives, villagers and representatives of NGOs and CBOs are the source for all primary data, while secondary data has been collected from the ASM project office and offices of PRIs.

Arthik Samata Mandal

Formed in 1977 Arthik Samata Mandal (ASM) was initially engaged in relief and rehabilitation work in the Nalgonda District of Andhra Pradesh. It has since evolved into an integrated developmental agency working amongst the economically backward communities. Although most of its programmes are women and child oriented, it is engaged in a wide range of development activities that include rehabilitation of the physically handicapped, formal and informal education, vocational training as well as agriculture, animal husbandry, fisheries, social forestry and environmental education. Empowering communities in order to enable them to pursue sustainable livelihoods is one of the goals of the organization.

To enable the community to play a participatory role in their own development, ASM has created opportunities for the local people to take part in the process of preparing their own development plans. Such participatory planning is done through various organizations such as:

- Antyodaya Gram Sabham (AGS);
- Antyodaya Women's Mutually Aided Cooperative Thrift Society (AWMACTS);
- Children Clubs (Bal Panchayat, Antyodaya Bal Sangham);
- Rayat Mitra Sangham (Farmer's Group);
- Youth Clubs;
- School Health Committees;
- Village Education Committees; and
- Village Health Committees.

Antyodaya Gram Sabham (AGS)

Members of AGS meet every month to discuss issues pertaining to their livelihood, health, education, sanitation, human rights, women's empowerment as well as the various government schemes and programmes for rural development. These meetings are well attended and there is a substantial presence of women. AGS has members among all castes and communities. There is an annual membership fee of Rs. 25. The members elect a President and other office bearers. Along with account books, vouchers and correspondence, records of all proceedings are maintained by AGS.

Although it works in close coordination with Arthik Samata Mandal, AGS is a self-governing agency. Interaction with AGS members revealed that they were keen to participate in the decision making processes and were eager to know about their rights and duties.

AGS is actively trying to make the local bodies responsible and transparent. It does so by social audit and mobilizing its members to attend Gram Sabha meetings. An information board provided by ASM at the villages is regularly updated. Information is collected on developmental schemes and projects from panchayat, mandal and other government functionaries.

Since Suryapet is a drought prone area, crop failure is almost a regular phenomenon. To meet exigencies the CBO helps its members by extending loan facilities up to Rs. 5,000 without charging any interest. It also facilitates obtaining government loans and benefits. Besides financial assistance, training programmes are organized for farmers in dire situations.

AGS works towards "Gram Swaraj" (Village Self-Rule). Assisted by ASM it promotes community participation in activities aimed at improving the quality of life in the villages. Some of these activities are:

- Cleaning of village drains to improve sanitation and cutting roadside bushes;
- Undertaking repair of the approach road to the village;
- Production of vermicompost for increasing the yield of crops and preparation of inorganic pesticides for crop protection in an environment friendly way. AGS also provides necessary technical know-how to farmers in these matters;
- Working with NGOs and government agencies in providing irrigation as well as drinking water facilities to the villagers;
- Participation in resolving village conflicts;
- Intervention in matters relating to gender justice; and
- Working towards making the local bodies responsible and transparent through social audit.

Antyodaya Women's Mutually Aided Cooperative Thrift Society (AWMACTS)

In order to economically empower women in the Nalgonda region, ASM has formed the AWMACTS in its project area. In 1997 ASM-Plan initiated the women's savings and credit society. Besides, it has formed women's Self Help Groups (SHGs) at the village level.

The SHGs meet every month to discuss their savings status and disburse loans to members. Each member holds a passbook and deposits Rs. 21 per month. Loans are given to members for buying cattle, to run small enterprises and meet expenditure on health. The group can sanction loans up to Rs. 5,000 and for bigger loans a member has to approach the federation unit at the Programme Unit Office. Members are charged an interest of 1.5 per cent per month.

These SHGs are engaged in:

- Income generating activities like making home based products such as pickles and spice mixtures;
- Providing financial assistance to poor and sick people;
- Information, Education and Communication (IEC) campaign on first aid methods, personal hygiene and sanitation;

- Immunization campaigns and birth registration in the villages;
- Campaigning against atrocities on women, child marriage and creating awareness on women's rights, encouraging women's participation at Gram Sabha meetings and motivating them to raise issues affecting them;
- Campaigning against child labour and encouraging child education; and
- Campaigning against sale of liquor.

Antyodaya Bal Sangham

The Children's Club comprises children in the age group of 6 to 13 years and includes all children of the village irrespective of their caste, community and economic status. The Club has various committees to look into matters such as health, education, environment, savings and communication. The committees have a leader each and the Club on the whole has a leader and a co-leader. They are responsible for maintaining records of the Club's activities.

Whether it is through posters and rallies to campaign for "badi bata"—a State Government programme to bring children back to school or creating awareness on safe drinking water or sanitation drive, the children of the villages have taken the lead in many a campaign in the villages of Suryapet. The coordinating NGO, ASM, provides the club members with booklets, posters and pamphlets for the campaigns.

Rayat Mitra Sangham (Farmers' Group)

The stated objective of the CBO is to train farmers in preparation of vermicompost and inorganic pesticides besides imparting knowledge in advanced methods of cultivation. However, interviews of those involved in the programme revealed that this transference of skill has not resulted in the desired output.

Antyodaya Youth Club

These Youth Clubs have played an important role in mobilizing the community to demand a transparent administration. In some areas, these clubs have exposed irregularities in implementation of government schemes by the Panchayats.

The Youth Club at Imampet Panchayat, for instance, in order to ensure transparency at Panchayat levels, conducted a social audit of the panchayat. They destroyed the poor quality rice distributed by the panchayat and brought this incident to the notice of the Mandal Office at Suryapet. Another Youth Club "Jago Banjarh" in Das village of Balemla GP kept a close watch on the functioning of the primary school in their village, especially the implementation of the Mid-Day Meal Scheme. Irregularities were brought to the notice of Mandal authorities. The headmaster's weeklong absence from the school was reported to the Mandal Education Officer.

Status of Gram Panchayats

Balemla Gram Panchayat: A Profile

Spread over an area of 12 sq. km. the Balemla Gram Panchayat consists of four villages—Balemla, Aregudem, Das, Rekya and two settlements—Kotta Thanda and Boota Thanda. The Panchayat is divided into 12 wards. Balemla panchayat has a population of 2,373 of which 1,159 are females. There are 230 children in the age group of 0-5 years and 533 between 5 and 14. The Scheduled Castes constitute 21 per cent of the population while 28 per cent of the people belong to the Scheduled Tribes. The Other Backward Classes form 51 per cent of the population.

Balemla has a literacy rate of 56.08 per cent. At 44 per cent, female literacy is significantly lower than male literacy, which is 67 per cent. There are five primary schools in the area. As many as 575 people live below the poverty line. Only 48 per cent of the households have sanitary toilet facilities. There is neither a Primary Health Centre (PHC) nor any charitable dispensary. There is, however, a medical sub-centre and a veterinary centre in the Balemla Panchayat office area. Nearly all households have access to safe drinking water within a distance of half a kilometre. Less than half of the households have electricity connections. Most families in the panchayat sustain themselves on agriculture. Five of the villages are accessible through proper roads. Suryapet Mandal is linked with the National Highway.

The Sarpanch heads the Panchayat. There is an Upa Sarpanch and 10 Ward members. All members of Balemla Gram Panchayat are educated. Both the Sarpanch—Linganaik as well as the Upa Sarpanch—Uma belong to the Telugu Desam Party (TDP) and have been elected for the first time. Except the four women members, all others were elected from unreserved constituencies. The Panchayat Secretary is a government official.

Gram Panchayat Activities

The activities undertaken by the Gram Panchayat (GP) include implementing welfare schemes of the government, such as—pensions for widows, the elderly and the handicapped, providing subsidized rations under the Annapurna and the Antyodaya schemes. The list of beneficiaries of these schemes is discussed and finalised at the Gram Sabha meeting, which is held three times a year. Health and immunization campaigns and creating awareness amongst parents of the need to educate children are some other tasks taken up by the Panchayat.

The essential infrastructure in the village is also maintained by the Gram Panchayat. This is done with grants from the State Government. Balemla GP has been responsible for:

- Construction of village link roads;
- Sending proposals to the Irrigation Department for providing irrigation facilities to the villages;
- Carrying out government campaigns on health awareness and organizing immunization camps;
- The GP monitors the working of government institutions such as the Integrated Child Development Services (ICDS) Centre and the primary school and functioning of the medical sub-centre; and
- The GP is responsible for relief and rehabilitation work in case of natural calamities or other emergencies. It also takes preventive measures and establishes contacts with local MLAs or MPs for securing help.

The panchayat, however, has not undertaken the creation and maintenance of a regular market. Its role in forest management is also nil.

Financial Status

Grants received by the panchayat under various government schemes are shown in Table 7.1.

Table 7.1: Grants received by Balemla GP

Scheme	Year	Amount (Rs.)
Sampoorna Grameen	2003-04	1,60,000
Rozgar Yojana (SGRY)	2004-05	1,80,000
	2005-06	1,80,000
Central Finance Commission	2003-04	1,40,000
Grants	2004-05	1,50,000
	2005-06	1,80,000
State Finance Commission	2003-04	80,000
Fund	2004-05	80,000
	2005-06	80,000

Balemla Gram Panchayat's own financial resources are confined to house tax and some amount of shared taxes, as shown below:

Table 7.2: Own Resources of Panchayat

	Year	Amount (Rs.)
House Tax	2003-04	9,461
	2004-05	10,500
	2005-06	10,800
Shared Tax	2003-04	15,000
	2004-05	16,000
	2005-06	16,000

Expenditure on salary, honorarium, allowances and miscellaneous office expenses are met from Gram Panchayat's own resources and the grants available from the State government. Expenses on salaries, honorarium and allowances increased from Rs. 9,500 in 2003-04 to Rs. 12,500 in 2005-06. Office expenses increased from Rs. 20,000 to Rs. 24,000 in the same period.

Interface with CBOs

The annual development plan of the villages in the panchayat is drawn up after consultation with the villagers in the Gram Sabha meetings. The CBOs contribute towards finalising the list of beneficiaries under the various welfare schemes. All CBO members participate in the Gram Sabha meetings and make their recommendations. These recommendations are taken into account by the Panchayat and verified before a final list is drawn up.

Imampet Gram Panchayat: A Profile

Imampet Panchayat has the distinction of being declared the best Gram Panchayat in Suryapet Mandal. Smaller than Balemla, the Imampet Panchayat consists of one village—Imampet and three settlements—Jatoth Thanda, Roopla Thanda and Bung Thanda. Spread over an area of 10 sq. km. it has 465 households with a population of 1,964. Of these, 987 are males and 977 are females. There are 167 children in the age group of 0-5 years while 442 are between 5 and 14 years. Scheduled Castes form 31 per cent of the population whereas Scheduled Tribes constitute 17 per cent.

The panchayat has only one primary school and medical facilities are almost non-existent. There are no medical sub-centre, PHC or any other charitable dispensaries in the panchayat area. All houses have access to safe drinking water within a distance of half a kilometre. However, only 85 out of 465 households have sanitary toilet facilities. Of the total households, 188 have electricity connections. Agriculture and sheep rearing are the main occupations in Imampet.

The panchayat has a Sarpanch, Upa Sarpanch and 10 other members. The Sarpanch, a member of TDP, Boina Anjaiah, is in his mid-thirties and is a matriculate. The Upa Sarpanch, Marapaka Istarama, a CPI (M) activist, has had no formal education. She is about 28 years of age. The panchayat has four women members.

The Gram Sabha meetings take place thrice a year. CBOs such as the Antyodaya Gram Sabham, Antyodaya Women Mutual Cooperative Credit Society, Antyodaya Bal Sangham, Youth Club, School Health Committee and Village Education Committee of the Aarthik Samata Mandal are active in the panchayat area.

Imampet Panchayat has been involved in the following activities:

- Interaction with State officials for undertaking construction of infrastructure such as roads and irrigation facilities;
- Ensuring regular supply of drinking water with the help of rural water supply authorities;
- Carrying out health awareness programmes on a regular basis;

- Helping in the construction of sanitary latrines and providing households with bleaching powder and phenyl for keeping toilets clean;
- Monitoring the functioning of the ICDS Centre or the balwadis and the primary school and propagating the government's Sarva Siksha Abhiyan. The balwadi and the primary school at Imampet were constructed with the initiative and under the supervision of the panchayat;
- Organising immunization camps;
- Implementing welfare schemes and programmes of the State and Central Government. Pensions to widows, the disabled and the elderly are distributed at the Panchayat Office by staff deputed by the Mandal Office. The beneficiaries are decided at the Gram Sabha meetings; and
- The beneficiaries of the Annapurna and Antyodaya schemes are given 10 kg of rice free and another 35 kg of rice at Rs. 3 per kilo.

The panchayat lacks a market infrastructure and so far no initiative has been taken on this account. The area is drought prone and although there is no disaster management system in place, relief work is undertaken in case of famines.

Financial Status

Grants received by the Imampet Gram Panchayat under various State and Central Government schemes are listed below:

Table 7.3: Sources of Revenue of the Gram Panchayat

Scheme	*Year*	*Amount (Rs.)*
Jawahar Rozgar Yojana	2003-04	2,00,000
	2004-05	1,75,000
	2005-06	1,70,000
Sampoorna Grameen Rozgar Yojana	2003-04	1,50,000
	2004-05	1,50,000
	2005-06	70,000
Central Finance Commissions	2003-04	52,000
	2004-05	67,000
	2005-06	90,000

But data on how much has been spent under what head is lacking. The National Rural Employment Guarantee Scheme in 2005-06 has already been started in this panchayat. It was encouraging to note that the Gram Panchayat provided employment to 472 families for 100 days at the rate of Rs.120 per day.

Table 7.4: Other Sources of Income

	Year	*Amount (Rs.)*
House Tax	2003-04	2,000
	2004-05	3,000
	2005-06	4,150
Shared Tax	2003-04	7,050
	2004-05	9,175
	2005-06	11,000

As Table 7.4 shows the amount collected from own source is very insufficient and are spent on maintenance of infrastructure. Separate funds are also available for construction of link roads, maintenance of village roads, construction of water tanks and providing irrigation facilities.

Interface with CBOs

Decisions are taken by the Gram Panchayat in consultation with the community at the Gram Sabha meetings. The meetings are open to all villagers and CBOs are expected to play a role. The CBO leaders and members take part in the finalization of the list of beneficiaries by the Gram Sabha.

After the projects are finalized, the beneficiaries and CBOs are involved in implementation of schemes. The elected representatives of the panchayat informed that only those with genuine needs get selected as beneficiaries. They also informed that the labourers of the village are given preference in construction work under Sampoorna Grameen Rozgar Yojana (SGRY).

The panchayat works in close coordination with CBOs when they undertake sanitation drives or organise health awareness programmes. It is because of such collaboration that Imampet was adjudged the best GP in Suryapet.

Sustainability of CBOs

Although the CBOs met regularly and actively participated in many development programmes, it was observed during field visits that they were far too dependent on the supporting NGO for guidance and intervention. The intervention of ASM was most sought after for obtaining government benefits. Internal feuds and rivalries within and between the CBOs prevented them from becoming cohesive organisations. Most CBOs lacked adequate funds. Members are often reluctant to pay the requisite fee. Nevertheless, the CBOs have become an integral part of the villages and are recognised by the community as such. At the same time it has to be admitted that most CBOs with the exception of Rayat Mitra Sangham, have the potential to carry forward their work with some support.

Interaction with Panchayats

Although the CBOs seek to make local bodies more accountable, the process is dogged by acute ignorance of rules and regulations which govern the Panchayats. The Panchayats, on the other hand, allege that even though they welcome interventions, advice and support of CBOs in implementing programmes for the community, they are kept out of decisions that involve utilizing grants received from the government.

According to Panchayat members, prior information is given to the villagers on all Gram Sabha meetings held by the Panchayat. This is done at least 15 days in advance of the scheduled meeting. As per rules, the meetings are to be presided by the Sarpanch and a government official representing the Mandal has to be present.

The CBOs have, however, a different story to tell. According to them, the meetings are often not held as scheduled or informed. There have been instances when the Gram Sabha meetings have proceeded without the requisite quorum, i.e. one-fifth of the total number of voters. This happened in Balemla Panchayat in 2005 and 2006. Mandal officers are similarly indifferent to these meetings. This further discourages the panchayats and the villagers. It was found that Gram Sabha meetings were mostly attended by those who had a personal interest at stake. The members of the Youth Club maintain that the meetings are never scheduled at a convenient time. Panchayat members were reportedly unhappy with the members of the Youth Club as the latter tend to raise uncomfortable questions.

The Panchayati Raj Act provides for the formation of sub-committees for effective and smooth functioning of rural administration. But in the areas where this study has been carried out, no such committee was found to be functioning.

Most Mandal and Village level officials cited financial crunch and staff shortage as the reason behind the ills. Says Mandal Development Officer, Suryapet, "The Mandals are not adequately staffed. Earlier, all the departments were under one unified Mandal but now they are separated which makes it more difficult to coordinate and integrate their activities." However, she admitted that local bodies would be more accountable and their functioning more transparent if the village communities took an interest and at least attended the Gram Sabha meetings in strength.

The CBOs have to be better informed and aware to be able to point out what is wrong with the system. They have to put in a greater effort in the task of motivating villagers to attend Gram Sabha meetings.

Change for the Better

Admittedly, the situation is not as bleak as it was earlier when CBO members felt intimidated by the Panchayat members and officials. With encouragement and interaction of the supporting NGO, the members have, over the years, gathered courage to speak up for the community to which they belong.

Community Governance: Best Practices

Two CBOs were found to be making useful contribution towards strengthening community governance and accelerating the pace of development. These cases are described below:

Antyodaya Bal Sangham, Balemla Gram Panchayat

Recognizing the potential of children as instruments of change, ASM has tried to involve them in their activities through Antyodaya Bal Sanghams. There are 70 such Sanghams in the area where ASM is active.

In order to strengthen these groups, ASM representatives hold monthly meetings with the members wherein they are informed on the rights of children, the importance of education and proper nutrition, the environment around them and how they could effect a change. Through training and motivation, children have been able to voice their demands and have been able to persuade authorities to recognize their rights to better services.

Till recently, one of the village primary schools at Balemla, functioned from tin sheds and had no toilets. The sheds were very uncomfortable during summers. But lack of toilet facilities was a greater problem. The issue was taken up by the leader of the Bal Sangham, Ramesh, with the Sangham Health Committee members, the Youth Club and ASM representatives. Later, with assistance from ASM, one common toilet and ten urinals, five each for boys and girls with provision for water were constructed.

For the construction of the school building, it was again children who took the initiative. They spoke to the village Sarpanch as well as the Mandal authorities. The Panchayat and the Mandal authorities agreed to partly fund the construction of the school building. The rest of the finance was provided by ASM-PLAN and Shanti Patient-Related Education and Direction (SPREAD), a donor NGO. The school building is seen as a major success in the village.

Besides these two major achievements, the club has been participating in campaigns on health and immunization. It is provided with posters, booklets and other campaign material by the ASM.

Antyodaya Gram Sangham (AGS), Imampet Gram Panchayat

AGS was instrumental in the setting up of a borewell in Imampet, a major step towards providing safe drinking water to the villagers. The suggestion for a borewell was initially rejected by the Panchayat on the ground that it was unaffordable. However, AGS led a campaign cautioning villagers against using water from the open wells as these were found to be polluted, mobilized support and the entire village community pressed its demand for a borewell. The panchayat then agreed to take up the matter with the Rural Water Supply Department which supplied the village with a motor pump. With additional finance from ASM and labour by AGS, the borewell dream soon became a reality.

The CBO has also undertaken the task of cleaning the irrigation canal, clearing bushes and repairing the village roads. In fact, at Imampet, the panchayat's image has been greatly enhanced by the CBO.

Conclusion

CBOs are ignorant of rules and regulations that govern PRIs and are, therefore, unable to make meaningful interventions. This problem can be resolved through adequate training. ASM can include CBO representatives in their training programmes for PRI functionaries. These can be followed by periodic orientations and assessments.

Better attendance at Gram Sabha meetings, especially of women will go a long way in enhancing community participation in governance. They need to be better informed and motivated. This can be done through better campaigning.

The CBOs should feel confident to interact and approach the Panchayat without the intervention of the NGO. So far, they are heavily dependent on the NGO.

The various sub-committees at the Panchayat level should get functional. This would provide better focus on the work that the Panchayat needs to do in the villages. The NGO can facilitate this by bringing the matter to the notice of the State Government.

Since most villagers in this area subsist on agriculture, organisations like the Rayat Mitra Sangham need to be strengthened.

Since Children's Clubs are fairly active and have taken several initiatives, it is imperative that they are encouraged. The NGO could open small libraries in villages for these children.

The Gram Panchayats as well as the CBOs could be trained to keep records more efficiently and systematically. This can also be achieved through proper training.

Women SHGs, especially those like the Antyodaya Women's Credit and Thrift Societies should increase their income generating activities.

SECTION II: URBAN

Introduction

This study is an attempt to make an assessment of the status of community governance and its impact on the people of Moulali Slum in Ward Council Number 17 of Ranga Reddy district of

Andhra Pradesh. The Action Programme for Slum Dwellers Federation (APSDF) has been working on various issues relating to women, children, health, education, sanitation and livelihood of slum dwellers in the twin cities of Hyderabad and Secunderabad and Rangareddy district of Andhra Pradesh in collaboration with Urban Local Bodies (ULBs) and Community Based Organizations (CBOs). The Municipality of Kapra of Ranga Reddy district, where this study has been conducted, constitutes the area of activities of the APSDF. Society for Promotion of Area Resource Centres (SPARC), Mumbai, has sponsored the activities of APSDF, with the main objective of improving the lives of slum dwellers. The slum dwellers are encouraged to strengthen ULBs by getting involved in the task of improving the living conditions of slums. Besides, support is given to the slum dwellers to form and nurture CBOs, so that they have their own organizations to pursue welfare programmes. APSDF has formed CBOs like Mahila Milan Groups to organize women and make them partners in achieving the objective of strengthening community governance. Though it seeks to build similar organizations for the youth and children, the focus now is on women's groups.

Methodology

Selection of the Slum

The Moulali slum (Rajeev Nagar and Navadoya Nagar basti) was selected for this study. Rajeev Nagar and Navadoya Nagar basti come under Council Number 17 in the Kapra Municipality. The Mahila Milan Groups, women SHGs of these areas were studied.

Data Collection

Both quantitative and qualitative data was collected. Qualitative data was sourced from interviews and focus group discussions (FGDs) with CBOs, elected representatives of the municipality, officials and representatives of NGOs. Quantitative data was obtained through questionnaires, printed material from APSDF and the municipality. Besides, direct field observations also constituted an integral part of data collection. Best practices of collaboration between the CBOs and ULBs in community governance were documented.

Profile of CBOs

APSDF originally started with implementing an action plan for the benefit of slum dwellers. It has Statewide programmes covering the districts of Hyderabad, Ranga Reddy, Adilabad, Karim Nagar, Guntur, Krishna, Nizamabad, etc. Since 1995, it has become more active in various slums of Hyderabad and Ranga Reddy districts. It started its activities on housing and sanitation problems, but now emphasizes on holistic development with a focus on women and child development. Integrated development activities include housing facilities for slum dwellers, health and sanitation, nutrition, childhood development, training for human potential development, formal and non-formal education etc. Apart from taking care of livelihood issues, APSDF aims at strengthening CBOs and improving local governance.

Working within the framework of community development, APSDF has made the local community a partner in the development process by enabling people to do their own investigation and analysis for preparing action plans for development and their implementation. The NGO has mobilized women's groups through Mahila Milans. It has set up the following CBOs:

- Ujeeva Mahila Milan Sangam;
- Indira Mahila Milan Sangam; and
- Mahila Milan Sangam.

Ujeeva Mahila Milan Sangam

To improve living conditions in the slums the NGO has formed Ujeeva Mahila Milan group, to work as a self-governing agency. Women of all castes and communities are members of this organization. It was started in 2004. It has 23 members who elect the first leader (President) and the second leader (Secretary). The Secretary maintains the proceedings of the meetings and other records. The group collects Rs. 3 from each member everyday and the subscription money is deposited in an account jointly run by the President and Secretary. The functionaries of APSDF also participate in the meetings. Various issues pertaining to livelihood, health, education, sanitation, human rights, women's empowerment and all other issues affecting slum life are discussed in the meetings.

The members of the Sangam appear to be confident and committed to the development of their community. They expressed their eagerness to learn about development programmes and are interested in taking part in decision making.

There is acute poverty in the area and women carry not only the burden of household work but they also have to work for income generation. APSDF has organized women to help them save and use their resources better. It provides them finance for minor economic activities. The CBO provides loans up to Rs.10,000 to its members to meet household emergencies, the rate of interest being 2 per cent per month.

The Ujeeva Mahila Milan Sangam is an economic and social movement in itself. Apart from economic activities, the group is involved in slum sanitation, health, education, environment, etc. It is also a part of the federation of AP Mahila Milan. About 1,800 women have joined the AP Mahila Milan in Andhra Pradesh and there are 90 groups with a total saving of Rs. 260 lakh.

It was found that the members of the group are not fully aware of the various government schemes for the benefit of women and children. Though they are in regular contact with the local Councillor, they rarely meet the Chairman of the municipality, nor visit the municipality office. They have not met the local MLA or other political leaders. The leaders of the CBO visit different offices at least once every month. The scope for people's participation in the affairs of municipal governance seems restricted. The representatives from this CBO are hardly ever invited to meetings of the municipality. The CBO has not yet gone for social audit of the municipality, but the members have started discussing these issues in their meetings. However, the NGO meets the municipal officials regularly.

Activities of the CBO

The CBO is active and committed to the development of slums. Besides meeting their individual and group needs, they undertake activities for the welfare of the community. Key activities are listed below:

- Provides loans to its members. It is involved in various other economic activities;

- Helps out the poor and sick people from the slums by extending financial support;
- Undertakes activities to create awareness on slum sanitation, clean environment and personal hygiene;
- Undertakes immunization campaigns in the slum with the help of the NGO and complements the government programme by creating awareness on birth registration, school enrolment etc.;
- Tries to generate awareness on the rights of women, atrocities against women, domestic violence and campaigns for strengthening women's participation in the local democratic process;
- Undertakes repair of roads and works to improve sanitation facilities;
- Campaigns for child literacy, against child labour and the sale of alcohol in the slum. Also campaigns against the known criminals of the areas and their activities; and
- Gets involved in all APSDF assisted community development programmes.

M.M. Sangam (Mahila Milan 'B')

As noted, APSDF adopted a strategy to use women as agents of social change. One of the organizations they created for women is M.M. Sangam. This Group was formed in 2005 and has 16 members. Membership is open to everybody and members elect their first leader and second leader, i.e. the President and the Secretary. At the time of this study, K. Ellama was the President and Sushila was the Secretary.

It collects Rs. 3 from each member daily and has a bank account. It provides loans to members at the rate of interest of 2 per cent per month. The maximum loan amount is Rs. 5,000. The loan recovery rate is 100 per cent. The loans cover household expenses, health and educational needs of the members.

The group meets every month and the Secretary maintains records like proceedings of the meetings, bank passbook, vouchers, etc. The Secretary has been trained by APSDF in record-keeping. The group supplies raw material for economic activities and provides support in marketing. Profits from these activities are used to meet individual and group needs and community development. The developmental activities include creating awareness on contagious diseases that affect slum dwellers, compulsory and universal primary education, road repair, sanitation and environmental awareness. APSDF assists the CBO with money and technical inputs.

Since it is a newly formed group, it does not have political linkages but its leaders have occasional contacts with politicians. They visit the municipality office and other government offices once or twice a month but are not called to the meetings of the municipality.

Activities of the CBO

- Works for the general welfare of the community with the assistance of APSDF;
- Takes care of the slum sanitation by cleaning roads, removing garbage etc.;
- Holds meetings and creates awareness on environmental cleanliness;
- Participates in government and NGO programmes on immunization and other health awareness programmes;
- Provides loans to its members, rate of interest being 2 per cent;
- Participates in resolving group conflicts in the slum;
- Takes up various awareness programmes like campaign against child abuse, atrocities against women and domestic violence; and
- Creates awareness on women's empowerment and works for promoting women's participation in the decision-making process.

Although its activities are supported and facilitated by APSDF, the group mobilizes its own resources through micro credit business and various other economic activities. After meeting its individual and group needs, it spends some amount of the surplus generated for the common cause of the slum community.

Indira Mahila Milan Sangam

This group was formed in 2004 by APSDF and has 25 members. It was set up as a change agent for sustainable development of the slum community. It functions under direct guidance and supervision of APSDF. It has a President and a Secretary and meets every month to discuss various developmental issues. Its leaders are members of AP Mahila Milan State Committee. APSDF has organized Mahila Milan Sangams in various parts of the State to mobilize women's savings. It has also organized SHGs at the basti, district and State levels.

The Indira Mahila Milan Sangam in Navodaya Nagar basti is quite active. Each member deposits Rs. 3 and the Sangam has a bank balance of Rs. 6,000. It provides loans up to Rs. 10,000 at 2 per cent interest rate per month for meeting household needs of members. A core sub-committee of seven members takes decisions on the sanction of loans at the Basti Committee level. The District or State Committees take decisions on larger loans. The group undertakes its own economic activities for which APSDF provides financial and technical help. The group is involved in matters such as health, hygiene, slum sanitation, primary education, women's rights etc. They pursue matters relating to registration of births, assist in the immunization programme, create awareness against major infectious diseases, universalization of pre-school and elementary education etc.

During the study it was felt that the group has not yet become self-sufficient in managing its activities independently. It does not directly interact with the municipality officials or local politicians. Group members are mostly preoccupied with their own needs rather than community development.

Activities of the CBO

- Provides loans to its members at a moderate rate of interest;
- Takes up income generation activities such as making Sabina powder, candles, acid, cement bricks etc.;
- Provides financial assistance to the poor and sick;
- Undertakes awareness campaign on slum sanitation, hygiene and health problems;
- Campaigns against domestic violence, atrocities against women etc. Works for women rights and women's participation in decision making process;
- Campaigns against sale of alcohol, promotes child rights and strives to drive out criminals;

Status of Urban Local Bodies

Ward Number 17 of Kapra Municipality

The bastis are spread over an area of 10 sq. km. and have a population of 25,000 of which 9,500 are males, 10,000 are females and 5,500 are children. There are 5,000 SCs, 4,000 STs, 6,000 Backward Castes, 5,000 OBCs and 5,000 others. The male literacy rate is 40 per cent and the female literacy rate is 30 per cent. There are 5 primary schools and 3 anganwadi schools. Poverty levels are high with 74 per cent of the households below the poverty line. Half of the households use sanitary toilets and have access to safe drinking water within a distance of half a kilometre. 82 per cent of the slum has electricity connections and road connectivity is good. The main economic activities are wage employment and some self-employment activities like driving auto rickshaws.

Ward is the basic administrative unit of the ULB. This study looks at Ward Number 17. There are 24 Wards in Kapra Municipality. Of the 24 Councillors, seven are women. Eight members are from the Congress, four from the Bharatiya Janata Party (BJP), 11 from the Telugu Desham Party (TDP) and one Councillor is an independent. This independent candidate is Srinibash Reddy, the Councillor of Ward Number 17, elected from a general seat. He is a first time member, has passed higher secondary and is a businessman. He maintains close contact with the CBOs and often calls them in meetings to discuss various developmental issues. The leaders of Mahila Milan groups participate in these meetings.

Major Activities performed by the Municipality

The responsibilities of ULBs with regard to slums may be divided into two categories—compulsory and optional. Under the former category come primary health, sanitation, primary education, drinking water, drainage and road. Under the latter comes various developmental projects and schemes to strengthen community life through different livelihood sustenance packages and building sustainable social and physical infrastructure. The staff consists of community organizers, community development officers and slum development officers/social workers at the local level. The Executive Officer of the municipality on the other hand, is in-charge of overall urban community development.

Various slum development programmes like Swarna Jayanti Shahari Rozgar Yojana (SJSRY), National Slum Development Programme (NSDP), Balika Samriddhi Yojana (BSY) and State government programmes on clean slum initiative, special nutrition and Voluntary Garbage Disposal Scheme (VGDS) are being implemented for the benefit of the urban poor.

Drinking water is an acute problem in the area. Under NSDP, the municipality provides drinking water and there is provision for individual water connections. The municipality also looks after drainage, sanitation and sewerage. It promotes pre-school education through Balwadi schools run by the local welfare societies and neighbourhood committees. It monitors the primary school run by the State government. Through a World Bank-assisted population project the municipality tries to meet the health needs of slum dwellers. It has established health posts and maternity centres where doctors and para-medicos work to provide health services for women and children.

The municipality implements various welfare and social security schemes, such as, Old Age Pension, Widow Pension, Adarsha Bastis, and Valmiki Ambedkar Yojana etc. The list of beneficiaries is finalized by the Councillor through a consultative process. It was observed that no initiative has been taken in the slum for adult education.

Infrastructure at the Ward Level

For the purpose of creation and maintenance of infrastructure at the ward level for the slum community, the municipality receives various grants from the State government and centrally sponsored NSDP Scheme. The Councillor prepares proposals and submits them to the municipality for various infrastructure projects, such as roads, Community Halls, Mahila Prashikshan Bhavan etc. As representative of the ward to the urban local body, the Councillor monitors the functioning of government-run institutions, such as Integrated Child Development Service (ICDS) Centre, primary school, health sub-centre etc.

Development Schemes implemented by the ULB

As mentioned above, the municipality undertakes various developmental activities at the Ward level. It gets funds from the State and Central Governments under SJSRY, Chief Minister Empowerment Yojana (CMEY), Development of Women and Child in Urban Areas (DWCUA), NSDP, Balika Samrudhi Yojana, Adarsha Basti Yojana, Integrated Low Cost Sanitation Scheme (ILCS), VGDS and Valmiki Ambedkar Yojana (VAMBAY) Scheme. Fund flow to Ward Number 17 in the last three years and the number of beneficiaries under different schemes are shown below.

The Ward Committee and the Councillor are responsible for planning the development of the Ward. According to the Councillor the planning is done in consultation with CBOs and other beneficiaries. Schemes being implemented in consultation with CBOs are NSDP, BSY, Adarsha Basti Yojana, Clean Slum Initiative Scheme and VGDS.

Status of CBOs in the Study Area

The status of CBOs, as revealed from the quantitative and qualitative data collected in the course of the study, has been described in the following section.

The CBOs hold meetings regularly. As they are in the process of learning, most of them require guidance and technical assistance in conducting meetings. The APSDF staff present in the meeting provide on-the-spot guidance whenever and wherever necessary. The group leaders have learned to maintain all the records like proceedings of the meetings, attendance register, Bank A/C, voucher etc. They are being trained by the NGO to undertake these activities.

From the FGDs it seemed that the groups maintain solidarity and work towards attainment of common objectives of improving the living conditions of people. The groups were found to be cohesive; the members and the office bearers of the CBOs care for each other. There seemed to be transparency in their functioning. If the group members can maintain this culture of interaction and togetherness, their sustainability will not be jeopardised.

The Mahila Milan groups in the bastis are active not only on women's issues; they also work towards overall development of the slum community. They get involved in activities like campaign

Table 7.5: Funds and Number of Beneficiaries Under Different Government Schemes

	2003-04		*2004-05*		*2005-06*	
	Amount in Rs.	*Beneficiaries*	*Amount in Rs.*	*Beneficiaries*	*Amount in Rs.*	*Beneficiaries*
SJSRY	100000	2	—	—	—	—
Rajiv Yuva Shakti Yojana					100000	
DWCUA	300000	1	—	—	—	—
PMRY	200000	2	200000	2	200000	2
NSDP	1000000	300	—	—	—	—
Balika Samrudhi Yojana		5 @ Rs. 500		5 @ Rs. 500		5 @ Rs. 500
Adarsha Basti Yojana	500000	10	500000	10	500000	10
VGDS		10 rickshaws		—		—
Integrated Low Cost Sanitation (ILCS)	1600000	400 families	60000	15 families	20000	5 families
Andhra Pradesh Urban Service for Poor (APUSP)			7000000			
Old Age Pension		50@Rs.100 pm		100@Rs.100 pm		120@ Rs.200 pm
Widow Pension		6@Rs.100 pm		—		20@Rs.200 pm
Handicapped Pension		10@Rs.100 pm		10@Rs.100 pm		10@ Rs.200 pm

against dowry, child marriage and atrocities against women. Their united effort in driving the *goondas* and rogues out of the bastis has received wide acknowledgement and recognition. This shows that the CBOs enjoy support of the slum community.

APSDF's support in terms of regular monitoring of the activities of the CBOs, social mobilization, facilitating exposure visits for the group members and guidance in resolving problems has contributed towards strengthening of the CBOs, which is essential for their sustainability. The capacity building training for the CBO members initiated by the NGO has also been very useful.

Interaction with the members and their leaders gives the impression that they are quite committed, concerned, confident and dedicated to their cause and are genuinely interested in bringing about change in their community. APSDF's guidance and feedback has made them confident. With the support of APSDF, the CBOs have been tackling development issues such as education, health, sanitation, infrastructure maintenance etc. A closer examination of the ground situation, however, indicates that the CBOs are in the formative stage and are still learning. They have become conscious and aware of the problems faced by slum dwellers. However, they lack confidence and are almost entirely dependent on APSDF for inputs, resources and guidance. They need at least 6 to 7 years of active support and guidance by the partner organization (APSDF) to consolidate their position and emerge as effective managers and leaders of the urban community.

Linkages between CBOs and ULBs: An Attempt towards Community Governance

The Ujeeva Mahila Milan has played a crucial role in the upliftment of the *basti* and has been instrumental in obtaining various government benefits for the people. This group has taken the initiative to keep the *basti* clean. It has worked towards minimizing the school drop-out rate and has initiated awareness programmes for the illiterate slum dwellers. It has initiated a campaign to generate awareness about infectious diseases. It has launched an AIDS awareness campaign in the *basti* and its neighbourhood. It has taken the lead in repairing roads and has secured benefits for residents for house construction under the VAMBAY scheme. The group has made a small but significant contribution towards community governance.

The other groups, Indira Mahila Milan Sangam and MM Sangam (B) were also found to be actively pursuing their developmental goals. MM Sangam (B) is new in the field and has a lot to learn, even though the group members are very committed.

An important bottleneck is finance. With almost no financial support from the ULB, the CBOs are heavily dependent on the NGO. Their own funds are extremely limited. The linkage between the CBOs and the ULB is weak. CBOs are not a part of the ULB's decision making process. They have not tried to make the local body more effective and efficient. The Councillor consults CBOs in the selection of schemes, but not in the disbursement of grants. It is difficult for slum dwellers to understand power politics and their ignorance makes them unaware of rules and regulations through which various projects and schemes are implemented by the ULB.

The 74th Constitutional Amendment Act which elaborates the functioning of ULBs, specifies the procedure for people's involvement in urban governance. In practice, regulations and provisions hardly exist and hence the vast majority of slum dwellers are left in the dark. Deviations are common in the procedure prescribed for calling Ward Council meetings. There is deliberate exclusion and ULBs under the influence of politicians decide their own issues. Attendance and participation of CBOs in the Ward Sabha is low because of various reasons and meetings are sometimes deliberately organized when people cannot participate.

Most of the rules, regulations and procedures are very complicated. The system provides little scope for transparency, accountability and pinning responsibility. For this, community participation and intervention on a larger scale is required. APSDF has just started giving training to CBOs on democratizing the urban local polity. It is making them aware of their rights to participate in each and every aspect of the functioning of the local bodies. APSDF has not, however, tried to rope in the representatives of the ULB in its programmes. It has to work harder to acculturalise the CBOs and the ULB in order to promote sound and viable community governance and build a closer relationship between the CBOs and the ULB. Community governance can be strengthened only by strengthening the relationship between the local political system and the community organizations. A close interface between the CBOs of the slum community and the ULB is yet to evolve.

Best Practices

The Ujeeva Mahila Milan Sangam has some outstanding achievements. It was promoted by APSDF to buttress its action plan for the benefit of slum dwellers and bring about changes in slums in the Rajeev Nagar Basti of Moulali Area. Moulali covers a large area on the outskirts of Secunderabad. The CBO has made some creative, meaningful and substantial contributions to the community and evolved a favourable culture for community governance. It has been chosen as the best in the slum community in the entire Ward.

It discusses issues such as livelihoods, income generation, the quality of life in slums, sanitation, health, hygiene, children's education, child and mother nutrition, violence and other atrocities against women, women's rights and government schemes for slum dwellers.

Households in the *basti* are scattered on a rocky terrain and the main road is in poor condition. When the Municipality did not take up the issue, Ujeeva Mahila Milan took the lead and got the road repaired after discussing the issue with the Councillor and APSDF. It raised money to construct 50 metres of the road at a cost of Rs. 20,000 and the *basti* residents contributed labour.

Women of the CBO have taken up issues such as STDs and AIDS and launched an awareness campaign. Education is another problem as most slum dwellers are illiterate and do not value education. This increases the drop-out rate. The CBO addressed this problem by counselling parents to send their children back to school. APSDF guided them in this process and they succeeded in getting 20 children readmitted.

Strengthening Community Governance: Some Suggestions

Community governance on the whole was found to be weak in the study area. The CBOs are quite active and vibrant in promoting community initiatives, but they are comparatively new and are yet to throw up leaders who can operate independently. APSDF has achieved a lot through its training and social mobilization programmes, but the CBOs need more time to be able to manage the programmes of community development. They also have to develop a strong link with the ULBs in their areas.

The linkage is poor because it has not been given the importance it deserves. None of the players—the ULB, APSDF or the CBO—have tried to improve links with each other. Along with training for CBO leaders, ULB functionaries also need to be trained on leadership, duties, good governance and the role of social capital in community development, social justice and community governance. Regular training sessions are necessary to achieve this.

In addition, the communities must be made aware about the structure and functioning of ULBs. Presently they do not have adequate knowledge on this. Further, women's participation in community life and the local political process has to be enhanced.

In order to make the ULB more transparent and accountable, the Ward committees must be activated and CBOs should be trained. To this effect, APSDF must also mobilize other groups like the youth, children and men, in addition to women. The CBOs and ULB must work together for development of the urban community.

There should be joint efforts to make people aware about the importance and need to participate. The livelihood issues of slum dwellers must be addressed on a priority basis. Health and hygiene in slums must be dealt with and primary education ensured jointly by the ULB and CBOs. Accountability and transparency must be ensured in the functioning of both. Development programmes and schemes must be implemented in a non-discriminative manner. Social audits should be encouraged. Gender equality is a must for balanced development. Women's rights and safety must be ensured. Illiteracy and ignorance must be removed through adult education. Issues relating to community development should be identified by the CBOs and they should demand government funding.

Conclusion

The present study examines community governance practices in a slum in the Kapra Municipality of Ranga Reddy district. It was found that the local CBOs play a significant role in community development and mobilization. APSDF has played a pioneering and pivotal role in making the CBOs effective. It promotes governance through women's groups but has not included other social groups. They have plans to include children as well as adult males and the youth in their programmes. Till now, however, the focus has been on women.

The study indicates the need to strengthen linkages between different groups. The poor do not participate in the implementation of schemes or in decision-making. CBOs have not yet acquired the competence to conduct social audits of ULB. APSDF has to play a greater role in this regard, as social audit is a must in ensuring good governance.

The ULB does not think it necessary to involve the NGO or CBOs in the execution of developmental activities. A composite training and orientation of the local community, CBOs and representatives of ULB must be taken up so that they can develop a shared understanding of the need for involvement in community development.

Strengthening the linkages among community members, CBOs and ULB, could strengthen the functioning of the ULB system in the area. Governance at the local level can be improved by enhancing their interface, minimizing their differences and bridging the gaps at various operational levels. The urban community in the study area, irrespective of various shortcomings, has evolved a culture of community governance, but the need of the hour is to strengthen it through a composite endeavour.

8

Bihar

Buddhadeb Ghosh, Madhulika Mitra and *Sucharita Dutta*

Introduction

The objectives of the present study are to document the experiences of an NGO and the CBOs sponsored and nurtured by it in the State of Bihar and to examine their relationship with the Panchayati Raj Institutions (PRIs) and government service providers.

Scope of the Study

The NGO selected for the Case Study on Bihar is Centre DIRECT located at Patna. Even though the activities of this NGO are spread over five districts of Bihar, the present study has been carried out only in Vaishali district. The Blocks selected are Mahnar and Mahua.

Data Collection

Data has been collected both from primary and secondary sources. Primary data for this study include the following:

- Survey reports and other documents available with the NGO;
- Interviews with the Executive Secretary of the NGO, project staff of study areas, BDO of Mahnar Block and Mukhiyas of two Gram Panchayats;
- Group meetings with Youth Volunteers of Mahnar Block;
- Participant-observation of two meetings of panchayat-level task force;
- Visit to villages and informal interviews with the villagers; and
- Questionnaire survey of 30 SHGs and 8 Gram Panchayats.

Socio-economic Profile of the Study Area

With a population of 8.29 crore, Bihar is the third largest State in India and second in terms of density of population (880 per sq. km.). Nearly 90 per cent of Bihar's population lives in rural areas. Both economically and socially, Bihar is one of the backward States of India. Its literacy rate is only 47 per cent, female literacy being only 34 per cent (Census of India, 2001).

As mentioned, two Blocks of Vaishali district were chosen for the present study, namely Mahnar and Mahua. There are 79 villages in these two Blocks. The demographic profile and social infrastructure of these Blocks are described below:

Table 8.1: Population Growth, 1991–2001

Block	*Population in 1991*	*Population in 2001*	*Population Growth 1991–2001 (%)*
Mahnar	38404	45439	18.34
Mahua	19135	26355	37.73

Source: Census of India, 2001.

Child Population

During the last decade, child population of the study area grew at a rate lower (15.93 per cent) than the total population. As a result, the share of child population to total population has declined from 20.08 per cent in 1991 to 18.66 per cent in 2001. In Mahua, this share was higher (19.57 per cent) than Mahnar (18.13 per cent).

Scheduled Caste Population

About 14.55 per cent of the total population of Bihar belongs to the Scheduled Caste (SC) communities. In our Study area, SCs constitute a much higher percentage than the State average. As Table 8.7 indicates, the SC population grew at a much higher rate than the total population between 1991and 2001. Though 7.66 per cent of the population of Bihar belongs to Scheduled Tribes (STs), there is no ST population in the study area.

Table 8.2: Scheduled Caste Population in the Study Area

Block	*% of SC Population to Total Population*		*Decennial Growth Rate*
	1991	*2001*	
Mahnar	18.44	19.66	26.94
Mahua	17.98	20.21	54.85

Source: Census of India 1991, 2001.

Literacy

Although literacy rate, especially female literacy rate in the study area was higher compared to the rest of the State (33 per cent), it is a matter of concern that nearly half of the total population and almost 60 per cent of women in these Blocks continue to remain illiterate.

Table 8.3: Sex-wise Literacy Rate in 1991 and 2001

Blocks	*1991*			*2001*		
	Person	*Male*	*Female*	*Person*	*Male*	*Female*
Mahnar	44.37	57.86	29.30	53.01	63.32	40.97
Mahua	42.04	59.36	23.18	55.94	69.86	40.91

Source: Census of India 1991, 2001.

Poverty Scenario

According to the BPL survey, 57 per cent of households in Mahnar and over 55 per cent of households in Mahua are below the poverty line (see Table 8.3). Despite the fact that BPL surveys are not always done properly, the figures indicate existence of high level poverty in the study area.

Table 8.4: BPL Households in the Study Area

Block	*Total No. of Households*	*No. of BPL Households*	*% of BPL Households to Total Households*
Mahnar	7193	4112	57.17
Mahua	3821	2122	55.53

Source: Centre DIRECT, Patna.

Infrastructure and Basic Amenities

Table 8.5 shows the number of primary schools in 9 Gram Panchayats of the two Blocks—6 GPs of Mahnar and 3 GPs of Mahua. There are 36 primary schools in the area. The average number of primary schools per GP and per village is 4 and 1.5 respectively.

Table 8.5: Primary Schools in the Gram Panchayats of the Study Area

Block/GP	*No. of Primary Schools*	*No. of Villages*	*Primary School Per Village*
Mahnar	26	13	2
Lawapur Mahnar	6	2	3
Lawapur Naryan	5	2	2.5
Hasanpur South	5	2	2.5
Hasanpur North	1	1	1
Alipur Hatta	4	4	1
Chamrahra	5	2	2.5
Mahua	10	11	0.91
Phulwaria	4	4	1
Mirjanagar	2	3	0.66
Hasanpur Osti	4	4	1
Study Area	36	24	1.5

Source: Centre DIRECT, Patna.

Health infrastructure in the study area is not up to the mark. All the nine GPs of the two Blocks have one sub-centre (health) each except Chamrahra, which has two sub-centres. Considering the population, most of the GPs have not yet reached the target of one sub-centre for 5,000 persons. Only Hasanpur South and Chamrahra have been able to meet the target. At the Block level, the situation of Mahnar is better than that of Mahua. Population served by each sub-centre is more in the latter Block (Table 8.6). There is no Primary Health Centre (PHC) in the study area, though the population of Mahnar Block is more than 30,000 and according to the national norm, there should be one PHC for every 30,000 population.

Table 8.6: Health and Other Infrastructures in the Study Area

Block/GP	*Population served by each Sub-Centre*	*% of Households with Access to Safe Drinking Water*	*% of Households having Sanitary Toilets*
Mahnar	6491	84.28	21.51
Lawapur Mahnar	7385	91.95	14.33
Lawapur Naryan	9630	70.69	22.80
Hasanpur South	4536	86.13	17.92
Hasanpur North	8389	86.43	19.76
Alipur Hatta	8936	86.42	28.00
Chamrahra	3281	87.05	24.98
Mahua	8785	87.23	26.35
Phulwaria	7884	90.90	29.41
Mirjanagar	8958	86.69	18.96
Hasanpur Osti	9513	84.94	30.67
Study Area	7179	85.30	23.19

Source: Centre DIRECT, Patna.

Among the basic amenities, water supply and sanitation are two important aspects. They are also directly related to environment and health conditions. According to the national goal of the International Decade of Drinking Water Supply and Sanitation (1981-1990), 100 per cent of the rural population was to be provided with safe drinking water. But none of the GPs in the study area have yet achieved the goal, though the situation has substantially improved. Table 8.6 shows that more than 85 per cent of the households in the study area have access to safe drinking water within a distance of half a kilometre. In all the GPs except Lawapur Naryan, more than 80 per cent of the households have access to this facility. The sanitation scenario is, however, very poor. Not even one-fourth of the households have sanitary toilets. Mahua is in a better position than Mahnar with more than 25 per cent of households having sanitary toilets. The above picture shows that there is an acute need for creating demand and providing facilities for constructing sanitary toilets in every household.

Centre for Documentation, Information, Research, Education, Communication and Training (Centre DIRECT)

Centre DIRECT, a voluntary and non-profit organization, was established for the promotion and dissemination of useful information on health, water and sanitation, promotion of non-formal and adult education and improving the lives of women and children, especially those belonging to the deprived classes through research, advocacy and training.

Centre DIRECT is one of the decentralized units of ADITHI (Bihar). It is registered under the Societies Registration Act, 1860. The organization has completed 13 years and although Centre DIRECT functions independently, it maintains a close relationship with ADITHI.

Geographical Area of Operation

The organization has adopted Sariya Block of Muzaffarpur district as its area of operation. But, in course of the last three years, it has undertaken many activities in various other Blocks and districts. It is now working in over 500 villages in 14 Blocks of Muzzaffarpur, Patna, Bhojpur, Vaishali and Samastipur districts of Bihar, as per details shown in Table 8.7.

Table 8.7: Geographical Area of Operation of Centre DIRECT, Patna

State	*Districts*	*Blocks*	*Number of Villages*
Bihar	Muzaffarpur	Paroo	15
		Saraiya	150
	Patna	Barh	40
		Athmalgola	32
		Belchhi	20
		Pandarak	45
	Bhojpur	Shahpur	17
		Barhara	25
	Vaishali	Mahua	29
		Patepur	27
		Mahnar	50
	Samastipur	Dalsinghsarai	15
		Bibhutipur	29
		Ujiarpur	08
Total	05	14	502

Source: Centre DIRECT, Patna.

Major Activities of the Organization

Major activities undertaken by the organization in the last three years under different programmes/projects are shown in Table 8.8.

Table 8.8: Current Activities of Centre DIRECT in different Districts of Bihar

Programme/ Project	*District*	*Coverage*		
		Men	*Women*	*Children*
Support to Gender Issue Project (SGI)	Muzaffarpur	0	400	1200
Swarnajayanti Gram Swarozgar Yojana (SGSY)	Muzaffarpur	0	1200	0
Swarnajayanti Gram Swarozgar Yojana (SGSY)	Patna	1000	600	0
SNID	Muzaffarpur	0		7500
Swawlamban (1st)	Bhojpur	0	1500	0
Swawlamban (2nd)	Bhojpur	0	1500	0
Swayamsidha	Vaishali and Samastipur	0	6000	0
Deep	Samastipur	0	1200	0
Kopal	Samastipur	0	71172	0
Village Planning Process	Vaishali	60255	67676	25000
Creation of Model Panchayat and Wards	Patna	0	3000	50
Learn to Govern	Muzaffarpur	0	250	0
Nirmal Gram Pariyojana	Vaishali	60255	67676	25000
Integrated Nutrition and Health Programme (INHP)	Patna	0	0	80000
ICDS Training Centre		0	200	0

Self-Help Groups (SHGs)

In the Sariya Block of Muzaffarpur district and Barh and Athmalgola Blocks of Patna district, Centre DIRECT is engaged in developing groups under SGSY. In these Blocks, 375 SHGs have been formed with a membership of 4,190 persons.

With the support of Women Development Corporation, they are organising the SHG movement for poor women in Mahua and

Patepur Blocks of Vaishali district under Swayamsidha Project. In Mahua, 100 groups have been formed and in Patepur 105, with an average group size of 15 members.

The Women Development Corporation of Bihar is also supporting other SHG movements of the Centre such as those in Bhojpur and Samastipur districts. In Bhojpur, 106 groups are functioning in 23 villages of two Blocks; and in Samastipur, 85 groups are operating. In all, the Centre has promoted 771 groups.

SHGs in Mahua Block

We studied the activities of SHGs in Mahua Block promoted under Swayamsidha Project since July 2004. By August 2006, 100 groups with 1,553 members had been formed in 24 villages spread over 7 Gram Panchayats. Inter-lending figures reveal that Rs. 14.90 lakh were used for consumption while Rs. 8.58 lakh were taken for productive enterprises. In all, 1175 members were engaged in individual enterprises. All SHGs conducted meetings fortnightly.

Grading: Only 10 out of 100 SHGs have been graded under SGSY, National Agricultural Bank for Rural Development (NABARD) etc. while grading under the Women Development Corporation has been done for all groups.

Training: Representatives of all the 100 groups have been trained in the principles of SHG, book-keeping, legal issues, and gender related issues etc. More than 50 per cent of the groups have been trained in Reproductive and Child Health and Community Health. Training has also been given on the methodology of managing clusters. Exposure visits have been arranged for representatives of 60 groups. Besides, Information, Education and Communication (IEC) material has been provided to all the groups.

A questionnaire survey was undertaken in 30 SHGs in 8 villages spread over 3 GPs, namely Phulwaria, Mirjanagar and Hasanpur Osti. From each of the three GPs three sample SHGs were chosen at random. These groups were formed at the initiative of Centre DIRECT. The important features, as revealed in the survey are as follows:

All the groups were formed between August and November 2004 with BPL women. Members of a group are residents of one locality of the village. Credit was made available to members both for consumption and for economic activities, the rate of interest being 2 per cent per month or 24 per cent per year. Recovery of loans is almost cent per cent. Only one SHG reported that one member defaulted in paying instalment. No group was found to be taking up any activity other than thrift and credit. Although some members in each group had taken loans to pursue economic activities, no such activity had been taken up on a group basis.

The groups received substantial assistance from the NGO in maintaining accounts and establishing linkages with banks. However, they reported that no assistance was forthcoming in respect of marketing of products or establishing linkages with the Panchayat/government office.

Linkage with the Panchayat and Government Agencies

The survey revealed that the groups had no contact with the local Gram Panchayat, government offices or with any political leader of the area. Women have been traditionally discouraged from taking part in public life. It is only through SHG activities that they have started getting a "feel" of the public sphere. Motivating women and empowering them to participate in public life is a major task and SHG-activists have to pay greater attention to this.

Gram Panchayat's Attitude towards SHGs

The survey shows that no attempt has been made by local Panchayats to get acquainted with the problems of SHGs or to involve them in development activities. What is more disturbing is that even SHG members do not take much interest in the activities of the Panchayat. There is a widespread feeling among SHGs that the Panchayat members are unaware of development schemes. There is also a lack of awareness among the Panchayat leaders about the need to support CBOs for local development. All this underscores the need for capacity building of the Panchayats.

Major Hindrance for Developing CBOs

It is through SHGs that poor women have learnt the first lesson on community governance. So far, lack of awareness and inexperience in addressing public concerns through an organized forum has prevented SHGs from turning into effective tools of change. If they can develop the skill of managing their own groups independently, they would probably acquire the capacity to participate in other spheres of community governance as well. As of now, SHGs of Mahua Block have not reached that stage.

Other Programmes

Other programmes taken up by Centre DIRECT for the development of women and children include advocacy meetings and workshops for gender sensitization, training of Integrated Child Development Services (ICDS) functionaries and establishing crèches and child care centres. In order to provide livelihood opportunities to women, the Centre has opened a training-*cum*-production centre at Muzaffarpur district. Women are trained in food processing, weaving and production of sanitary towels. After training some women have formed SHGs for receiving assistance under SGSY. The SHGs producing sanitary towels are selling their products under a brand name.

By far, it is the UNICEF sponsored Village Planning Process (VPP) that provides a platform for convergence of the activities of the CBOs and NGOs with the government service providers, which appears to be the most innovative initiative of Centre DIRECT. A detailed study of this programme is presented later.

An Assessment of the Activities of Centre DIRECT

The distinctive mark of this organization is its commitment to the cause of development of women and children and safeguarding of their rights. It defines women's empowerment in terms of their self-respect, self-confidence and self-dependence. Its activities under different projects are aimed at creating awareness among women and imparting appropriate knowledge and skill to them, so that they can stand on their own feet. It also seeks to enhance participation of women in associational activities to facilitate not only their own development, but also to contribute in social development. The organization, therefore, promotes and supports CBOs of women. As noted, they are putting in a lot of effort in promoting SHGs and in capacity building of the groups. Development and strengthening of Village Panchayats is another important area of work for the organization.

The kind of services that an NGO like Centre DIRECT provides cannot be expected from the government's development agencies. For example, various poverty alleviation schemes envisage SHGs as the basic institutional unit for generating self-employment, to facilitate savings and to enable the poor women in accessing credit. But there is no institution that can take up vital tasks such as creating awareness among the community members, developing women's leadership, imparting appropriate knowledge and skill to the members and establishing linkages between the groups and other agencies like government offices or banks. By providing such services in the remote rural areas, the organization is filling a vital institutional gap. If the CBOs have to play an important role in women's empowerment and local development, they would need support and such support can be extended by the NGOs. It will also be seen from the case study of the VPP that Centre DIRECT is contributing towards making the village panchayats of Mahnar district nodal institutions for coordination of development activities in the local areas. This is an important intervention, indeed, the effect of which will be noticed in future. Unlike many NGOs, Centre DIRECT does not consider panchayats as rival institutions. It works with these institutions of local democracy and provides support to them, so that they may provide leadership in coordinating planning, implementation and monitoring activities for local development.

One aspect of the style of working of this organization deserves special mention. It has been noticed in many cases that whenever a new project is launched in an area, two important activities are taken up before actual work starts. First, a benchmark household survey is done. This helps immensely in not only formulating the strategy of actual operation, but also in monitoring and evaluating the project activities. Secondly, appropriate training programmes are arranged for the field staff before they are asked to take up the advocacy or mobilization work at the village level. Since untrained or ill trained staff may do more harm than good, this kind of professional attitude for building capacity of the project staff is quite commendable.

Like other NGOs, Centre DIRECT is yet to solve the complex question of sustainability both of its activities as well as the 750 SHGs that they are nurturing. The organization is, however, aware of this problem, that is why in Mahua Block it attaches immense importance to clusters. Not only have all the

SHGs been brought under the umbrella of clusters, various programmes are also being undertaken to build their capacity. The sponsoring NGO claims that it is possible to make the clusters self-financing with subscriptions from each group. It is too early to judge how far this claim is justified. As of now, both the groups as well as the clusters are heavily dependent on the NGO. There is another year left for the present project to end in Mahua. Within this period, the self-management capacity of the CBOs has to be built. The groups will need some more years of nurturing. If another project is not available to enable the NGO to do this, the local panchayat and the District Rural Development Cell (DRDC) or the Block have to come forward. Therefore, the NGO has to enter into effective collaboration with the permanent institutions of the State, namely the local panchayat and the Block officials/DRDC to ensure sustainability of the SHGs. As of now, such an effort is not in sight. The project VPP, which will be discussed in details later, is also in operation in Mahua Block. Unfortunately, the SHGs have not yet been integrated in the overall scheme of the VPP. VPP will be a good framework within which the question of sustainability of the SHGs and other CBOs can be linked. It seems that the NGO has not yet given sufficient thought to this possibility.

Status of Gram Panchayats

Panchayati Raj in Bihar

Bihar is considered to be one of the non-performers in respect of institutionalization of Panchayati Raj. Ironically, it is one of the few States in India, which enacted a Panchayati Raj legislation within a few months of achieving independence in 1947. Under the Bihar Panchayati Raj Act, 1947, the Gram Panchayats and their judicial arm—Gram Kuchehries started functioning from 1948.

In 1961, following the report of the Balwant Rai Mehta Committee, an Act was passed to set up a three-tier system of Panchayati Raj with the Gram Panchayat at the village level, Panchayat Samiti at the Block level and Zila Parishad at the district level. But no serious attempt was made to implement this Act. As a result, the two tiers above the Gram Panchayat were not set up in all the districts till 1980.

During the long period of 36 years between 1964 and 2000, panchayat elections were held only twice—in 1971 and then in 1978. In 1981, all the newly set up Zila Parishads were superseded. The Gram Panchayats and Panchayat Samitis were allowed to exist, but elections to these bodies were not held. The terms of Mukhiyas of Gram Panchayats and Pramukhs of Panchayat Samitis were extended every six months by executive order, till a judicial pronouncement brought this practice to an end in 1997.

In 1992, the 73rd Constitution Amendment was passed, making it mandatory for each State to set up a panchayat system and hold fresh elections to the local bodies immediately after the expiry of the present term or by 1994 whichever was earlier. Bihar enacted a new Panchayati Raj Act in 1993 to bring its panchayat system in conformity with the constitutional provisions, but chose to ignore the mandatory provision of holding the elections, till the Supreme Court gave a direction in 2000 to hold elections immediately. Thus, the first elections to the constitutionally designed three-tier panchayat bodies were held in April 2001.

Composition of Panchayats

Panchayats in Bihar, like in other States, consist of Gram Panchayat at the lowest level, Panchayat Samiti at the Block level and Zila Parishad at the district level. While a Gram Panchayat is headed by a Mukhiya, a Panchayat Samiti and Zila Parishad are headed by Pramukh and Adhyaksha respectively. In a Gram Panchayat, there is one elected member for every 500 voters.

Provision for Reservation

After the 73rd Amendment, when the State Panchayat Act was passed, elaborate provisions were made for reservation of seats for the backward castes. In all the three tiers of panchayats, seats were reserved for Scheduled Castes, Scheduled Tribes and Backward Classes in accordance with the proportion of these three categories to the total population. One-third of the total seats (both from reserved and unreserved categories) were reserved for women. When panchayat elections were held in Bihar in 2001, after a gap of 23 years, 44,815 women entered the panchayats, of whom 9,286 were from the SC category.

In 2006, Bihar's Panchayat Act was amended by an ordinance. The amendments raised the quota of reservation for women to as much as 50 per cent, both in respect of seats of members and the offices of chairpersons. This made the representative character of Bihar's panchayats more gender-sensitive. The second panchayat elections, held in June 2006, followed the above principle of reservation for women.

Panchayats of the Study Area

During the first term of the new generation of panchayats established after the elections of 2001, not much effort was made by the State government to develop these bodies as real institutions of self-government. Insufficient devolution of functions, finances and functionaries crippled the PRIs. No serious efforts were made to build the capacity of elected representatives, a large number of whom were women or belonged to the disadvantaged groups. In order to get an idea of the status of the Gram Panchayats in the study area, information was collected from 8 GPs—6 from Mahnar and 2 from Mahua. The result of the survey is described below:

Size of the Panchayats: Except two GPs of Mahnar, namely Hasanpur Osti and Hasanpur North, all other GPs have a sizeable population ranging from 6,500 to 9,500. Number of households range between 1,000 and 1,400 in most of the panchayats.

Functions of Panchayats: Even though the Act provides that 31 functions would be devolved to the GPs, in reality no devolution of functions has taken place. However, the GPs have been involved in some agency functions of the State government. In the study area, the GPs were found to be involved in activities relating to the following:

- Beneficiary selection in various social assistance schemes like Widow/Old Age Pension, National Family Benefit Scheme;
- Beneficiary selection of targeted public distribution scheme like Annapurna, Antyodaya;
- Management of ICDS centre, sub-centre, primary schools etc.; and
- Construction/maintenance of roads.

It is surprising that the GPs have not been involved in drinking water supply or sanitation. However, Mukhiya of Gorigama and Chamrahar GPs of Mahnar district told us that they would take up construction/maintenance of tubewells from the Twelfth Finance Commission Funds available to them.

Finances: It was not possible to get accurate financial data from the panchayats. However, it appeared from discussions with the Mukhiyas that the finances of the GP are in poor shape. The Act gives powers to the GPs to raise resources through holding tax, profession tax and some fees. But these powers are not properly utilized. The GPs depend on grants of the State government. As of now each GP gets funds to execute the National Rural Employment Guarantee Scheme. Besides, the GPs receive funds sanctioned in terms of the recommendations of the Twelfth Finance Commission. The Gorigama Panchayat received a sum of Rs. 1.76 lakh from these two sources in 2007-08. It may receive more funds from these sources after they spend the amount.

Staff and Office: In Bihar, the Secretary is the only staff of the Gram Panchayat. Even he is not available on a full-time basis, as one Secretary is required to serve more than one GP. The offices of the GPs are also not well organized. Most of the GPs have permanent office buildings, but offices are opened only when the Secretary comes. Normally Mukhiyas work from their homes.

Profile of Members: It is clear from Table 8.9 that most panchayat members are in the age group of 31-45 (56 per cent), while a sizeable number of members are below 30 (32 per cent). Members above the age of 45 are few (11 out of 96 or 11 per cent). Of the 96 members of 8 panchayats, only 21 or about 28 per cent are illiterate. All others have received education above the primary level.

Relationship with NGOs/CBOs: In the study area, most common CBOs are SHGs of women. In a few GPs, Mahila Samitis and Youth Clubs also exist. In one GP a cooperative society was also found. Though there should be regular interactions between these organizations and the panchayats, this was not the case in the study area. Collaboration between NGOs/CBOs and the GP for a common development programme does not take place. It is, however, possible to bring all these institutions in a common development programme, as has happened in the implementation of the VPP.

Gram Sabha: As Table 8.10 shows, attendance in Gram Sabha meetings is very low, ranging between 2 per cent to 7 per cent. Moreover, there has not been any appreciable rise in attendance over the last three years. One good feature is that, in general, gender bias does not seem to be pronounced in most of the Gram Panchayat areas.

Table 8.9: Profile of Members of the Panchayat

Gram Panchayat Name	Number of Panchayat Members	Age			Sex		Educational Qualification		
		30 years or less	31-45	More than 45 years	M	F	Illiterate	Up to IV	V and above
Phulwariya	11	5	5	1	6	5	2	-	9
Lawapur Naryan	14	6	6	2	6	8	7	-	7
Alipur Hatta	14	6	8	-	7	7	2	-	12
Mirjanagar	12	6	6	-	5	7	-	-	12
Hasanpur North	14	2	8	4	6	8	6	-	8
Chamrahra	11	4	5	2	5	6	3	-	8
Lawapur Mahnar	13	2	9	2	5	8	-	-	13
Hasanpur South	7	-	7	-	5	2	1	-	6

Source: Centre DIRECT, Patna.

Table 8.10: Attendance in Gram Sabha/ Ward Sabha Meeting

Name of GP	*Voters*	*2003*				*2004*				*2005*			
		M	*F*	*Total*	*%*	*M*	*F*	*Total*	*%*	*M*	*F*	*Total*	*%*
Phulwariya	4251	130	15	145	3.41	109	30	139	3.27	100	75	175	14.12
Lawapur Naryan	6711	NA	NA	NA	NA	75	50	125	1.86	125	75	200	2.98
Alipur Hatta	5863	75	70	145	2.47	100	79	179	3.05	120	75	195	3.33
Mirjanagar	5700	75	50	125	2.19	96	50	146	2.56	125	79	204	3.58
Hasanpur North	5346	75	48	123	2.30	80	61	141	2.64	105	70	175	3.27
Chamrahra	4058	69	23	92	2.27	48	37	85	2.09	175	45	220	5.42
Lawapur Mahnar	4721	50	47	97	2.05	75	70	145	3.07	120	75	195	4.13
Hasanpur South	2450	47	37	84	3.43	50	75	125	5.10	90	75	165	6.73

Source: Centre DIRECT, Patna.

Case Study

Village Planning Process

As mentioned, Centre DIRECT is implementing a UNICEF-sponsored project in Mahnar Block of Vaishali district. By all standards, this is an innovative project, for it presents a model of institutional integration for local development. A detailed study of the project is presented in this section.

Village Planning Process: Principles and Objectives

The Village Planning Process (VPP) is an exercise in planning and implementation of activities for development. It is a process, not an event. It is a process *with people*, not *for the people*. Participation is thus both a means and an end of VPP.

Its primary objective is to promote collective responsibility of the government service providers, panchayats and NGOs/CBOs and the local communities to work in partnership mode. By creating and heightening awareness of the community in areas of health and education, the "process" seeks to strengthen demand of related services and to ensure an effective response to these demands.

The VPP covers the entire community of the village, but its focus is on women, children and other disadvantaged groups, because the need for development is highest among these groups. The specific objectives are to create a visible impact on the following:

Health

- Immunization
- Breast feeding
- Delivery by trained midwife
- Vitamin A for children
- Diarrhoea management

Child Protection

- Preventing child marriage
- Preventing exposure of children to hazardous labour
- Taking precautions against HIV/AIDS

Nutrition

- Growth monitoring of children
- Supplementary nutrition for children
- Use of iodized salt

Education

- Universal enrolment and preventing drop-outs before completing primary education.
- Ensuring attainment of minimum level of learning through the following interventions:
  - Monitoring teachers' attendance;
  - Ensuring acceptable standard of teacher-child ratio;
  - Ensuring mid-day meal;
  - Ensuring toilets and drinking water facilities in school; and
  - Improving physical infrastructure of schools.

Water and Sanitation

- Access to potable drinking water for each household
- Sanitary toilets for each household

The Programme and its Partners

There are two major components in this method of development intervention of VPP. The first component is to prepare a comprehensive plan after taking stock of the existing situation for which a survey of each household of a village is done. The second component is to follow up the implementation of the plan. The supporting NGO is expected to play a proactive role in the planning stage and a supporting role during the follow-up stage.

There is a conscious attempt to institutionalize the process of preparing plans and their implementation. Several strategies are adopted to ensure this. First, a group of youth volunteers are raised and trained to carry on the activities of monitoring and implementation of the plan in each village. Second, the existing CBOs are made partners in the process. Third, the local Gram

Panchayat is made an integral part of the whole process. The service delivery agencies at the local level, namely the Anganwadi centres, health centres, schools etc. are made partners in both the planning process and the implementation of the plans.

The Strategy

The development strategy adopted in the VPP is very simple and practical. It is simple because it aims at optimizing benefits from the delivery system that is already available in the villages. It seeks to create demand for the services by raising awareness of the community and strengthen the supply mechanism. The latter is done by enhancing the accountability of the service providers.

The activities involved in the project can be accomplished on a continuous basis under the leadership of the local Gram Panchayat with support from the field offices of the departments of the State government. This ensures convergence of the development activities within the village by bringing all the service providers on a common platform.

Implementation of the Project in Mahnar Block

UNICEF is supporting the VPP in four Blocks of Vaishali district. For overseeing the programme, there is a nodal NGO at the State level. Besides, an NGO has been identified in each district for implementation. Centre DIRECT is the NGO in charge of implementing the programme in Mahnar Block.

The work on VPP in Mahnar began in September 2005. The Block has 50 villages clustered into 14 Gram Panchayats with a population of a little over one lakh. The social infrastructure appears to be quite developed with 60 primary schools, 22 middle schools, one basic school and two high schools. There are 87 Anganwadi centres, one PHC and 18 health sub-centres. Yet, the Block remains backward in respect of enrolment of children, drop-out rates, infant mortality rate, fertility rate and gender disparity. Two factors are responsible for this—lack of sufficient awareness among people and inadequate services from the delivery system.

VPP in the present form is an additional intervention for development of the social sector. But, it is not an additional scheme meant for creating physical infrastructure or for providing services or other resources. It seeks to strengthen both the demand and the supply side by giving emphasis on participative planning, awareness generation, community-level institution building, strengthening the existing delivery system and establishing a system of regular monitoring, coordination and evaluation. The structural arrangement at various levels for accomplishing these objectives is as follows:

District: A District Level Task Force (DLTF) consisting of the Chairperson of the Zila Parishad, District Magistrate and other district level functionaries of various line departments like District Health Officer, District Education Officer, District Social Welfare Officer etc. along with the representatives of the nodal NGO and the implementing NGO.

Block: Block Level Task Force (BLTF) consisting of Block Development Officer (BDO), Block level functionaries of line departments, Chairpersons of Gram Panchayats along with the representative of the implementing NGO.

Gram Panchayat: Chairperson of Gram Panchayat, Auxiliary Nurse Midwife (ANM), ICDS supervisors, headmasters of schools, representative of the implementing NGO.

Village Level: Village Information Centre supported by youth volunteers, school teachers, SHGs and other CBOs.

The NGO team consists of one Block coordinator, three area supervisors, one data analyst and facilitators. At the time of conducting village planning exercise there were 42 supervisors. Now that the planning exercise is over, there are 7 supervisors, one in charge of two Gram Panchayats. Besides a large number of youth volunteers have been raised in various villages. They have been trained by the implementing NGO and now work at the village level on a voluntary basis.

The work started with a series of training programmes. The Block level project staff of the implementing NGO was exposed to a 21-day training programme by the nodal NGO. Participants were trained in the procedure of plan preparations, Participatory Research and Action (PRA) tools and techniques of social survey. Following this, a similar training programme was held by the implementing NGO for local facilitators. Thereafter 357 volunteers were trained.

The planning team consisted of the area supervisors of the implementing agency and three trained facilitators, at least one of whom was a woman. Additional facilitators were deployed for bigger villages with population of more than three thousand. The team would work in a village for five days continuously. The hectic five-day schedule laid stress on familiarizing the community with the objectives of the project through rallies, meetings, posters and slogans. It included selection and survey of households, testing of iodine content of salt, collecting health information of children in the village, interacting with school headmasters and teachers and analysis of the collected data. Separate meetings were held with women on health matter.

The base-line survey brought a wealth of information on various issues proposed to be addressed. These were as follows:

- Households having toilets with water facilities;
- Households using hand-pumps as source of drinking water;
- Households using iodized salt;
- Percentage of women receiving ante-natal care;
- Percentage of pregnant women using Iron and Folic Acid (IFA) tablets and provided with Tetanus Toxoid (TT) injection.;
- Percentage of deliveries by trained mid-wife/Percentage of institutional delivery;
- Percentage of women having knowledge of HIV/AIDS;
- Percentage of people washing hands by soap or ash after meal or after defecation;
- Children having birth certificate;
- Children exclusively breastfed for six months;
- Children completely immunized as per schedule;
- Children provided Vitamin A during last six months (> 9 months);
- Children provided ORS during diarrhoea;
- Children availing pre-primary education;
- Children going to school;
- Children working;
- Adolescent girls taking weekly IFA tables; and
- Adolescents having knowledge of HIV and AIDS.

Apart from the above information, data was also collected on the various facilities available in the villages and their present condition, such as schools, Anganwadi centres, health sub-centres, sources of drinking water, condition of the hand pumps/wells, arrangements for immunization etc. With such information, it was possible to identify the gaps, prioritize the problem areas and prepare the action plan. Local school teachers, anganwadi workers, health workers and panchayat representatives also joined in this process of participatory planning.

After the village planning exercise in Mahnar Block was over, the project entered the second phase. The major focus of this phase was on strengthening the post-Planning follow-up process through strengthening of the existing institutions of service delivery and bringing coordination between them.

To involve the village community in regular monitoring of plan implementation, a novel method was adopted. In each village a 'village display board' was set up at a prominent place. This board was updated regularly—at least every fortnight—by the youth volunteers. Apart from vital statistics of the village such as child population, names of important government functionaries, the village plan etc., it also listed out various problems ranging from defective tubewells, number of children suffering from Vitamin A deficiency, number of child marriages, number of vacant posts of teachers in the local school etc. The Board also informed the public about which official to approach for specific problems.

At Mahnar, the panchayats could not be involved in the planning phase, because they were completing their terms and new elections were on the cards. But, in mid-2006 elections were over and the newly elected Panchayati Raj bodies took charge. This provided a unique opportunity to involve the Gram Panchayats in the implementation of the action plans. The process began with a one day orientation of newly elected PRI representatives on the VPP. Special care was taken to familiarize the Mukhiyas on the objects and methods of VPP.

Thereafter, the BDO issued an office order forming a Panchayat Support Group (PSG) in every GP. The PSG is headed by the Mukhiya of the Gram Panchayat and the members of the Village Level Support Group are its members. The Village Level Support Group consists of GP ward member, ANM, ASHA/Sahaiyka, Headmaster of the school, Presidents of Village Education Committee and Village Water and Sanitation Committee, representative of youth volunteers and the facilitator of the implementing NGO. Within a GP, there are several such village support groups. All of them are invited to the meetings of the PSG. In the case of youth volunteers, they are represented in the PSG by their captain. In each GP, the volunteers choose one from among themselves as their captain. The role and the activities of the PSG are as follows:

Planning

- To develop an action plan based on the plans of action developed under VPP for different villages catering to the most common issues affecting most communities and at the same time to take up critical issues affecting specific communities;
- Combined planning of activities at the panchayat level and demarcating overlapping areas to minimize repetition; and
- Incorporating the planned activities into the Panchayat Plan.

Implementation

- Implement planned activities;
- Distribute and share responsibilities of implementation; and
- Put up efforts to achieve the VPP milestones.

Monitoring

- Develop a sense of accountability and responsibility amongst partners to deliver services effectively;
- Provide feedback and suggestions based on observation and on-site inspection to achieve sectoral as well as community objectives; and
- Raise issues concerning the action plan and seek remedies from the group itself.

Sensitization and Support

- Generate a sense of support and coordination amongst sectors;
- Inculcate a feeling of oneness amongst partners;
- Seek support from communities to achieve the milestones; and
- Mobilize community for owning up the process of development.

Acting as a Pressure Group

- Act as a pressure group on the delivery system to ensure quality service delivery in the context of the plan developed at the village level.

Meetings of the PSG

The ISS researcher attended two meetings of PSG on 20th and 21st September, 2006 at Gorigama village and Chamrahar village respectively. Mukhiyas of the respective Gram Panchayats chaired the meetings. The meetings were attended by the Ward members (many of them were women), Anganwadi Sevikas, ASHA, Head Teacher and other teachers of schools, Secretary of Village Education Committee, youth volunteers, the facilitator of VPP and the staff of the implementing NGO. Some villagers also attended the meetings. The problems raised at these meetings and decisions taken to solve them are described in the following paragraphs.

There were complaints from teachers and headmasters of schools regarding lack of sanitary toilets and defective tubewells. The Mukhiya promised that he would soon visit all the schools within his GP and ensure construction of toilets and install/repair tubewells in the schools. He also promised to construct the boundary wall of one school, as requested by one of the headmasters. There were complaints regarding shortage of teachers and need for additional classrooms in some schools. It was decided that the panchayat would bring such problems to the notice of the higher authorities, because they could not be resolved locally.

A number of Anganwadi workers complained about the lack of proper infrastructural facility at the Anganwadi centres. The panchayat, the Mukhiya assured, would discuss this matter and prepare schemes for drinking water and toilet facilities in these centres. It was decided that other issues relating to administration and vacancies for the post of Sahayikas would be raised at the Block level Task Force meeting.

In one GP, PSG took decisions to hold birth registration camps in some villages and fixed the dates for such camps.

The Youth volunteers (YV) and the facilitator reported about the progress made in different sectors and also offered suggestions to improve performance with regard to birth registration, immunization and adoption of hygienic practices.

Lessons from the VPP of Mahnar

From the above description of the VPP of Mahnar Block, one may draw the following conclusion:

- Different types of institutions are operating in the villages to provide various kinds of services to the rural people. These include government service providers, panchayat, NGOs and the CBOs. Coordination between them may optimize the use of resources being invested by each of them. For, such coordination would make integration of activities of different types of institutions possible. This would also ensure that none work at cross purposes and each complements the other's efforts in reaching the common goal of development.
- Integration of the activities requires a common programme. Such common programme may be built around a continuous process of participatory planning and monitoring.
- The local panchayat may take the lead in providing a common platform for the government service providers (health centres, anganwadi centres, schools etc.), NGOs, CBOs and the local panchayat to achieve the development goals through a continuous process of planning, implementation, and monitoring.
- Initially, an NGO may play a useful role in institutionalizing the above process and also in the process of capacity building of CBOs and the panchayat.

Conclusion

The need for involvement of the community in governance issues is felt more keenly at the micro level of the village community. No doubt, at this level both panchayats and the agencies of the higher level government are at work. Yet between them, they cannot address many vital issues concerning development of women, children and other disadvantaged groups. Moreover, if Civil Society Organizations (CSOs) are strong and active, they may minimize damages resulting from the government's failure to act or perform well.

This is the *raison d'etre* for the growth and development of civil society institutions. Most important among them are the community based organizations which have an important role to play in development. But lacking in organizational capabilities, resources and capacity, they need the support of NGOs as well as panchayats.

However, the support provided by the sponsoring NGOs to the CBOs cannot go beyond the project period and in most cases, such period is too short. Generally, within that period, the CBOs, particularly the SHG-type CBOs, cannot acquire the capacity to manage their group activities independently. Accordingly, sustainability of such CBOs becomes suspect once the NGO-support is withdrawn. The present case study also could not provide a satisfactory answer to this problem.

The other area of concern is the weak linkage between the CSOs and the panchayats. Other than the area where the VPP is on, there is practically no realization on the part of panchayats about the need for collaboration between them and the CBOs. Needless to say, the orientation of the panchayat leaders needs to change. In the case under study, no evidence of any attempt to build a nexus between the panchayats and the CBOs was found, except in the project of village planning being executed in Mahnar.

At the micro-level of the village community, it is the Gram Panchayat that has to provide strategic leadership in establishing this process, because this institution is the representative government of the area. There are certain key principles that have to be observed by different actors for improving the quality of governance at the level of the village community. These have been described below:

The panchayats and the local agencies of the higher levels of government must recognize the contributions of CSOs in local development and should provide necessary support to enable them to make such contribution. The concern of panchayats should extend beyond the services they provide directly. They should play the enabling role of empowering the CBOs. The NGOs and the CBOs have to give up the practice of working in isolation. They must learn how to work on a common programme under the leadership of the local panchayat without sacrificing their own institutional identities. In matters of common interest of the village community, all the local institutions should remain transparent and accountable to the Gram Sabha, which is the assembly of all adult people of the area.

9

New Delhi

Arvind Kumar Pandey

The present study intends to look into the functioning of a Plan-supported NGO, namely Community Aid and Sponsorship Programme (CASP), the CBOs supported by it and the linkages between them and the urban local government. The study was conducted in the slum areas of Madanpur Khadar, Badarpur and Sangam Vihar of Delhi.

CASP-Plan and CBOs

The Community Aid and Sponsorship Programme (CASP) was started in 1976 to work for children's rights. CASP-Plan's Delhi Project began in 1986 to work for children who are from poor families, those in difficult circumstances, or those who are physically or socially handicapped. The focus of CASP-Plan has been on community mobilisation in certain portions of the slum settlements of Madanpur Khadar, Badarpur and Sangam Vihar.

Project Area Profile of CASP-Plan

Badarpur: Badarpur is a mix of urban and rural settlement and is situated in the southern part of Delhi, touching the border of Haryana State. It is spread over 200 acres of land and has a population of about 2 lakh. The area is characterized by inadequate water and sanitation facilities, poor housing conditions, inadequate health services (government hospital is at a distance of 17-18 km), though private doctors have established their clinics to provide basic curative services. There are 6 primary schools and 2 secondary schools in the area. Government as well as private transportation facilities exist and the frequency is quite good. The Government has provided electricity in the area. Badarpur area consists of Sapera Basti, Tajpur Pahari, Bilaspur Molarband Extension and Mohan Baba Nagar. CASP-Plan started working in 1995 in eight locations of these four communities.

Sapera Basti: Sapera Basti is an authorized colony located between Tajpur Pahari and Bilaspur on the Jaitpur Road near Badarpur Border in South Delhi. Sapera Basti consists of about 200 families of snake charmers, *been* players (a traditional flute) and drummers. These traditional occupations of the community are gradually dying. Threatened by animal activist groups and having no other skill at their disposal, the snake charmers temporarily migrate to neighbouring States to give performances. When they are in town the men have no constructive work to do; they are idle for several months in a year while women perform the household chores. Literacy level is very low among women and average among men. The community follows conservative traditional practices. Education of children is not a priority as a result of which children are not sent to school. Girls are the worst victims of this tradition.

Tajpur Pahari: Tajpur Pahari is a semi-urban area, with a population of 10,000. The slum is spread over 10 acres. The colony is unauthorized and most of the residents are from Rajasthan, U.P. and Bihar. Most residents are daily wage earners in the nearby factories. Literacy level is very low.

Bilaspur Molarband Extension: Bilaspur Molarband Extension is a rural and a semi-urban slum, which has population of about 50,000 (10,000 households). The area is spread over 15 acres and came into existence in 1978-79. Residents are migrants from different States of the country like M.P., Bihar, U.P. and Rajasthan. Residents belong to the economically lower strata. Most of them are daily wage earners, cart pullers, hawkers, vendors, helpers etc. The area does not have legal supply of electricity. Sanitation and housing conditions are poor.

Mohan Baba Nagar: Mohan Baba Nagar is a semi-urban slum. This slum came into existence in the decade of 1980s with approximately 2000 households and a population of more than 10,000. Residents are migrants from different States of country like M.P., Bihar, U.P. and Rajasthan. Most of them are wage earners, vendors, helpers, hawkers etc. Basic amenities like water supply and sanitation are inadequate and people have low level of awareness on different issues affecting their development.

Madanpur Khadar: Madanpur Khadar is a relocation colony in southeast Delhi built by the Government to relocate people from unauthorized slums from various parts of the city. The area is divided into two colonies. The first colony, known as Phase II–B Block which contains 923 plots, of which 534 are currently occupied. The second colony, known as Phase III, contains 2,352 plots, of which only 956 are currently occupied. CASP-Plan has divided the region into five roughly equal areas. MK1, MK2 and MK3 are in Phase III while MK4 and MK5 are the two Blocks of Phase II.

The prime inhabitants of the colony are natives from various States like West Bengal, Uttar Pradesh, Bihar and Rajasthan. They speak different languages and have very different backgrounds. Majority of them are Scheduled Caste Hindus. There is a Muslim population in certain pockets, which is not very high in number. The area faces many developmental challenges like unavailability of basic services—health, education, transportation, financial services and sources of livelihood. For most families, relocation was traumatic. The main source of income for many is employment in factories of Okhla, working as vendors and wage labourers in the nearby vegetable market. The source of income was depleted after relocation due to unreliable transportation from JJ Colony involving higher cost. Most of the males remained unemployed. Some have managed to keep their jobs in Okhla, while others are employed in construction work or petty vending. In addition to homemaking, many women and girls work as maids in nearby posh colonies of Delhi. They travel a considerable distance everyday.

The area has a primary and middle school, but the nearest higher secondary school is approximately 5 km away. Many children who were attending schools during the pre-settlement phase have dropped out due to transportation difficulties and the need to supplement family income. In a way they are in a much worse situation now than they were prior to relocation. Health problems like malaria, typhoid, and other water-borne diseases are rife in the area (diarrhoea, dysentery, etc.) Children have been the most affected.

Residents of both colonies, especially Phase III prefer to identify themselves on the basis of their earlier habitations (like from Nehru

Place or from Alaknanda). This has been a major obstacle for community organization and also a source of tension. The refusal to abandon the identity of their former community may be a response to the trauma of their forced relocation. Drug peddling is becoming an increasing problem, especially in one specific location in Phase III.

Sangam Vihar: 1,00,000 people live in the disadvantaged Sangam Vihar community which is the largest unauthorized colony of Asia. The colony came into existence in 1984 and is inhabited by people who have migrated to Delhi from various States in search of livelihood. Most of the people from Sangam Vihar work as factory labourers or as daily wage earners. When CASP-Plan initiated its developmental interventions in the area, most of the residents were illiterate or had very low level of education. Education facilities in the area were quite dismal. Although a few schools existed, they were located far away and hence were difficult to access due to lack of public transport facilities. Since Sangam Vihar is an unauthorized colony there is no provision of electricity, water supply, bituminized roads, hospitals etc. Today some parts of the area have been electrified and water is supplied through private vendors. The community is handicapped because of low level of awareness regarding health, education and rights of the child. They are also unaware about the Government policy and facilities for rehabilitation and treatment of the physically and mentally disadvantaged. Moreover, most of the families have very low incomes and opportunities for improved livelihoods. Housing facilities and urban infrastructure including transportation are woefully inadequate or totally lacking. Health facilities are practically absent within easily reachable distances. Severe congestion due to a very high density of population has led to unsanitary conditions.

Activities of CASP-Plan

Table 9.1 summarises the kind of developmental activities CASP has taken up in the slum areas. These range from acute problems of health to education faced by the slum population. Table 9.2 documents the types of Community Based Organizations (CBOs) with whom CASP works.

Table 9.1: Developmental Activities of CASP-Plan (Delhi)

Health	*Education*	*Social and Food Security*	*Citizen Empowerment*	*Physical Infrastructure*
Immunisation of children	Universal enrolment of children	Encouraging savings	Creating gender sensitivity	Promoting/ supporting CBOs, Mahila Samitis, Youth Clubs, etc.
Popularisation of breast feeding	Eliminating drop-outs		Empowerment of children	Creation of alternative schools/non formal schools etc.
Nutrition of children	Mid-day meals in schools		Capacity building to empower them for their rights	Information centres
Diarrhoea management			Dissemination of information on schemes	Monitoring Sub-centres/PHCs
Birth registration				
Immunisation of pregnant mothers				
Nutrition of pregnant mothers				
Prenatal/postnatal check-up of mothers				
Personal hygiene				

Table 9.2: Area-wise break-up of CBOs and SHGs with whom CASP works

Badarpur	Nav Jagriti Sangathan Saheli (SHG)	Nav Prabhat Abhibhawak Sangathan	Nav Yuvak Sangathan (SHG)
Sangam Vihar	Bal Panchayat	Nav Prabhat	Nai Disha (SHG)
Madanpur Khadar	Bal Panchayat		

CASP-Plan is working in these areas mainly through CBOs and three Bal Panchayats, Nav Jagriti Sangathan and Nav Prabhat Abhibhawak Sangathan. There are some Self Help Groups such as Nav Yuvak Sangathan, Saheli and Nai Disha. In this case the organization has made a distinction between Self Help Groups and CBOs. According to CASP, a variety of Community Based Organizations has been formed in Sangam Vihar and Badarpur areas as well as in Madanpur Khadar. CASP provides technical, managerial and financial support to the CBOs. Some of the groups have been registered as Cooperative Societies with the Registrar of Society whereas others are trying to register.

Bal Panchayat

Bal Panchayat is a forum of children, by children, for children. It works towards making children aware of their rights and responsibilities towards the community and society. Bal Panchayat has been created in certain portions of Sangam Vihar and Madanpur Khadar. Children from Below Poverty Line (BPL) and non-BPL families are members of the Bal Panchayat.

Nav Jagriti Abhibhawak Sangathan

In Badarpur, community-based clinical services are an integral part of the Sangathan's programmes for reproductive and sexual health, AIDS awareness, elimination of dowry and the caste system, motivating school drop-outs etc. 100 drop-outs are now attending the Sangathan's training classes. The organisation also offers micro-credit facilities.

Nav Prabhat Abhibhawak Sangathan

This is a very old CBO. The organisation helps people in the community to build their own capacity. It networks with the government and NGOs for resources to sustain health services for its members. It manages the activities of mentally retarded children. This is a Sangathan of the parents of mentally retarded children. It is in the process of registration.

Nav Yuvak Sangathan

This SHG was set up on January 1, 2005 in Badarpur through a CASP-Plan initiative. It has 15 members, men and women, both from BPL and non-BPL families in the area. The Sangathan offers micro-credit facilities and maintains close links with banks. On March 31, 2006, the Sangathan had Rs. 27,000 as capital. Members get credit at 2 per cent per month simple interest.

Saheli

CASP-Plan helped set up Saheli with 12 members on January 18, 2006. All the members are women from the Badarpur area. Saheli offers micro-credit and bank finance facilities. It had a capital of Rs. 4,800 in 2006.

Nai Disha

CASP-Plan helped set up Nai Disha in Sangam Vihar on April 24, 2005. As on March 31, 2006 it had a capital of Rs. 10,000. It offers loan facilities to members for economic activities. Nai Disha has 12 members, men and women, who are trained by CASP-Plan to keep accounts.

The ISS team conducted Focus Group Discussions (FGDs) with the members of two CBOs—Nav Jagriti and Nav Yuvak Sangathan.

FGD 1

Nav Jagriti was formed under the initiative of CASP-Plan. The SHG members were trained by CASP-Plan and a government agency, the Central Labour Welfare Board. They have become vocal about their rights and are likely to continue to function even after the NGO support is withdrawn, the members felt.

FGD 2

The Sangathan, set up in January 2005 under a CASP-Plan initiative, has so far opened only its bank account. The members seemed to be united and self-reliant, they invest their own savings to run this SHG and plan to continue their work should the NGO withdraw. They have a good rapport with the NGO, but are disappointed with the sitting councillor. In fact, they think they elected the wrong candidate as councillor, based on "caste" biases. They are also dissatisfied with the current state of welfare schemes—Mid-Day Meal Scheme, primary education, ICDS centres, old age pension, pension for the physically handicapped and Sarva Shiksha Abhiyan.

FGD 3

Each of the nine children who attended the FGD were clear about the objectives of CASP-Plan and Bal Panchayat initiatives in their area; in fact, these children were better informed than non-member children. The members of Bal Panchayat are from CASP-Plan's remedial centre and non-formal education centres, which are tuition centres for children from government-run schools. Not only do their parents encourage them to attend these remedial classes, these children also seemed determined to attend even classes run by another body, should the NGO stop its centres.

FGD 4

The six children in this group, studying in class 5 and 6, said they have gained confidence after attending the classes run by the CBO and are learning to become electricians, radio or electronic repair mechanics. They are aware that the government provides free school bags, books and nutrition. These children have been encouraging other slum children to attend classes. Some children left the Bal Panchayat, saying that the Bal Panchayat authorities seemed to be very hard task masters. They are, however, eager to continue their activities should CASP-Plan withdraw. The CBO is fruitfully linked with the NGO, but not with the local government body.

FGD 5

CASP-Plan started Nai Disha and provided training to its members. Seven members were present at the FGD. They seemed to be united and took consensual decisions. However, the group couldn't take any decision regarding its President. So CASP took the initiative and chose its President. The group has rapport with the NGO working there, but no links with the local government agencies and wants to keep functioning should the NGO withdraw.

FGD 6

Fifteen boys and girls, all Bal Panchayat members, participated in this discussion. They are familiar with issues of children's rights and duties, are enthusiastic about Bal Panchayat activities, and have been able to persuade members of their group to abide by group norms. Most of them are school children, studying in class 7 to class 10. One of them, Neelam Garg, now in class 12, taught at the remedial classes run by the CBO for two months during her summer vacation this year, without any remuneration. The children want to continue their activities even if CASP-Plan withdraws from their locality.

FGD 7

Eight boys and girls, all Bal Panchayat members, participated in this discussion. The children organise awareness camps and rallies on social issues and enact street plays. They also publish a community newspaper *Apni Duniya* and a monthly magazine *Bal Darpan*. The reporting, scripting, editing and layout for *Bal Darpan* are all handled by the Bal Panchayat children under the supervision of CASP-Plan. The children have become confident and ambitious and some of them are determined to work for the community. If the concerned NGO withdraws, the members want to continue their activities under the supervision of some other organisation.

Outcome of FGDs

Mutual trust exists between the members of these groups. Conflict is resolved democratically, through a consensual approach. They are strongly linked with an NGO, but not with local government bodies. The CBOs have been successful in generating awareness in the local community and people now voice their genuine demands. Some groups are uncertain if they can continue after CASP-Plan withdraws, though they want to continue their activities. The group members convince non-participating members to utilise community services, through the medium of drama, exhibitions and posters.

Sustainability of CBOs

Members of CASP-Plan attend meetings of CBOs regularly. Though CBOs work under the close guidance of CASP-Plan, they maintain proper records of activities and financial transactions and are capable of conducting meetings on their own. Some of the CBOs have helped mobilise economic resources at the grassroots level and try to raise the standard of living of their community, particularly the deprived sections. The communities, in turn, support these organisations and understand the need for healthcare, education and family planning. In other words, the CBOs are heavily NGO dependent for funding as well as resolving internal conflicts. The NGO also chalks out plans for future action of the CBOs. In certain cases, however, the CBOs have registered and are working with the Municipal Corporation of Delhi to sustain themselves. For example, Nav Jagriti got registered itself under the name of Jan Jagriti Samiti and has been working on the MCD schemes on sanitation, tree plantation, etc.

Status of Urban Local Self Government Institutions

Before 1992, the municipalities did not have a Constitutional status and thus urban local areas were directly under the jurisdiction of State governments. However, the Constitution (Seventy-Fourth Amendment) Act of 1992 redefined the role, powers, functions and financial authority of Urban Local Government Institutions

(ULGs). The 12th Schedule confers the following responsibilities on ULG:

- Urban planning;
- Regulation of land use and construction of buildings;
- Planning for economic and social development;
- Roads and bridges;
- Water supply;
- Public health, sanitation and solid waste management;
- Fire services;
- Urban forestry;
- Safeguarding the interests of the weaker sections of society, including the handicapped and mentally retarded;
- Upgrading and improving slums;
- Alleviating urban poverty;
- Providing urban amenities and facilities such as parks and playgrounds;
- Promoting cultural, educational and aesthetic facilities;
- Burial and cremation grounds, and electric crematoria;
- Cattle pound, prevention of cruelty to animals;
- Vital statistics, including registration of births and deaths;
- Public amenities, including street lighting, parking lots, bus stops and public conveniences; and
- Regulation of slaughterhouses and tanneries.

Delhi (total area 1,483 sq. km.) comes under three civic agencies:

- The Municipal Corporation of Delhi (MCD), the biggest of the three, covers 1,397.29 sq. km. (94.22 per cent of Delhi State) in 12 zonal segments, urban and rural and 134 Wards. The MCD has obligatory functions (public health and sanitation, water supply, street lighting, roads and bridges, traffic engineering, maintenance of mortuaries and cremation grounds, etc.) as well as discretionary functions (taxes, etc.).
- The New Delhi Municipal Committee (NDMC), covering 42.74 sq. km.
- The Delhi Cantonment Board, also covering 42.74 sq. km.

The focus of our study is on South Delhi district and Kalkaji subdivision.

Table 9.3: Developmental Activities of Urban Local Bodies in Sangam Vihar, Badarpur and Madanpur Khadar

Health	*Education*	*Livelihood**	*Citizen Empowerment*	*Physical Infrastructure*
Immunisation of children	Universal enrolment of children	Extending credit facilities	Dissemination of information on development schemes	Promoting/ supporting CBOs, SHGs, Mahila Samitis etc.
Nutrition of children	Mid-day meals in schools	Others		Primary school
Birth registration				Anganwadi centres
Immunisation of pregnant mothers				Veterinary centres
Pre-natal/ post-natal check-up of mothers				Roads
Birth control				
Sanitary toilets				

Delhi State Government Welfare Schemes for South Delhi's Poor and Slum Dwellers

Old Age Pension: Rs. 400 per month is given to 18,000 persons, those with an income of less than Rs. 48,000 per annum.

Widow Rehabilitation Scheme: Provided to nearly 250 women, who are also encouraged to earn their livelihood.

Handicapped Welfare: Monthly stipend of Rs. 50 to Rs. 70 for handicapped children studying in class 1 to class 8 and Rs. 125 for those studying in class 9 and above.

National Family Benefit Scheme: A one-time grant of Rs. 10,000 has been given to nearly 40 widows who are 64 years of age, or more.

Widow's Daughter's Marriage Scheme: A one-time grant of Rs. 20,000 for the marriage of a widow's daughter.

The Central Government's Urban Poverty Alleviation Schemes

Prime Minister's Rozgar Yojana (PMRY): Provides employment to educated youth through setting up of micro enterprises in industry, service and business. In Sangam Vihar and Badarpur, loans of Rs. one lakh each have been given to 180 beneficiaries. To be eligible for a loan, neither the applicant's spouse nor parents should have an annual income exceeding Rs. 40,000.

Swarna Jayanti Shahari Rozgar Yojana (SJSRY): From December 1, 1997, the three Urban Poverty Alleviation Schemes – Urban Basic Services for the Poor (UBSP), Nehru Rozgar Yojana (NRY) and Prime Minister's Integrated Urban Poverty Eradication Programme (PMI UPEP)—were merged under SJSRY. Funded on a 75:25 basis by the Centre and the State, SJSRY contains two special schemes: The Urban Self Employment Programme (USEP) and the Urban Wage Employment Programme (UWEP).

Urban Self Employment Programme (USEP): Under this scheme, women below the poverty line are trained in a particular skill. Skill improvement classes are conducted in Mirabai Polytechnic in South Delhi. In South Delhi, 400 women are being trained, but in Sangam Vihar, only four or five women have benefited. According to the Deputy Commissioner's office, people of Sangam Vihar and Badarpur are not aware of this programme. The UWEP on the other hand has not made much headway.

Case Studies: Nav Jagriti

Before this CBO was set up in 1996, the staff conducted several meetings with different groups of people. At first, only young people came forward to monitor pre-school centres, assist in income-generating activities, including remedial education, community development works, health projects for the under-five, prevention and treatment of RTIs, social mobilisation through street plays, FGDs and *melas*.

With the help of the CBO, the youth volunteers started a peer group education training on HIV/AIDS. The health coordinator provided technical and managerial support and coordinated the programmes. Now this CBO can maintain and supervise community clinics, generate awareness and mobilise emergency referral services. It runs community-based pre-school centres, and Non Formal Education (NFE) centres with the help of pre-school teachers and NFE teachers. It conducts Early Childhood Care and Development (ECCD) activities and pre-school based activities for children up to three years old.

A mobile clinic functions four days a week (half-day a week at one centre) in collaboration with the Population Foundation of India. Women are assured of privacy and safety so that they can avail of these services. Health *melas* and street plays organised to create awareness in the community have proved effective and enrolment at the clinic has increased.

The CBO is exploring issues of sustainability through various means such as collaboration with other NGOs /government bodies, generating revenue by increasing service fees for quality services, holding specialised camps in collaboration with other agencies and coaching to generate revenue. To provide quality care, the intervention has adopted three strategies: (i) A client-centred approach; (ii) emphasis on quality; and (iii) gender-sensitive services.

Conclusion

With the help of CBOs, CASP-Plan has established a network of small, isolated actors so that they can work together to exchange experiences and ideas, learn to look at the bigger picture and generate pressure on the government and political bodies. The existing programmes have changed attitudes and raised awareness levels in all the three localities: Badarpur, Sangam Vihar and Madanpur Khadar.

CBOs have followed up with drop-outs and provided free remedial classes, funded by CASP-Plan and helped people learn how they can increase their income and avail of loans. The organisation has done commendable work in areas of women's empowerment, child rights, health and local self-government, and CBOs have worked to raise awareness on issues of health, sanitation, education and evil social practices, especially among low-income and migrant groups.

The performance of urban local bodies has been unsatisfactory—poor health and sanitation facilities, no regular garbage clearance, irregular water supply and no slum improvement work. According to CASP-Plan, urban local bodies provide no financial assistance for its welfare activities.

The role of CBOs and other SHGs is crucial—they act as facilitators for slum-dwellers. CBOs and ULBs can play complementary roles in achieving participatory governance at the community level, but links between ULBs and CBOs are very weak. The ULBs are not inclined to share any information with CBOs on their functioning or financial resources. The CBOs must keep trying to work with ULBs. The latter should take CBOs into confidence while devising development programmes. The CBOs can strengthen the ULBs and other local institutions through meaningful participation in the developmental programmes launched by ULBs. Wherever the CBOs have worked in collaboration with urban local bodies such as sanitation programme in Sangam Vihar the service delivery has improved on a sustained basis.

We need to move from policy-driven changes to making real-life changes at the grassroots. Networking among NGOs and NGO collaboration with the State, can throw up plenty of local models of success.

10

Tamil Nadu

K. Subha and *B.S. Bhargava*

Introduction

Dharmapuri district with an area of 9,344 sq. km. was formed on October 2, 1965 with ten talukas. It has a population of 28.56 lakh (2001 Census) and a total literacy rate of 53.01 per cent (male 61.5 per cent, female 44.1 per cent). The percentage of SC population is 15 per cent but that of ST is only 2 per cent as per the 2001 Census. It is also interesting to note that the sex ratio is only 935, slightly higher than the national average. Dharmapuri has 2,260 primary schools, 555 middle schools and 115 senior secondary schools. Several Non-Governmental Organizations (NGOs) have been active in Dharmapuri district but the study conducted by the ISS team has focused on the developmental activities of the Plan partner MYRADA.

The Mysore Resettlement and Development Agency (MYRADA)-Plan Dharmapuri Project has been implemented in 542 villages, including 300 sponsorship villages, in Dharmapuri and Krishnagiri districts of Tamil Nadu. The project, which originally had the objective of resettling bonded labourers and homeless families, began in 1984-85 in 50 villages of one of the most backward Blocks, Thally.

The project was implemented mostly with the help of women's Self-Help Groups (SHGs). A non-formal technical training centre for children was established in 1997. The project supported more than 5,800 children and their families. In 1989-90, the project entered into partnership with Plan International to work for children, their families and communities and enrolled 500 children in the sponsorship programme.

Approach and Methodology

The data used in this study was collected from a two-month long fieldwork. The primary data was collected through interviews with stakeholders, focus group discussions with the villagers and field visits. Secondary data was collected from the MYRADA-Plan District Office at Dharmapuri, Community-Managed Resource Centres (CMRCs) and panchayat offices.

Table 10.1: Number of Respondents Interviewed

Respondents	*Numbers*
Village Leaders	4
Volunteer (Self help Affinity Group or SAG trainer)	3
GP Secretaries	2
Farmers	1
Gram Panchayat Elected Representatives	4
Project Unit Staff	2
Parent-Teacher Association (PTA) President and members	4
Total	20

Twenty persons were interviewed. These included village leaders, Gram Panchayat secretaries and elected representatives of two panchayats.

Activities of MYRADA

From its inception in 1968 until 1978, MYRADA worked to resettle Tibetan refugees. From 1978 to 1979, at the invitation of State governments, MYRADA started working with the rural poor, managing 16 projects in 12 backward districts of Karnataka, Andhra Pradesh and Tamil Nadu.

Self-help Affinity Groups (SAGs)

Table 10.2 depicts the spatial distribution of SHGs and the number of members of SAGs in different parts of Dharmapuri district. When cooperatives broke down and the banking system could not meet

Table 10.2: SAG Coverage Details as on June 30, 2006

Sl. No.	*Sector /Resource Centre Area*	*Number of SHGs*	*Number of Blocks*	*Number of Panchayats*	*Number of Villages*	*Number of Members*
1.	B. Agraharam	2	9	45	132	2485
2.	Bettamugilalam	2	2	28	45	754
3.	Denkanikottai	3	19	59	182	3058
4.	Dharmapuri	2	16	55	175	3212
5.	Eriyur	1	8	49	99	1915
6.	Hosur	1	12	34	82	1498
7.	Kadamadai	1	21	45	220	4177
8.	Kamanadoddi	2	12	31	77	1292
9.	Kambainallur	1	9	24	89	1603
10.	Kelamangalam	2	12	29	106	1860
11.	Krishnapuram	2	16	53	141	2660
12.	Odasalapatti	2	7	17	65	1195
13.	Palacode	2	26	80	164	3178
14.	Pauparapatti	3	12	48	148	2905
15.	Pennagaram	1	10	65	183	3505
16.	Salivaram	2	13	35	90	1668
17.	Shoolagiri	1	27	94	198	3608
18.	Thally	1	25	63	127	2060
	Total	31	256	844	2323	42633

the needs of the poor, MYRADA experimented with an alternative credit system in 1984-85. MYRADA did not provide the credit, but set up Credit Management Groups (CMGs), formed on the basis of affinity between group members. These groups were both flexible and responsive to the needs of small clients, yet large enough for banks to have transactions with.

In 1987, the National Bank for Agriculture and Rural Development (NABARD) gave MYRADA a grant of Rs. 10 lakh from its Research and Development funds to promote and study this pilot experiment. Most of the investment went into building the capacity of CMGs, later renamed as SHGs. When SHGs became popular and a part of the government's anti-poverty programme, MYRADA went back to focusing on affinity to unite group members.

Federation of SAGs

To strengthen individual groups, a federation of 10 to 20 functional SAGs, located close to each other, is set up. One such Federation has been set up at Dharmapuri. The role of such federations is to provide fora for interaction and networking, resolution of conflicts among members of SAGs, disseminate information to SAGs, take up community action programmes that cannot be accomplished by individual SAGs and lobby with the government and other institutions in support of the poor.

Each SAG is represented by two members, at least one of whom must attend the federation's monthly meetings to present monthly reports of their groups and the action plans for the next month. Member SAGs coordinate credit programmes. Criteria for SAG enrolment in a federation is that each member SAG should have a record of proper functioning for at least six months, have up to 20 active members and should have its own bank account.

Resource Centre

The Resource Centre Management Committee (RCMC), comprising representatives of CBOs, mainly SAGs, manages Resource Centres (RCs) set up by MYRADA-Plan. Each RC has up to 120 CBOs as members. Each CBO pays a monthly fee and is assessed annually to ensure that it maintains certain standards of performance and maturity, or else it loses its RC membership. Each RC has a separate office, a separate account, a financial management system and a full time RC Executive Manager (generally someone with at least 10 years' experience working in MYRADA). The Manager reports to the RCMC and is supported by community resource persons selected by the CBOs.

It is the RCMC's responsibility to create links between SAGs, the government and private sector institutions, including banks and Sanghamitra, the micro-finance institution of MYRADA; build capacity; resolve conflicts; disseminate information on agriculture, markets, health and employment opportunities; organise health camps, set up programmes for poverty alleviation, programmes for the aged, children, street children, the physically handicapped and orphans and to offer internet services.

Sources of Income

Sources of income of the Resource Centres are admission and annual membership charges of CBOs, fee for services, external consultancies and training, rental for use of space and equipment and donations. Services to non-members include arranging field visits, especially to government and NGO training institutes, offering a tally package to maintain shop accounts in the area, marketing and support for senior citizens.

Children's Club

Children's Club members are between 7 and 16 years old. The members save money to run their own organisations. They focus on education, sports and health issues, provide books and stationery for "bright" children, run a library, arrange one field trip a year and celebrate birthdays of members. The members have made their own membership rules. These include the following—each child must attend school, be disciplined and clean, attend their weekly meeting and be on time and take responsibility to educate other children on their rights and responsibilities.

The members help maintain classrooms and sanitation facilities in school, and encourage every child in the village, including drop-outs, to attend school. They also plant and protect trees, maintain the village environment, ensure proper utilisation of the library, toys and games and mobilise contributions from members and their parents. Two children selected from each Children's Club represent their club at the federation. At federation meetings, children discuss the activities of their club, as well as various other subjects concerning environment, land and people of the country etc.

Grassroots Developmental Works of CBOs

The 73rd Constitutional Amendment Act, 1992 provided a three-tier system of Panchayati Raj for all States with a population of more than 2 million, thus promoting people's initiatives in self-governance and popular participation in developmental activities. The CBOs provide support to the Gram Panchayats (GPs) in implementing such development projects as health awareness camps, providing access to health care services, promotion of use of toilets etc.

CBOs participate in Gram Panchayat elections, encourage participation in Gram Sabhas (GSs), question and assess the development works of GPs and help GPs conduct surveys of people below the poverty line.

Children's Club members participate confidently in meetings of the school development monitoring committee and share their opinions in the presence of adults. They also approach the GPs with their problems.

Weaknesses of CBOs

Sustainability of CBOs is an area of concern. RCs were created to address this problem. It was thought that with the support of RCs, it would be possible for the SAGs to manage their group activities even after MYRADA withdrew from the scene. But it seems that the groups will still face various problems, some of which are as follows:

- Though the poor have access to institutional credit, marketing opportunities for local products are limited.
- Few women participate in SDMC meetings and some SAG women members hesitate to attend the Gram Sabha as they face resistance from their husbands.
- CBO members do not take much interest in the functioning of GPs. With a few exceptions they do not lend support to

the GP in organizing Gram Sabha. SAG members interact with the GP only to get their names included in the Below Poverty Line (BPL) list.

- Some SAG members are interested only in savings and lending, not in village development work and are not involved in the implementation of development work done by the panchayats.
- Since most children are first-generation learners, parents are not adequately supportive of their educational needs.

Case Studies

Institution-building is a core MYRADA activity. Institutions such as SAGs ensure the involvement of people in the process of their own development and in taking control of their own lives. The following case studies illustrate the role of SAGs in confidence-building and empowerment activities.

SAG Meetings

When MYRADA-Plan started work in Kelamangalam, a panchayat town in Dharmapuri district, people did not cooperate in organising SAGs, nor did the women join these groups. Most women of Kelamangalam work as coolies in the neighbouring village, Thamandarapalli, where MYRADA had already initiated the process. The women visited the homes of SAG members in Thamandarapalli and saw for themselves the benefits of organizing SAGs. On May 13, 1995 the women of Kelamangalam formed a SAG. Named as Maramma, the group started with 35 members from different castes and communities: OBCs, SCs, STs, and Muslims etc. Three years later, Maramma was divided into two for better management: Maramma with 14 members and Om Shakthi with 15 members.

Maramma SAG borrowed Rs. 2.4 lakh from the Swarnajayanti Gram Swarozgar Yojana (SGSY), which gives assistance to rural BPL families for self-employment. Out of this 12 members took loans to purchase cattle. They now supply 80 litres of milk per day to Krishna Dairy in Athibele, at the rate of Rs. 8 per litre, and earn Rs. 17,000 to Rs. 18,000 per month. The other members used the loan money to construct houses. Besides, Maramma SAG got a revolving fund of Rs. 25,000, from which five members took Rs.

5,000 each for agricultural purposes and for purchasing sheep. When these five members repaid the loan, other members became eligible for loans. Maramma SAG saved Rs. 70,000.

Om Shakthi SAG also got an SGSY loan of Rs. 2.6 lakh, in 2003. Thirteen members took loans to purchase cattle and two members to construct houses—Rs.35,000 for each member. Each member also received Rs.10,000 as subsidy. The members with cattle, supply milk to Nilgiri Dairy (Andhawadi). Om Shakthi SAG members got Rs. 25,000 as a revolving fund, which was shared between five members to start flower business, sheep rearing and cattle rearing. The SAG took Rs.1.5 lakh from Sanhagmitra to repair old houses. Each member got Rs. 30,000. They pay a monthly premium of Rs. 1,500 to the bank. Om Shakthi SAG has saved Rs. 90,000.

Maramma and Om Shakthi are also involved in developmental works. These two groups along with the villagers contributed Rs. 3,000 and took the remaining amount from MYRADA to construct the compound of the village school. MYRADA helped the school form a Parent-Teacher Association (PTA). SAG members are a part of the PTA. Each of the three SAGs gave Rs. 1,000, and the villagers together gave Rs. 7,000, to the PTA.

Om Shakthi SAG has helped three orphans with books and clothes. Initially, for want of a proper place, SAG meetings used to be held in temples. With the cooperation of MYRADA, SAG got Rs.2.28 lakh to construct a community hall. They contacted the local MLA and got a power connection for the hall.

Women's Empowerment

Manjula of Shankarapura village studied up to Pre-University Course (PUC). Soon after, she fell in love with Chandrashekar, whose family was well off but did not approve of the match. Manjula's parents sold four acres of their land to get money for the wedding and Chandrashekar's family agreed to the marriage. Within 10 months of the marriage, however, when Manjula's pregnancy was full term, Chandrashekar died of an electric shock. Manjula delivered a son. To support herself and her child, she worked in a shop, but was forced to leave her job as the villagers, particularly women, gossipped nastily about her.

In 2003, Manjula got a job as a library in-charge, at a salary of Rs. 700. She organised 12 members from her street and started a

SAG. A Children's Club leader, Basha, introduced Manjula to MYRADA. MYRADA-Plan appointed her a Children's Club promoter and later referred her for Training of Trainers (ToT). After ToT, she began training women's groups. Today she is respected not only by the people of her own village but also by people of other villages. Her son is now in the 2nd standard. Thus Manjula's association with MYRADA as well as her engagement in economically meaningful activities made her empowered.

Mixed Group Discussion (SAG and Panchayat Members)

Bennangooru village comes under the Navajyothi CMRC which works in 45 villages, with 14 panchayats and 210 SAGs. Bennangooru village has five SAGs. A mixed group discussion was conducted in Bennangooru village on July 21, 2006 with 22 participants.

Outcomes

Before the MYRADA intervention, villagers were not involved in developmental work; women were confined to their homes; there was no income-generation programme and the local credit market was monopolized by the money lenders who used to charge interest at the rate of 10 per cent per month.

MYRADA intervention changed the life of the villagers. Women joined SAGs, started saving and got loans at the rate of 2 per cent interest per month. Most children go to school, and all five SAGs got loans of Rs. 6 to 8 lakh for economic activities. Women participate in MYRADA-Plan programmes for antenatal check-ups. They are now sufficiently aware of health issues such as breastfeeding, nutrition and safe delivery. One SAG member said: "After forming SAGs, we got loans for agriculture and to buy cattle and sheep".

GP President Venkatachalapathi said, "Women's participation in the GS has increased. Women concentrate on basic needs such as water, street lighting, drainage, roads etc. They participate in GP elections and some have been elected with the support of SAG members."

The village school is situated on the main road, which is an accident-prone area. In 1996, worried parents and villagers decided to construct a compound wall at a cost of Rs. 50,000 around the school to protect the children. Each SAG gave Rs. 1,200, the GP

President gave Rs. 1,000, and the teachers also pitched in, making a total of Rs. 25,000. The balance was contributed by MYRADA, and the wall was constructed. The PTA, villagers and teachers contributed Rs. 10,000 and MYRADA contributed Rs.10,000 towards school developmental works. Rupees 20,000 is kept in the bank as a fixed deposit.

SAG members and MYRADA saved a huge old tree near the bus stop and built a concrete platform around it as well as benches for passengers. The community contributed the money and the work was done by men's SAG. The GP President and the community contributed Rs. 8,500 and MYRADA provided the material to drill borewells and construct a *pucca* floor around them.

SAG member Lakshmamma said: "For Women's Day celebration (March 8), we invited the High Court Judge, the Deputy Superintendent of Police (DSP), Members of the Legislative Assembly (MLAs) and MYRADA's Project Officer with the help of the GP president. We collected Rs. 600 from each SAG to buy gifts for the chief guests, while the GP president paid for the food and *shamiana*. SAG members from four surrounding villages also participated."

After the formation of the Children's Club, children have become more interested in education and sports. The extra income earned from selling vegetables grown in kitchen gardens is utilized for children's education. Some SAG members have opened their own shops to sell flowers, vegetables etc.

Children's Clubs Federation (CCF)

More than 300 members of Children's Clubs in the area are foster children. There are 15 CCFs in the area, one in each cluster or sector. Each Children's Club sends two representatives to the CCF.

Children's Club in Kundamaranapalli Village

Kundamaranapalli village, with 184 households, has one Anganwadi, one panchayat union, one primary school, and one high school with 167 students. It also has the Netaji Children's Club with 25 members who elect a "promoter" from among themselves and hold weekly meetings to discuss skills, health sports, etc. The Netaji Children's Club members dream of making their club the best in Dharmapuri.

Outcomes

Children's Club members provide support to their parents in household works—getting water, cleaning and growing vegetables in the kitchen gardens in the vacant homestead lands. The children use the income they get from selling vegetables to buy notebooks, pens, etc., and set aside a bit to go for camps and excursions.

For instance, Vinay Kumar grows brinjal and Ambrish grows beans—both earn Rs. 30 a month—while Satish grows pumpkin and brinjal earns Rs. 45 a month. In 2005, the children visited the Vidhana Soudha, the Iskcon (International Society for Krishna Consciousness) temple, and the Vishveswaraiah Museum in Bangalore.

Members visit the homes of children who have dropped out of school, and persuade parents to send them back to school.

Members went for a *jatha* (small band of volunteers on a mobilisation campaign) to create awareness among villagers on health, education, pulse polio programme etc.

The Children's Club members also conduct village surveys and go to the GP office to discuss problems with elected representatives. As a result of such initiative, the village street lights and taps get repaired. GP members give priority to the children's work. Children conducted a survey to ascertain the infrastructural facilities available in the villages.

In 2004-05, the club members complained to the Block Development Officer that the veterinary doctor did not regularly visit the hospital. The doctor was suspended and a new veterinary doctor was appointed who has proved to be very punctual.

Members attend the MYRADA-Plan three-day training camp every year and learn such skills as paper-cutting, paper-folding, doll-making etc.

Children's Club in Kelaipasandra Village

Kelaipasandra village has 100 households (SC/OBC/BC), one overhead tank and four borewells out of which but only one is in good condition. For primary school education, the children of this village go to nearby villages, Kothanuru and Benaspalli. The village school has 450 students from 6th to 10th class. The village has three Children's Clubs: Bhagat Singh Children's Club, Ramakrishna Children's Club and Rajiv Gandhi Children's Club.

Outcomes

The Bhagat Singh Children's Club, formed on January 1, 2004, has 25 members. The club sends its representative to the monthly panchayat meetings; shares its report on activities in the monthly SAG meetings, participates in the government's mass literacy awareness campaigns and mobilises resources to support education of poor children. It helped raise contributions for the victims of the Kargil War, the Gujarat earthquake and Orissa floods.

At their weekly meetings, members discuss village needs, such as streetlights and repair of taps and then approach the GP President. Their suggestions are taken seriously and acted upon.

Members participate actively in the pulse polio programme and eye camps. They take the help of the PTA to convince parents of school drop-outs to send their children back to school. They were successful with four drop-outs: Kavitha, Nagaraj, Nagamani and Murali. The children visit the village library once a week to read and help the panchayat maintain the library. They work on kitchen gardens. The children arrange sports events on Republic Day and Independence Day every year.

Community Governance in Collaboration with Local Government

Three out of four residents of Bennangooru village are farmers and the rest are labourers (coolies). The farmers grow maize, rice, ragi, groundnut, tomato and beans. Only 10 per cent of these have irrigation facilities, the rest depend on rain.

Before the GP was set up, village leaders were in charge of village development. Now the GP collects house tax—Rs. 11 for a small tiled-roof house and up to Rs. 150 for a bigger house, collected annually. There is one overhead tank, with a capacity of 100,000 litres of water. Public taps are free, but for an individual tap connection, villagers have to pay Rs. 1,000 as deposit and Rs. 30 as monthly charges. (In Bennangooru village, only 10 houses have individual tap connections.)

The SAG concept has helped villagers. They can now send their children to school and afford three meals a day. Confident and aware, the villagers have taken up developmental works. When MYRADA withdraws from this area, the villagers will still be able to get work done through the Jana Jagruthi Resource Centre.

The village has five women's SAGs. Initially, Muslim women did not join the groups, but since the year 2000 they have also formed SAGs. Awareness among villagers has grown.

GP members are involved in school developmental work and cooperate both with SAGs as well as members of the Children's Club who meet once a week. MYRADA has started Scouts Programme in the school. Children participate in sports and cultural activities, and have won State-level awards.

The GP gets a newspaper under the government's Arevalikum Akshara Jyothi programme. Villagers read the paper and get books from the library. Incidentally one village has provided same space for the location of library. Villagers are aware about birth and death registration, done through the Village Accounts Officer, who issues a certificate within a reasonable period of time. MYRADA ran a night school for five years, and now many of the villagers can sign their names and also read to some extent. A bus stand was built with the help of the GP, MYRADA and SAG groups. The men's group contributed labour for the construction of the bus stand.

Sustainability of CBOs

It is clear that MYRADA-Plan interventions have helped develop individual capacity, enhanced group cohesiveness for developmental activities and encouraged the involvement of people, including children, in identifying problems and finding solutions. As a part of the withdrawal strategy, institutions have been set up that will ensure sustainability and self-reliance and contribute to the creation of a vibrant rural civil society. However, there are some problems that need to be addressed.

In most areas, men still dominate and object to the involvement of women in village development activities. In remote areas, many are illiterate and unable to understand the concept and benefits of SAGs. Although CBOs are involved in income-generating projects like manufacturing soft toys, nylon rope, garland, greeting cards, tamarind processing etc., they do not have established markets for the products.

Status of Panchayats

The State has a long history of local self-government, both rural and urban. Following the 73rd Constitutional Amendment Act,

1992, the Tamil Nadu Government enacted a legislation in 1994 to create the three-tier Panchayati Raj System.

A Gram Panchayat (GP) can be set up in villages with a population of more than 500; if the population of these villages is less than 500, there is a common GP for two or more villages. A GP can have between five and 15 members. Ward Members and the GP President are elected directly by the villagers for a term of five years. The GP Vice President is elected from among the elected GP Ward members. GPs get financial resources directly from the State and Central Governments.

The Gram Sabha is an important element of the panchayat system. It provides an opportunity to every adult to participate in the affairs of the panchayat. All registered voters are members of the GS. Under the Act, the GP must convene the GS at least four times a year. The GP President is the presiding officer of GS meetings. GS approval is necessary for the panchayat's budget proposals and its annual plan. The audited statement of accounts of the GP has to be placed in the GS meeting. Beneficiaries for government schemes are to be selected only in the GS. Officials from government offices related to development are observers in the GS and report the proceedings to the Inspector of Panchayats.

Each development Block has a Panchayat Union (PU). The PU Chairperson and Vice Chairperson are elected by Panchayat Council members, who are elected directly by the people.

There is one District Panchayat (DP) for every district and members are elected directly by voters. The DP Chairperson and Vice Chairperson are elected indirectly by and from among DP members.

The major sources of revenue for the panchayats are the house, profession and vehicle taxes. Revenue is also generated from fees paid by markets, cart stands and remunerative enterprises. The government gives a grant matching the revenue collected from house tax. PRIs are not economically strong. Most of their resources come from the Centrally sponsored or State sponsored development schemes and the Central Finance Commission Grants. Thus, their autonomy is limited. Yet, PRIs have brought governance closer to the people, especially for the marginalised sections of society. The elected representatives are approachable and the GS is a forum for registering the voice of the common people.

The Tamil Nadu Government plans to give more powers to local bodies and to train panchayat members. NGOs and CBOs may strengthen the panchayat system by providing support to them in various ways. They may also make useful contribution in building capacity of the panchayat leaders.

Traditional Panchayats in Tamil Nadu

Traditional panchayats and caste panchayats still exist in different parts of Tamil Nadu. In many rural areas, such panchayats have been operating side by side with formal panchayats (statutory panchayats). At many places, village communities thought of formal PRIs as an imposition. They had their own structural arrangements to manage their community affairs by following norms evolved over a period of time. These arrangements were, however, feudal, elitist, patriarchal and caste-based. In some rural areas, traditional panchayats and statutory panchayats overlap and have developed "functional linkages" with each other. Sometimes, this "synergy between the traditional panchayat and the formal panchayat has enabled the formal panchayat to perform very well" (G. Palanithurai, *Synergisation of Traditional Panchayat with Formal Panchayati Raj System in Managing the Community Affairs*, Gandhigram, 2003).

Case Studies of Presidents/Vice Presidents: Kundamaranapalli and Mallasandra GPs

Profile of Gram Panchayats

Table 10.3: Profile of Kundamaranapalli GP

Sl. No.	*Particulars*	*Total Number*	
1.	Number of villages	8	
2.	Number of elected representatives	9	
3.	Population	4,842	
		Male	Female
		2,420	2,422
4.	Schools	6	

Table 10.4: Profile of Mallasandra GP

Sl. No.	*Particulars*	*Total Number*	
1.	Number of villages	8	
2.	Number of elected representatives	103	
3.	Population	3,222	
		Male	Female
		1,705	1,517
4.	Schools	6	

The population of Kundamaranapalli is 4,842, of whom 2,890 are voters. The GP area has 780 houses, four primary schools, two high schools, two balawadis, five factories and four borewells. Roads are being upgraded. Five "watermen" are responsible for supplying drinking water to villagers. Tax collection is 100 per cent. This GP area has eight villages, and is divided into two Blocks—Bennangooru Block with 1,392 voters, Mallasandra Block with 1,318 voters. GP collects house tax and profession tax. GS is held four times a year: January 26, May 1, August 15 and October 2. Participation by women has increased after SAGs were formed. The Panchayat has five accounts: (a) GP Fund (Rs. 1 lakh) to pay honorarium and salaries of GP President, members and the GP staff. (b) Funds from Eleventh Finance Commission for providing water facilities; (c) SGRY money for roads, drainage, community building and repair; (d) State Government Scheme for group house construction for SC/ST and other poor people; and (e) Water Supply Account. The GP collects tax to be utilised only for water supply.

Chinnamma: A Member of SHG and a GP President

Thirteen years ago Chinnamma joined a MYRADA SHG in Kundamaranapalli. She participated in training programmes, started saving and helped women of backward classes. In the 1996 panchayat election, the seat of the president of the GP was reserved for SC women and the villagers selected Chinnamma as their candidate. Though not very knowledgeable about GP activities, Chinnamma got 664 votes and became GP President.

After her election, Chinnamma acquainted herself with the functions of the GP and then plunged into developmental works. In the 2001 elections, Chinnamma again contested the elections and won with 760 votes.

Under Chinnamma, the GP is functioning well. She collects information on BPL families with the help of SAGs. Earlier, the GP gave priority to street lighting, sanitary works, etc. but now the focus is also on rain water harvesting, prevention of child marriage etc. The GP executes various government schemes for welfare and development of girl children.

There was a library in the village. Though the local language is Tamil, most of the books in the GP library were in Telugu. MYRADA provided Tamil books and now villagers have begun using the library.

A number of NGOs including MYRADA are working in the area and the GP has close links with them, particularly with MYRADA. With the support of the latter, it has been possible to construct a community hall and provide financial assistance to the school.

Chinnamma is a strong advocate of decentralization. According to her it improves the delivery of basic services and enables villagers to solve their problems locally. "But I am unhappy to find that the panchayat gets little cooperation from different government departments' she says.

Ravi, Gram Panchayat Vice President

After getting a Diploma in Mechanical Engineering, Ravi actively worked for the Arevaliku Government Scheme—an adult education programme to benefit 288 villagers and the Rajiv Gandhi Water Project. Thereafter, villagers encouraged him to contest the GP elections, and he was elected Vice President.

Talking about infrastructure, Ravi said that the panchayat had provided borewells, drainage and taps, but since the borewell water was contaminated, villagers contracted various diseases and stopped using it. Ravi provided water from his own borewell to villagers, as a result of which his own three-acre land became dry.

After MYRADA-Plan introduced SAGs in the village, the groups, with the help of the community, provided borewells, constructed a community hall and school compounds, and formed PTAs. Money for school development was put in a joint bank account in the name of the headmaster and GP President.

Both Ravi and Chinnamma encourage women to participate in the GS meetings, which are held four times in a year actively. Other villagers also involve themselves in developmental works and discuss their needs such as roads, electricity, cleaning of ponds etc. with their MLA.

> *"While electing GP representatives",* Ravi feels *"we should choose capable candidates. If a capable person is elected, then it will be easy to do a lot for development of the area."*

Bennangooru : Gram Panchayat President of Mallasandra GP

The GP President has had a difficult personal life. For quite some time he was out of the village working in distant places for livelihood. In 1987 he returned to his native village, Bennangooru. In 1988 he purchased land and constructed a house in the village and started his own hotel business. The villagers belonging to all communities recognised his virtues and in the 1999 election, they elected him to the post of GP President. He was re-elected in the 2001 election.

The President not only has a rapport with the officials but also SAG members. He also has gained confidence of local MLA and MP. As a result the government officials always discuss GP schemes with the GP President before implementation. GP is involved in implementation of SJSY under which loans and subsidy are given to SHG groups after being graded as per instructions of the government. In 2006, five MYRADA sponsored SAGs got loans.

Sometimes GP gets funds from the MP and MLA. Such funds are utilized for building SC/ST houses, roads, borewells and school buildings.

Conclusion

MYRADA has promoted people's institutions in the district of Dharmapuri. These institutions are emerging as a power base, capable of taking decisions affecting their lives. This process of empowerment has enabled many women to become elected panchayat members and benefit from the system.

Participation of SAG members has increased GS attendance. The quality of discussion in the GS has improved. Collaborative developmental activities between SAGs, PUs and panchayats have increased, resulting into avoidance of conflicts between different institutions.

Cooperation between CBOs and the panchayat was evident in the study area. Efforts should be made to include capacity-building programmes for elected panchayat members. The panchayats could have regular meetings with the CBOs to evaluate their development programmes. The CBOs can monitor the development works in their areas and report to the panchayats. These interactions will strengthen their relationship and improve the functioning of PRIs. Therefore, a formal CBO panchayat collaboration should be established to speed up development.

11

Karnataka

K. Subha and *B.S. Bhargava*

Introduction

Mysore district of Karnataka was the capital of the Wodeyar Empire and is now emerging as an information technology hub. The new highway and infrastructure corridor up to Bangalore will bring in more investments and jobs. The population of Mysore district is 2,641,027 as per the 2001 Census. Literacy rates for males and females are 62 and 49 per cent respectively. Taluk HD Kote was selected for the purpose of this study.

HD Kote is located south-west of Mysore. It is predominantly rural and people are mostly engaged in agriculture and animal husbandry. Table 11.1 gives a demographic profile of the taluk.

There are several Non Governmental Organizations (NGOs) in the taluk including Mysore Resettlement and Development Agency (MYRADA), Swami Vivekananda Youth Movement (SVYM), Jeetha Vimukthi Karmikaru (JIVIKA) and the Spoorthi Centre. MYRADA is the largest NGO in the taluk.

Approach and Methodology

The study was conducted using participatory research and evaluation methodologies and the case study approach. A questionnaire was used to interview the main stakeholders, Block members, panchayat members and residents including a sample of women, men and adolescent children.

Table 11.1: Demographic and Socio-Economic Profile of Taluk HD Kote

Gram Panchayats	32
Hoblis (Revenue Circles)	5
Area	1618 sq. km.
Population	2,42,615
Males	1,23,042
Females	1,19,573
Rural	2,30,572
Urban	12,043
SC	55, 818
ST	11, 321
Sex Ratio	1000: 972
Cultivable area	69,996 ha.
Irrigation source	Kapila dam
Households with sanitary toilets	44,715
Households with access to safe drinking water within 0.5 km	12,198
BPL households	14,755

Research methodology included desk study of documents, in-depth structured interviews with selected stakeholders, questionnaire survey, Focus Group Discussions (FGDs) and field visits.

Out of 32 Gram Panchayats (GPs), four were selected for the study—Annur, Matakere, Bidarahalli and Hebbalaguppe. In these GPs the team met women's groups, the president, vice president, secretary of GPs and village leaders, held FGDs, and attended meetings of Children's Clubs, federations and boards of directors of MYRADA.

Secondary data was collected from the MYRADA-Plan district office, HD Kote project office, selected community managed resource centres and panchayat offices. In addition to the structured tools of data collection, interviews with concerned and knowledgeable persons were also conducted.

Role of MYRADA

An account of the history of MYRADA, its mission, objectives and the mode of functioning has been given in the chapter on Tamil Nadu. As mentioned in the previous chapter, MYRADA gives special emphasis on building people's own institutions. To achieve this objective, it has created several CBOs and has tried to strengthen them by developing their self-management capacity. In HD Kote, there are two types of CBOs—Self-help Affinity Groups (SAG) and Children's Clubs. There are 674 SAGs and 214 Children's Clubs in the area.

Self Help Affinity Groups (SAGs)

In 1984-85, MYRADA promoted credit management groups for providing credit to the rural poor. In 1987, these groups were renamed as Self-help Affinity Groups (SAGs). In the same year, NABARD provided a grant of Rs.10 lakh and this grant was utilized for capacity building of the groups.

SAGs are involved in borrowing and giving loans and a few have got a revolving fund from MYRADA or the Zila Panchayat. SAGs generally work closely with the concerned GP. All SAG members have ration-cards and some have Birla Sun Life Insurance Policy. Even though, the focus of the groups is on credit management, MYRADA puts much emphasis on enhancing the self-management capacity of the group members.

Federations

Federations are the next level of SAGs. There are 23 federations of SAGs in the Taluk. They strengthen individual groups and review their operations. Federations also help in resolving conflicts, disseminate information to SAGs, take up community programmes and lobby with the government for pro-poor programmes. Each federation can have between 15 and 25 SAGs and two members from each group are nominated to the federation. These members elect the office bearers. To join a federation, a SAG must have the following:

- Stable and voluntary membership of up to 20 members;
- Regular meetings;
- Existence for six months before joining the federation;
- Regular savings;
- A well-managed common fund and a bank account in the group's name with regular transactions;
- Maintenance of books and accounts;
- Rules for governance; and
- Rotational leadership.

At least one of the two representatives from each SAG should attend the federation's monthly meeting regularly to ensure continuity. In the meeting they present a monthly report of their SAG and an action plan for the coming month. The representatives also report to their SAGs on the proceedings of the federation. Member SAGs coordinate credit-plus activities and programmes.

Community Managed Resource Centre (CMRC)

There are six CMRCs in the Taluk, each managed by the Resource Centre Management Committee with representatives of CBOs, mainly SAGs. Each centre covers a specific area and up to 120 CBOs can join a Resource Centre as members. However, these CBO have to attain certain standards of performance and maturity before joining a Centre. The CBOs pay a monthly fee to retain membership and are assessed or rated yearly to ensure that their standards have not declined.

The Centres have their own office, account and financial management system. Each is managed by a full time person who, till now, has been a MYRADA employee with at least 10 years of experience. This person is the executive head and is supported by several community resource persons selected by the CBOs. Each Centre has evolved according to local needs.

Each Centre keeps information relevant to SAGs, the public, youth, government and NGOs. They build linkages between SAGs, financial institutions, insurance companies, the government and the private sector. The Centres also provide capacity building, audit and conflict resolution services. They provide daily information on farm prices, health and employment. The Centres organize health camps, animal health camps and run poverty alleviation programmes. They oversee programmes related to the aged, children, street children and handicapped.

MYRADA has set up the Centre of Institutional Development and Organizational Reforms (CIDOR) to enhance the capacity of CMRCs. CIDOR acts as training centre to CMRC. They also support SAGs by auditing their activities. They assist in resource mobilization.

Non-members especially the government, NGOs and CMRCs are also provided services by CMRCs.

Children's Clubs

The clubs work for the rights of children by creating awareness among them about education, sports and health. Some of them run libraries and their members save money to help run the clubs. The clubs also create awareness among adults about child rights, hygiene and family planning. The clubs have addressed various social issues such as casteism. Clubs support talented students by providing study material. They also arrange a study visit for members once a year to book fairs. These clubs have their own rules and regulations. Membership is open to children between 7 and 16 years of age. Children should be disciplined, punctual and clean. All have to attend weekly meetings.

Children's Club Federations

Above individual clubs, there are federations to which two members are selected from each club. Each member presents his/her club's activities in federation meetings. Children are involved in creating awareness about the environment, planting and protecting of trees, ensuring discipline and maintenance of classrooms, sanitation in schools, ensuring 100 per cent attendance in schools, personal hygiene, utilization of the library and toys, raising contributions from club members and parents and motivating the drop-outs to rejoin school.

Developmental Works of CBOs

The members of CBOs have been elected to PRIs. Besides, CBOs also play a part in developmental activities and work with GPs to implement village-level schemes. They mobilize resources to conduct health camps, provide sanitation facilities and conduct trainings on accounting. Children's Clubs also take part in these activities and present their issues to the GPs. CBOs also monitor the work of the GP.

Weaknesses of CBOs

The greatest problem is how SAGs will sustain themselves after MYRADA phases out of the region. Even though in some cases SAGs help the GP in implementing the developmental activities, the members are very dependent on MYRADA not only in terms of financial stability but also for chalking out the action plan for them. The CMRCs are a step in this direction but they have not developed to a point where they can be self-sufficient.

As discussed above the CMRC tries to address various issues ranging from finance to conflict resolution and providing information regarding the government schemes. In other words the CMRC under the guidance of MYRADA is still involved in the practice of 'handholding'. Hence if the NGO exits, the CMRC as well as SAGs may not be sustainable.

Status of Panchayats

Karnataka has a three-tier structure as envisaged by the 73rd Constitutional Amendment. There are Gram Panchayats (GPs) at the village level, Taluk Panchayats (TPs) at the middle level, and Zila Panchayats (ZPs) at the district level. Their functions have been specified in three schedules in the Panchayati Raj Act of 1993 and these institutions are responsible for implementing 29 developmental subjects. Though funds and functionaries have been transferred, they are still not financially viable to fulfil their obligations.

Functions of Gram Panchayats

GPs have the following functions:

- Revising and collecting taxes, rates and fees periodically;
- Providing sanitary latrines to at least 10 per cent of households every year and achieving full coverage as early as possible. Construction and maintenance of adequate number of community latrines;
- Maintaining water supply system;
- Ensuring universal enrollment of children in primary school;
- Achieving universal immunization of children;
- Ensuring prompt registration and reporting of births and deaths;
- Construction, repair and maintenance of public roads;
- Removing encroachments on public roads and pubiic places;
- Providing adequate number of street lights and paying

electricity charges regularly;

- Culling of rabid and stray dogs;
- Maintenance of all community assets;
- Maintenance of records relating to population census, crop census, cattle census, census of unemployed persons and census of persons below poverty line; and
- Earmarking of places away from the residential areas for dumping of refuse and manure.

Revenue of Panchayats

Within the limits of the Panchayat area every Gram Panchayat can levy taxes on buildings and land that is not subject to agricultural assessment. They can also levy tax on entertainment other than cinema shows, vehicles, advertisements and hoardings, pilgrim fees, market fees, fees for registration and grazing of cattle and entry charges on vehicles for public events. There exists a Gram Panchayat Fund comprising taxes, fees and other locally generated income. All payments to the GP from the government and gifts also go into this account.

The State Government gives an annual grant of Rs. 5 lakh to each GP to enable it to meet electricity charges, maintain water supply, sanitation and other facilities.

In 2002, the State Act was amended to allow setting up of Ward Sabhas that had the power to approve the panchayat budget and programmes, select beneficiaries, and prepare a plan of action. Provisions have been made to ensure that SCs, STs, backward classes and women participate in the Ward and Gram Sabhas. Candidates have to declare their assets and the State Election Commission manages the elections. PRIs have been brought under the purview of the Lokayukta (Ombudsman at State level).

The State government has decided to transfer 176 State schemes to the district sector with additional funds. The government is also considering the idea of creating a separate cadre for panchayats.

These steps are expected to transfer sufficient finances, functions and functionaries to the PRIs. In the given situation, participation of local communities becomes even more crucial in ensuring good local governance.

Profile of Selected GPs

Annur GP

This covers 12 villages and consists of 18 elected members with six women, four of whom belong to SAGs. The total population is 6,005 of which 3,003 are males and 3,002 are females. There are 42 SAGs and three federations, six lower primary schools, five higher primary schools, one high school and nine Anganwadi centres in this GP.

Bidarahalli GP

This GP covers a population of 8,385, of which 4,155 are females and 4,229 are males. There are 1,714 BPL families. The GP has five primary schools, four higher primary schools, one high school and seven Anganwadi centres. Most people are self-employed with agriculture and petty business being the main occupation. Some are daily wage labourers while others are engaged in their traditional occupations. The panchayat has contributed Rs.10,000 to three SAGs and they help the panchayat in household survey and collecting BPL data. There are 49 SAGs in this GP. The panchayat has 20 members, out of which 8 are women. Out of 8, 6 women members are from SAGs.

Hebbalaguppe GP

Hebbalaguppe comprises four villages and has 17 members with seven women, three of whom are from SAGs. There are 11 SAGs and three Children's Clubs. There are three lower primary schools, two higher primary schools and one high school, four Anganwadi centres and one private high school. The total population is 6,187 with 3,235 males and 2,952 females.

B. Matakere GP

This Panchayat covers 22 villages and has one elected representative from each village. There are eight women, five of whom are from SAGs. The GP has 15 primary schools, one high school and 10 anganwadi centres. The total population is 9,924 with 2,285 families.

In the four GPs which were selected we could not identify any active caste/traditional panchayats. MYRADA has trained 864 newly elected PRI members. Through such training programmes, the knowledge and skill of the members has improved in respect of such subjects as development programmes that panchayats are supposed to implement, mobilization of local resources for development, rights and responsibilities of members etc.

The Gram Sabha meets once in three months. Panchayat members inform SAGs and the CMRC members about these meetings to help in motivating people to attend the Gram Sabha. Women's participation is high, at 50 per cent. Gram Sabhas discuss, among other things, issues like drinking water, electricity, sanitation, street lights, BPL lists and selection of beneficiaries.

Tax collection is around 50-60 per cent and is done collectively by the panchayat members, the secretary and village leaders. MYRADA also emphasizes the importance of paying taxes in time at its SAG meetings. The Panchayat conducts an annual social audit called *Jamabandi*, executed by the president, vice president, elected members, secretary and nodal officer.

MYRADA's intervention has improved public awareness about development and helped in successful completion of village development programmes. The Panchayat discusses new projects with MYRADA. It can be said that in this area PRIs, NGOs and CBOs are working together.

Weaknesses of the PRIs

The elected members are unaware of schemes launched by the State and Central Governments. Ward Sabhas are not conducted regularly in any of the GPs. Villagers are not aware of the *Jamabandi* process. SAG members feel meetings are dominated by the influential people in the village and they choose beneficiaries for housing schemes. The fact that there is one secretary for two GPs also hampers development because he/she is not always available. The secretaries do not always share information with elected representatives. The panchayat's tax collection is very low.

The allotment of funds under various heads during 2005-06 in the selected panchayats was as follows:

Table 11.2: Allotment of Funds under Different Sources to Selected Gram Panchayats, 2005-06

(in Rupees)

Gram Panchayat	*Sanitation*	*Water, Borewell Pump Repair, Watchman Salary, Electricity*	*Road Construction*	*Housing*
Annur	2,00,000.00	1,50,000.00	4,50,000.00	—
Bidarahalli	31,501.00	5,00,000.00	—	8,00,000.00
Hebbalakuppe	70,000.00	1,50,000.00	85,000.00	—
B. Matakere	3,60,000.00	6,49,688.00	—	—
SGSY, NREGS and NRHM grants to these GPs				
Gram Panchayat	*SGSY*	*National Rural Employment Guarantee Scheme*	*National Rural Health Mission*	*Library*
Annur	1,25,000.00	20,000.00	—	—
Bidarahalli	6,00,000.00	30,000.00	—	12,500.00
Hebbalakuppe	20,000.00	60,000.00	—	—
B. Matakere	2,70,000.00	25,000.00	10,500.00	—

Source: Panchayat Records.

Case Studies

Ankala Parameshwari SAG

The Ankala Parameshwari SAG was started in the year 1991 under MYRADA's guidance. It has 15 members. Initially, its members used to save Rs. 5, but they now save Rs. 500 a month. Members take loans ranging from Rs. 5,000 to Rs.35,000 a month for their traditional occupations or for setting up a new business.

Rajamma, a SAG member said she lost her husband early and took a loan of Rs. 2,000 from MYRADA to start a small business of manufacturing leaf plates. When she repaid this, she took another loan of Rs. 25,000 and started a kerosene dealership. Nagamma took a loan to start a curry powder business and now she makes 50 kg curry powder a week and earns Rs. 1,000-1,500 a month.

The SAG has helped members get loans at lower rates and has thus improved their socio-economic conditions. They sent Rs. 500 to support widows of the soldiers who died in Kargil. They also helped some cancer patients.

Vinayaka SAG

The success of SAGs inspired the unemployed youth of Tharanimanti and Beechanahalli villages to form a SAG for men called Vinayaka in July 2000. It started with 20 members but five left soon after. Since then, they have accumulated savings of Rs. 90,000 and got a loan from a bank. Loans are given at 2 per cent interest up to a maximum of Rs. 35,000.

All SAG members have toilets built with the support of MYRADA and the GP. The panchayat has also constructed toilets for 114 families for which it gave Rs. 2,000 per person and MYRADA, Rs. 750. The community or concerned individuals contribute labour. One of the SAG members took a loan of Rs. 35,000 to start a flour mill.

Akshaya Community Resource Centre

The federation under the Akshaya Community Resource Centre comprises 35 SAGs. At a meeting, one of the representatives of a SAG was well informed about the government schemes regarding sanitation and incentive to have girl child. He in turn shared this information with others saying that in his GP there is a scheme for providing financial assistance of Rs. 1,200 to each household for construction of toilets. Besides, government assistance is provided to the mothers if they give birth to a girl child at the rate of Rs.1,000 if born in hospital and Rs. 500, if born at home. In addition, the government deposits Rs.10,000 in the bank in the girl's name under the Sanghamitra scheme, which she can withdraw once she turns 18.

The federation monitors activities of the associated SAGs and mediates in conflicts. It also helps them in book keeping and recovery of loans. It trains members and arranges exposure visits. It tries to formulate plans of action for strengthening the groups. Earlier MYRADA used to fund the training programmes. But this practice has now been stopped. In order to make training self-financing, the federation charges Rs. 100 from SAGs as annual membership fees. Members of the federation are confident that they can continue working even after MYRADA withdraws.

Akshaya Community Managed Resource Centre (ACRC) is one of six centres of its kind in the HD Kote taluk. It has 35 SAGs and provides services for their growth and sustainability. There are also three federations, 14 children's Clubs and one Children's Club federation. The directors meet on the first day of every month to discuss SAG development issues, such as, strengthening the self-management capacity of the groups, their finance, resource mobilization, audit, life insurance, Children's Club and federation meetings, training and the Sanghamitra scheme. The board members felt confident about the sustainability of the centre.

The CMRC has its own bank account. With the help of a local NGO called SVYM, ACRC conducted health awareness programmes and camps. The St. Mary's School of Nursing has been running for the last one year in the taluk and the Board members requested it to reduce fees for SAG members.

ACRC supports member SAGs in auditing, linkages, dissemination of information and other matters. It is being developed in such a manner that in course of time it becomes substitute for MYRADA. CIDOR, an independent unit of MYRADA, will, however, continue to provide support to CMRCs once the parent NGO leaves the area.

Children's Clubs

The Shanthi Children's Club falls under the Kalpavruksha CMRC, Saragoor in Hebbalakuppe village. There is a school in this village offering education up to class 7. The club has 18 members and they are also members of the school parliament. These members attend the School Development and Monitoring Committee (SDMC) meetings.

The Nanjundeshwara Children's Club comes under the Kamadhenu CMRC and has 16 members. It is located in Tharanimanti village. The village has a school offering education up to class 7. The children meet weekly in the community hall. They have selected two members to represent the club at the federation. Club members actively participate in health camps and sanitation activities.

The activities of these clubs indicate that children collectively work towards attaining their rights to recreation, participation and development. The children are trained in leadership skills, public speaking, vision building and human values and they are not hesitant to speak up in the presence of teachers and adults.

The clubs distribute stationery to poor children, have savings, guide parents about hygiene and organize entertainment programmes for their members. They try to get drop-outs back into school and participate in *jathas*. This helps improve the village literacy levels.

Major Findings

In HD Kote, MYRADA, CBOs and Panchayats work in a well coordinated manner to implement development schemes. For instance, Children's Clubs and SAGs are involved in the pulse polio programme. MYRADA and the Zila Parishad jointly fund toilet construction while the community or beneficiary contributes labour. MYRADA trains local PRI representatives and runs an HIV and AIDS awareness programme for school children.

The NGO has raised awareness about child rights through paintings on primary school buildings. It has helped in increasing the number of teachers employed in schools and even pays their salary in some cases.

Adolescent girls get vocational training on livelihoods. Farmers are given training on preparation and use of vermicompost. The

GP helps SAGs get bank loans and this in turn helps the poor. SAG members train children who are members of the club and federation. SAG members have also acquired considerable standing in society, which enables them to have a say in selecting panchayat candidates.

Women have taken up health issues at federation meetings and regularly attend health-related training sessions. They have assumed leadership roles outside the family. Women can manage their SAG's finances and their spouses have begun to accept their new status.

Children have developed letter writing skills and communicate with sponsors.

Linkage Between MYRADA and the Government

The Mysore ZP has released funds for rain water harvesting to GPs (14 GPs × Rs. 39,000) for implementation through MYRADA in certain government schools. The NGO has trained the SDMC President and Secretary Head Master (HM) to monitor the project. The panchayat has standing committees on social welfare, health, education, planning and development and public works.

The Department of Women and Child Development has improved the Anganwadi centres that has in turn improved their attendance.

The sustainability of CBOs (SAGs, CMRCs, Children's Clubs and Federations) has to be viewed with reference to their performance, participation, decision-making power as well as their ability to function effectively. MYRADA has run several programmes towards this end such as capacity building for SAG members, providing linkages with banks and government departments. Federations and RCs are well trained to disseminate information. The representation of women in PRIs has increased and they now are able to manage institutions and deal with banks and micro finance institution. This has raised their socio-economic status.

The government and PRIs have recognized the importance of SAGs and the government is replicating SAGs through the Stree Shakthi Project and other schemes. The CBOs have also evolved their own administrative structure.

Conclusion

The study has shown that individuals together with their organizations play a central role in the process of empowering the rural community, socially, economically and politically.

MYRADA has made a significant contribution to improving the living standards of people, their livelihood and their participation in governance and has been able to involve them in the development process. The Karnataka Government is also furthering the cause of decentralized governance. In this context, it is desirable that the civil society organizations should make positive contribution in strengthening participatory democracy at the grassroots level.

MYRADA, as the study shows, has already moved in that direction and there is a lot of scope for further thinking and action. This should perhaps be a part of MYRADA's policy. One of the important aspects in relation to PRIs appears to be the capacity building programmes for the elected members. This will enable them to perform their roles more effectively and efficiently. Further, it would be better if MYRADA organizes pre-election discussions to create necessary awareness among the communities under their functional jurisdiction.

Social and economic development is no longer the sole responsibility of the State. It should be shared by the civil society institutions as well. The popularity and mass appeal of MYRADA is evident. 'Unifying for the purpose of development' was reflected clearly in this study as MYRADA is supplementing the efforts of the Government and PRIs.

12

Uttar Pradesh

Manju Panwar

The study focuses on the interlinkage between the local government institutions in rural areas of Maharajganj, Uttar Pradesh and Community Based Organizations formed by an NGO called Gram Niyojan Kendra in the areas of basic service delivery. While preparing the report, both primary and secondary source materials have been used. The focus group discussions and interviews have been carried out in two Gram Panchayats, namely Mauva and Trilokpur.

Gram Niyojan Kendra (GNK)

It was started by a handful of committed social workers in the year 1977 to support the underprivileged and marginalised groups of society. GNK's main objective is to reduce vulnerability of children and women to prostitution by helping them become aware of their rights, raising their literacy levels, improving their general health and generating sustainable employment opportunities.

GNK conducts training programmes on human resource development, promotion of environment protection and development of women and children. GNK is well known for its action research on issues related to sexual exploitation of women for flesh trade and trafficking. GNK has conducted a national level study on girls/women in prostitution in India, a first of its kind on the subject. The study highlighted the traditional practice of sending young girls for sex trade to distant places to earn additional income.

Study Area

In recent years, GNK has been working with Plan International in Nautanwa Tehsil, Maharajganj district, Uttar Pradesh. Maharajganj is one of the 100 most backward districts of India and is situated on the border of India and Nepal. The district was constituted in 1989. According to Uttar Pradesh Development Report, 2000, Maharajganj, which lies in eastern Uttar Pradesh, is one of the most backward districts. As per the Census of 2001, the total population of the district is 21,67,041 with a sex ratio of 933. In so far as literacy rate is concerned the male literacy rate is 65 per cent but the female literacy rate is only 28.64 per cent. The percentage of SC population to total population is 10. Agriculture is the main source of livelihood here. The farmers grow two crops annually as the soil is very fertile and there is enough water for irrigation. Yet, the yield is low and family incomes continue to be limited. Hindus are in a majority here and the caste system is well entrenched. Early marriage of girls, discrimination against girls and gender-based violence are major social problems that plague the region.

Status of Community Based Organizations (CBOs)

GNK-Plan have been working in this Block through three CBOs:

- Self-Help Groups (SHGs);
- Babu Bahini Manch (BBM); and
- Village Development Committees (VDCs).

Self-Help Groups

The main objective of forming SHGs is to build the capacity of rural poor women in entrepreneurship, so that they can take up some gainful activities for extra earnings. SHGs are also instrumental in empowering women socially.

Meena SHG of the Mauva Gram Panchayat was formed in the year 1999. Out of a total of 13 members, only two belong to the higher caste and the rest are OBCs and STs. Every member has been contributing Rs. 30 monthly and can take a loan for various purposes such as purchasing medicines, paying fees for school going children etc. Their inter-loaning rate is Rs. 2 per month. By March 2007 the group had Rs. 42,000 in its kitty.

All SHG members agree that with the formation of the group their vulnerability to moneylenders has decreased. SHG is like a mini-bank for them, from where they can withdraw money as and when required.

With an aim to generate income, the SHG started renting utensils for marriages and other occasions. However, this activity of renting utensils for Rs.100 per day has not generated sustainable income for the group.

The monthly meetings of the SHG are a hurried affair. Although all women said they had learnt to sign after they joined the SHG, the register showed many thumb impressions. When questioned, the women said they did not have the time to sign.

Out of 13 members, only three have taken a loan from the SHG and none have returned it so far. This indicates that rules and regulations of the SHG are not being implemented properly. Further, the recording of proceedings and maintenance of accounts is being done by GNK-Plan volunteers. This indicates that the women are dependent on GNK-Plan for running their SHG.

Since its formation, Meena SHG has received a loan of Rs. 25,000 only once from the bank. As its accounts were not up-to-date, the SHG was not eligible to get more loans from the bank.

With the support of GNK-Plan and Gram Panchayat, Meena SHG constructed a balwadi, which benefited the entire village. Small children of the village were often vulnerable during heavy storms. After getting support (Rs. 40,000) from GNK-Plan, the women decided to, construct the Balwadi. The women convinced the president of the Gram Panchayat to grant them a piece of land. They collected Rs. 5,000 from the villagers for construction of the Balwadi. They built the Balwadi on their own without hiring labourers.

It is primarily the president, secretary and the treasurer of the SHG who run the organization. Members appeared inexperienced and hesitant during discussions. They said that they did not have a sense of belonging to the SHG as the three office bearers controlled it.

Women from the Mina group also participate in the Gram Sabha. They raise issues like construction of toilets in the schools. However, the women complained that their voice was rarely heard and the president of the panchayat did not like giving clarifications.

Besides, some members had problems attending meetings as their husbands objected to their participation in the SHG. As far as support from the GP is concerned, some women felt the president of the GP was biased against them.

Babu Bahini Manch

Babu Bahini Manch (BBM) is a group of children who are trying to make a difference in their own little way. The group largely consists of boys and girls between 10 and 14 years. While "Babu" stands for brother/boy, "Bahini" stands for sister/girl. BBM's approach to development was mentioned in the Sub-Group report entitled 'Girl Child in the Eleventh Five Year Plan (2007-2012)' by the Ministry of Women and Child Development, Government of India.

BBM names its elected leaders Junior Doctor, Junior Teacher, Junior Musician, Junior Communicator and Junior Captain. These elected members perform their responsibilities with the help of other children. While the Junior Doctor ensures presence of all eligible children on Immunization Day, the Junior Teacher helps other children continue their studies by motivating their guardians.

The office bearers maintain records of all procedures and have been trained for this by GNK-Plan volunteers. Each member contributes Rs. 2 to corpus of the Manch. Their total savings up to March 2007 was Rs. 2,500. They recently started a magazine *Bacchon ki Muskan* (Smile of Children) wherein children contribute articles, poems on social issues and jokes.

All the leaders of BBM meet every month to discuss problems in their respective areas. Gradually, the children have gained confidence to meet and invite government officials to their functions and activities. They have also learnt how to tackle difficult situations. The president of the GP had made encroachments on a portion of the playground and refused to vacate when approached by the children. Leaders of BBM, along with volunteers of GNK-Plan, wrote a complaint to the Sub-Divisional District Magistrate (SDM) against the president. When the GP President came to know about it, he not only retracted himself from the playground but also gave a donation to BBM. Activities of BBM include the following:

- Attempts to reduce the high rate of school drop-outs by encouraging parents to send their children to school;

- Performs skits on different issues like education, child labour, safe drinking water and girl's education at the village and tehsil level;
- Prevents gambling among children;
- Campaigns for the Pulse Polio Abhiyan;
- Celebrates Netaji Subhas Chandra Bose's Jayanti (23rd January) and Environment Day;
- Educates parents about the disadvantages of early marriage; and
- Creates awareness about child rights.

GNK-Plan has tried to develop the capacity of children in creating awareness among villagers on social issues. The strong linkage between GNK-Plan and BBM has helped make BBM an effective body and has facilitated its efforts to tackle social evils in the community.

Village Development Committee

The main objective of the VDC is to cooperate and coordinate with GNK-Plan volunteers and other CBOs to help develop the village in a holistic manner. Each VDC consists of 10 to 12 members including the President, Secretary and Treasurer. Active women of the village are also made members of VDC.

Activities of VDC

- Monitors the attendance and presence of teachers in schools;
- Ensures attendance of students during vaccination campaigns;
- Ensures issuance of birth certificates to children;
- Motivates people to construct toilets in homes;
- Raises issues like child marriage, declining sex ratio, low education among girls in various for age groups; and
- Participates in the Gram Sabha meetings and encourages women to participate too.

Conclusion

Except for the BBMs, all other CBOs appeared entirely dependent on GNK-Plan. They were neither contributing to strengthening the Panchayati Raj System nor civil society in the village. Neither the members belonging to CBOs nor those of GP were aware about the main provisions of the Uttar Pradesh Panchayati Raj Act.

The Status of Panchayati Raj System

The State of Uttar Pradesh brought in Panchayati Raj just after independence through the UP Panchayati Raj Act, 1947. After the recommendations of Balwant Rai Mehta Committee, a three tier system of panchayats was set up through the enactment of Kshetra Samitis and Zila Parishad Act, 1961. After the 73rd Amendment Act, 1992, the UP Government amended the earlier Act and passed two laws in conformity with the new amendments. Like other major States, Uttar Pradesh also has a three tier Panchayati Raj System. So far as the effective devolution of functions and functionaries is concerned, the State government has devolved functions of twelve departments. Efforts were on to transfer the village level functionaries of eight departments.

The average size of a Gram Sabha in the State is 2500. It is supposed to be convened at least twice a year. The GPs are required to put the entire accounts including audit with full details to the Gram Sabha.

Status of Panchayats in the Study Area

Trilokpur and Mauva of Nautanwa Block were the two GPs under review.

Trilokpur Gram Panchayat

This GP has a population of 2,216, one primary school, toilets, drinking water and a road. The main occupation of the villagers is agricultural labour. CBOs like SHGs, VDC and BBMs have been functioning in this GP.

The President of this GP is Kushboon Nisha, a tribal. But she is the president only on paper. Her husband does all panchayat related work. After interacting with the members of Gram Sabha and other CBOs in the village, it was learnt that most people referred to her husband as the President.

Neither the President nor her husband was aware about the

various rural development schemes, the only exception being Indira Awas Yojana (IAY) and Sampoorna Grameen Rozgar Yojana (SGRY). Both Nisha and her husband were found to be dependent on the Gram Sachiv for Panchayat work. Nisha was not even aware about the SHG in her village.

Resources

Trilokpur GP receives grants under various schemes. Under SGRY, it received Rs. 1,67,874 from 2003-04 to 2005-06 for road construction. Under Swarnajayanti Gram Swarozgar Yojana (SGSY), three SHGs were formed in the year 2003-04, for which Rs. 3, 50,000 was received. Under IAY, 13 houses were constructed during 2004-05. No grant was received by the GP under IAY during 2005-06. Nor did it receive any grant under the Eleventh Finance Commission and State Finance Commission. Trilokpur GP mobilized Rs. 1,200 on its own by imposing house tax in the three years from 2003-04 to 2005-06. It did not receive any funds from the State government as assigned/shared tax. There was no income from non-tax revenue.

Although the GP President was not aware of the annual development plan, her husband claimed that all works done in the village were decided by the Gram Sabha.

Mauva Gram Panchayat

With a total population of 1,921 this GP has facilities for primary education, sanitation and a link road. The main occupation of the villagers is agriculture. In this GP too, the President is a woman. Subhawati, who belongs to the ST category and is a mere rubber stamp. Organizations like the SHG, BBM and Yuva Kalyan Samiti have been functioning in the village. With the support of CBOs and GNK-Plan, these have done a good job in constructing toilets in maximum houses. It has been nominated for Nirmal Puraskar.

Resources

This GP has received grants under various schemes like SGRY and IAY. Under SGRY, it received Rs. 1,77,627 from 2003-04 to 2005-06 for construction of roads. Under SGSY, four SHGs were formed in the year 2004-05 for which Rs. 2,49,000 was received. Under IAY, 15 houses were constructed during 2004-05. It received no grants under the Eleventh Finance Commission and State Finance Commission.

It collected Rs. 1,800 as house tax from the village in the last three years starting from 2003. However, it received no funds from State government as assigned or shared tax. There was no income from non-tax revenue.

As in the previous case, in this GP also all work was done by the President's husband. The President was not aware of the six sub-committees of the GP. The Gram Sachiv said the committees existed only on paper. Both the president and the Gram Sachiv were ignorant about micro-planning.

Despite a woman President, women's participation in the panchayat and Gram Sabha remains limited. Although GNK-Plan has conducted workshops on PRIs, focusing on roles and responsibilities of women leaders, these have not made a substantial impact. Besides, women in the village still don't visualize themselves as decision-makers.

Funds, Functions and Functionaries

As per 243G of the Constitution of India, panchayats are autonomous institutions and are expected to prepare plans for economic development and social justice, including 29 subjects listed in Eleventh Schedule of the Constitution. In the mid-term appraisal (Tenth Five Year Plan) details of triple Fs (funds, functions and functionaries) of each State have been given. According to this appraisal, in UP, out of 29 only 12 functions have been transferred to the panchayats. Only six functionaries are functioning at the panchayat level. Interaction with BDOs, Gram Pradhans (President of GP) and Gram Sachivs revealed that they were not aware about the three Fs.

District Planning Committee is an important element of the panchayat and has a major role to play in development planning of the district. However in Maharajganj, DPC is not functioning.

No linkage was found to exist between the GPs and the CBOs.

Presidents of neither of the two GPs were aware about the functioning of the VDC. One of them was not even aware of the existence of an SHG in her village. Although both the presidents attended BBM meetings, they did not contribute in any way to their activities. GNK-Plan has trained GP presidents but not on a sustainable basis.

Sustainability of CBOs

After interacting with the GPs, CBOs and representatives of GNK-Plan, the following areas of concern emerge as far as sustainability of CBOs is concerned:

- Linkage between GNK-Plan and CBOs was found to be weak.
- The BBMs were conducting their monthly meetings regularly. There was also enthusiasm and determination among members to do something meaningful for the development of the village. However, other CBOs were more dependent on GNK-Plan to initiate meetings.
- BBM registers indicated that children were skilled in noting the proceedings. It seems they can function without the support of GNK-Plan. But in case of SHG and VDC, all the documentation and maintenance of records was done by GNK-Plan volunteers.
- There is lack of mutual trust and unity among members of CBOs. Mutual differences make it difficult to reach a consensus.
- Due to the constant change of volunteers of GNK-Plan, they could not establish a rapport with the CBO members. GNK has also not given sufficient attention to the functioning of VDCs.

Linkage between CBOs and Gram Panchayat

Both CBOs and Gram Panchayats are engaged in providing basic services such as provision of drinking water, construction of toilets, drains etc. CBOs are dependent on the NGOs. The panchayats on the other hand are dependent on the higher tiers of government. Nonetheless, the panchayats have a legal status unlike that of CBOs or NGOs. The sustainability of CBOs is at stake once NGOs withdraw from the area. One possible solution is to interlink with the panchayats for providing basic services. However, the field level experience gives a mixed picture.

SHG and Gram Panchayat

As mentioned earlier, presidents of both the GPs were entirely dependent on their husbands for panchayat work. The women presidents did not attend any of the SHG meetings. GPs do not consult SHGs in planning and implementing programmes and schemes related to the development of the village. Even though, Gram Sabha meetings should have one-fifth quorum, it was often lacking. The women are not aware of the Gram Sabha. Members of SHGs in the two GPs that were studied did not even know who the GP members were. Some women were confused between the terms GP and Gram Sabha. It may be concluded that due to the absence of a linkage between the GP and SHGs, the latter has not been able to emerge as a pressure group in the village.

BBM and Gram Panchayat

The BBMs have managed to establish a better link with the GPs. The GP Presidents participated in functions like Independence Day, Children's Day, etc., organized by the BBM. Members of BBM of Mauva panchayat said they had established a good rapport with the woman president's husband, who has also made contributions to the Manch's corpus.

However, the role of BBMs could be strengthened if they learnt more about the Gram Sabha and participated in them. As children, however, they have a limited role in the Gram Sabha.

VDC and Gram Panchayat

It was observed that the VDCs and GPs had no interaction on any issue. The VDCs had limited interaction with the Gram Sabha too. Their queries in the Gram Sabha were confined to construction of roads or the panchayat office. None of the VDC members raised social issues such as child marriage or low education of girls etc.

None of the CBOs were found to be aware of terms like 'accountability' and 'transparency'. Take the case of SHG members in Mauva, who said that they had been warned not to ask the GP President about schemes and programmes run in their village. Gram Sabha meeting is the only platform where accountability and transparency within the Sabha is examined by the community. But these meetings are never taken seriously. Even the fuctionaries never care to understand the significance of these meetings. Though the BDO claimed that he attended the Gram Sabha meetings regularly, the GP members and members of CBOs said they never saw him.

According to the Panchayati Raj Act, Uttar Pradesh, there are six sub-committees which should be constituted at the GP level. These are: (1) Education Committee, (2) Planning and Development Committee, (3) Construction Committee, (4) Health and Welfare Committee, (5) Administrative Committee, and (6) Water Conservation Committee. Neither CBOs nor GPs were aware about these sub-committees. The BDO, who was aware of the committees, was not interested in operationalising them.

Social mobilization of CBO members is necessary for a strong linkage between the GPs and CBOs. Members also need to be educated about the different roles of the GP and the Gram Sabha. Even the GNK volunteers were confused about the difference between the two.

Similarly, the UP Government has implemented the Right to Information (RTI) Act. Public Information Officers (PIOs) have been appointed as heads of concerned departments. Presidents of GPs act as PIOs, but only on paper. The role of the assistant PIO has been given to the Gram Sachiv. But interaction with GP members, Gram Sabha members and CBOs revealed that they were not aware of this Act.

There is an urgent need for intensive training of elected representatives. Due to lack of awareness, the GP members are dependent on the Gram Sachiv and have little involvement with panchayat related work.

Case Studies

Babu Bahini Manch (BBM)

BBM of Mauva GP has been winning accolades for its remarkable work in community governance. BBM's approach to development has also been appreciated by the Ministry of Women and Child Development.

Child marriage is one of the major social problems in the area. Most BBM members have vowed to marry only when they come of age and never to take dowry. They perform role-plays on social issues like illiteracy, child labour, child marriage etc. to create awareness among the masses. BBM has also been publishing a magazine entitled *Bacchon Ki Muskan* (Smile of Children).

Recently BBM has started a campaign against corporal punishment. 18 members of the local group of BBM, who were trained as comic trainers became ToT and conducted a number of campaigns against corporal punishment. The children created stories in comic form and the local Bhojpuri singers composed songs using these stories and a real people's campaign started against corporal punishment.

Similarly, BBM has done commendable work in the Nautanwa Tehsil in creating a successful strategy towards gender equality and has brought about attitudinal changes of adolescent boys and girls. These children meet and discuss issues on health, sanitation, child rights, and family life education. BBM has achieved remarkable results in the following areas:

1. It has been instrumental in bringing the girl child back to school.
2. The practice of early marriage of girls has been challenged in the area where BBM works. Parents have started asking the opinion of their daughters before getting them married.
3. It has taken up the practice of sending girl children for flesh trade. The Department of Women and Child Development felt that the model should be replicated throughout the country.

This has been documented by the Eleventh Five Year Plan.

Mechanism for Effective Community Governance: Some Suggestions

It was observed that CBOs in Maharajganj were not capable of running their own activities without the help of NGOs and their linkages with the GP were very weak. Here are some suggestions to strengthen community governance:

1. Adequate social mobilization should be done by GNK-Plan so that CBOs understand their roles and responsibilities. Once CBOs are formed, it is important that monitoring and evaluation is done regularly.
2. There should be separate training for women elected representatives and they should also be given reading

material in the language they understand. GNK-Plan can involve folk media to spread awareness on the relevance of Panchayati Raj.

3. The six sub-committees need to be made functional so that GP members can participate in the development process of the village.
4. In order to make CBOs more independent, GNK-Plan has to put in extra effort and build capacities of the members.
5. In order to bring in transparency and accountability, it is desirable to conduct meetings of GP and government officers like BDO, Gram Sachiv together. Members of CBOs may also be invited in these meetings. In this way, linkage between Gram Panchayat and CBOs will be strengthened and holistic development of the village can be ensured. GNK Plan should play the role of a facilitator in these meeting.
6. One of the provisions of the State Panchayati Raj Act is that Panchayats are expected to prepare plans for economic development and social justice at their respective level. But this seems doubtful considering the pressure of five Gram Panchayats on one Gram Sachiv. Interaction with Gram Sachivs revealed that only two Gram Panchayats should be assigned to one Gram Sachiv to ensure effective functioning.
7. Networking between and among CBOs and Panchayats should be done at micro and macro levels for strengthening community governance.

Conclusion

The linkage between CBOs and Gram Panchayat has been found to be weak. This can be strengthened with constant monitoring of CBOs. CBOs were quite active and assertive but not effective and this is primarily due to a lack of understanding on their part.

Due to lack of awareness and patriarchal nature of society, elected women representatives are dependent on their husbands for panchayat related work. They have no say in panchayats.

Non-functioning of sub-committees at GP level has also weakened the system of local governance. GNK. Plan can ensure transparency, responsiveness and accountability in local governance by playing the role of a facilitator in bringing coöperation, coordination and trust among CBOs, Gram Panchayat and government officials. Except BBM, no other CBO was found to be performing satisfactorily. GNK Plan has to work harder to strengthen relationships between CBOs and PRIs for deliverance of good governance.

13

Uttarakhand

Jitendra Kumar

Introduction

This report evaluates the process and impact of community governance on the people of Basunga, Ganeshpur and Led Gram Panchayats in Bhatwari and Dunda Blocks of Uttarkashi district, Uttarakhand.

Shri Bhuvneshwari Mahila Ashram (SBMA) has been working on various socio-economic issues for the last three decades in the Garhwal region of Uttarakhand. SBMA has focused on security of livelihoods, strengthening civil society and local governance and believes that mobilizing people through Community-Based Organizations (CBOs) is an effective way of ensuring livelihood security for villagers. SBMA has also been supporting pre-school activities for children. It has appointed health workers called 'sanjeevanis' to support the village health system.

In recent years, SBMA has also attempted to strengthen the Panchayati Raj Institutions (PRIs) in the Garhwal region through its CBOs. These activities of SBMA have been sponsored by Plan International, a leading international NGO.

This evaluation report is an attempt to examine the synergy between CBOs and PRIs for effective local governance.

The concept of community governance implies collective decision-making — the entire community is responsible for resolving any issue or problem. Widespread participation, cooperation and coordination are required among different individuals and groups in community governance. The local government is an important player in providing leadership role in establishing and maintaining the governance process.

Three Gram Panchayats (GPs) — Basunga and Ganeshpur from Bhatwari Block and Led from Dunda Block—were sampled for this study. Although SBMA started its work in Bhatwari Block in 1991, it has been supported by Plan International in this endeavour since July 1997. SBMA started its work in Dunda Block in the year 2004.

From these villages, four categories of CBOs—Mahila Mangal Dals, Nanda Kishori Samoohs, Bal Panchayats and Kisan Sewa Samitis were chosen for the study.

Both primary and secondary data were collected for this study. Primary data were collected by conducting interviews and through focus group discussions with CBOs, panchayat members, villagers, officials and the representatives of NGOs. Secondary data were collected from SBMA.

Two best practices illustrating the partnership between CBOs and PRIs were also documented as part of this study.

The findings of the evaluation were presented in a workshop held on August 23, 2006 at Dehradun. The workshop included representatives of CBOs, PRIs, SBMA and government officials along with ISS researchers.

Status of Community Based Organisations (CBOs)

Mahila Mangal Dal (MMD)

The main objective of forming MMDs is to empower women. SBMA has formed several MMDs with a membership fee of Rs. 20 per month. The MMDs discuss issues related to education, health, sanitation, human rights, women's participation in panchayats and relevant rural development schemes and programmes.

The MMD in Ganeshpur Gram Panchayat was established in 1996 and today has 31 members. In Basunga Gram Panchayat, the MMD started working in 1998 and has 21 members. The MMD connected to Led Gram Panchayat was initiated in 2006 and has 43 members.

The MMDs, in addition to organizing cultural events and creating awareness on health issues, strive to mobilize women to participate in Gram Sabha meetings as mentioned above. SBMA provided a grant of Rs. 15,000 to the group from its Public Health

Safety Fund (PHSF) in five installments. The MMD also gives to its members loans up to Rs. 500 at the rate of 2 per cent per month for treatment of children and pregnant women.

Some MMDs have initiated sanitation programmes in villages; prevented ruin of crops; imposed fines for cutting trees and motivated people not to cut trees. The MMDs also prepare vermi-compost for increasing yield in an environment-friendly way; rent utensils to villagers during different ceremonies and provide financial assistance to sick people. The women's groups have started immunization campaigns and birth registration in the villages, tried to ban the sale of liquor in the vicinity of their residence, distributed free medicines, encouraged women's participation in the Gram Sabhas and motivated them to raise issues affecting their daily life in the Sabha.

Recognising the commitment of one MMD, the Forest Department gifted a tent to the group for use during activities. It was due to the MMD's efforts to improve sanitation that Basunga Gram Panchayat was awarded Rs. 2 lakh from the government as Nirmal Gram Puraskar for translating the concept of total sanitation into a reality.

Nanda Kishori Samooh (NKS)

The main objectives of NKS are education of girls, upgradation of their skills, health care and self-defence. Besides, NKS works to build the confidence of girls so that they are equipped to shoulder the responsibilities of motherhood and become part of MMDs.

In Ganeshpur Gram Panchayat, the NKS, established in September 2004, has a total of 22 members. In Basunga Gram Panchayat, NKS started in 2005 and the members total to 22. In Led Gram Panchayat, NKS started in April 2005 and has 13 members. NKS has girls in the age group of 12 to 18 years. Members of NKS meet once in a month and each member contributes Rs. 10 to the group corpus. A total of 140 groups— with a membership of 6,000 — Five have been functioning in the area where SBMA works. These groups have been taking up various social issues without any outside support.

Activities of NKS include (i) spreading awareness about HIV/ AIDS in the village through street plays; (ii) helping the Gram

Panchayat in organizing health camps for testing haemoglobin levels; (iii) motivating newly married couples to plant saplings to commemorate their marriage; (iv) urging the community to understand the importance of education; (v) helping SBMA start stitching-tailoring centres in villages; (vi) campaigning for immunization; and (vii) campaigning for girls' education.

The NKS girls have played an important role in the film 'Nanda' based on social issues like dowry and education. These girls have also requested Gram Panchayats to include them in Gram Sabha meetings so that they can raise issues concerning young girls.

Bal Panchayat

The main objective of a Bal Panchayat is to help children develop into healthy and responsible citizens. Bal Panchayats also help in encouraging children's education and facilitating better health care for them. Bal Panchayats make children aware of their rights and attempt to eradicate child labour.

In Ganeshpur GP, the Bal Panchayat started in 2004 and today has 30 members. In Basunga, Bal Panchayat started in 2004 and its members total to 26. In Led, the Bal Panchayat started in 2005 and it has 24 members. A total of 135 Bal Panchayats—with a membership of 3,300—are spread in 140 villages where SBMA works. Bal Panchayats have children aged 5 to 12 years. There is no caste based or economic discrimination.

The Pradhan, Sachiv and Treasurer of a Bal Panchayat maintain the records of the group. The children are trained to maintain accounts and write down proceedings of the meeting. In order to make the Bal Panchayat financially viable, each member contributes Rs. 5 to the corpus funds. In May 2006, one of the Panchayat's bank balance was Rs. 150.

Every year, through the medium of *nukkad nataks* (street plays) and other cultural programmes, members of Bal Panchayat present their community development activities at the district and State level. They also invite the Chief Minister, Governor and the MP/MLA for these programmes. These programmes not only develop confidence in the children but also improve their personality. The members of the Bal Panchayat have also requested the President of the Gram Panchayat to include them in the discussion meetings of the Gram Sabha.

Although the Bal Panchayats have not got any financial support from SBMA, children have received books, posters, pamphlets and other publicity material on child rights.

The activities of Bal Panchayats are diverse. They try to ban entry of stray animals into the fields and impose a fine of Rs. 20 on anyone who defies the ban. One of them collected Rs. 1,800 by imposing such fines. They also played a very important role in campaigning for liquor prohibition and collected money for tsunami victims. They try to create awareness on gender equality. One of them could set up a library with the help of Panchayat and forest department.

Kisan Sewa Samiti (KSS)

The main objective of KSS is to empower farmers—socially, economically and politically. KSS helps farmers become aware of latest technologies. In Ganeshpur, the KSS started in August 2001 and has 51 members. In Basunga GP, KSS was established in 2001 and has 10 members. In Led, KSS was initiated in April 2006 and has only two members. Annual membership of KSS is Rs. 50. A series of courses on training and capacity building have been carried out by SBMA for KSS members in recent years.

Farmers have been provided with improved seeds, fertilizers etc. by SBMA. Problems of farmers are discussed in the Gram Sabha meetings. These groups have been formed at the cluster and the district level, where Kisan Federation operates. There are 15 clusters of KSS in the region where SBMA works. Each cluster has 20 to 30 members. Each cluster nominates two members to the Federation. There are 30 Federations operating in the region. It was learnt in course of the study that due to lack of proper training and paucity of funds, the KSS has not been very successful.

A review of above mentioned CBOs shows that these groups have been able to address some social problems of the villages. However, groups like KSS have failed to deliver, largely due to inadequate training, resource crunch and lack of interest among the group members.

On the other hand, by participating in Gram Sabha meetings CBOs have succeeded in ensuring that their members become a part of the Panchayati Raj system. If their understanding of the provisions of the Panchayati Raj Act can be furthered, the CBOs could contribute substantially more to the cause of promoting good local governance.

Status of Panchayati Raj System

Even though the State of Uttarakhand was carved out of undivided Uttar Pradesh in 2000, it does not have its own act on Panchayati Raj system. It is still guided by the Kshetra Panchayats and Zila Panchayat Act, 1961 and UP Panchayati Raj Act, 1947. But these Acts were modified by the Uttarakhand State government in 2001 and 2002 respectively. Like Uttar Pradesh, Uttarakhand has a three tier Panchayati Raj system consisting of Gram Panchayat, Kshetra Panchayat and Zila Panchayat. It is distressing to note that each Panchayat does not have a secretary of its own. One Secretary is being shared by three Panchayats in the State. Many Panchayats do not even have office rooms of their own.

The Gram Sabha meets twice a year to select beneficiaries. Provisions have been made in the Act for six Standing Committees but no action has been taken so far. In 2006-07, official orders were given to transfer 14 out of 29 subjects of the 11th Schedule. In other words no effective devolution has taken place. Further there is no separate budget for Panchayats. So one Panchayat does not know how much it would get per year!

Status of Gram Panchayats

Basunga GP

This GP lies in Bhatwari Block and has a population of 450, boasts of a school, electricity, sanitation and road facilities. The main occupation here is animal husbandry and agriculture. Groups like MMDs, NKSs, Bal Panchayats and the Village Education Committee are operating in this GP.

Although Basunga GP has had limited success in providing drinking water to the villagers, it has played an important role in implementing the Total Sanitation Campaign (TSC) with the support of the MMD and villagers. The GP was awarded the Nirmal Gram Puraskar from the President of India for its complete coverage of total sanitation. The GP has constructed a link road with the help of grants received from the Central and State Governments.

For the development of the village, the GP receives tied grants under various schemes, like the Sampoorna Grameen Rozgar Yojana (SGRY), Indira Awas Yojana (IAY), from Eleventh Finance Commission and State Finance Commission. Under SGRY, it received Rs. 106,000 from 2003-04 to 2005-06 for construction of roads and a Panchayat office. No grant was received under Swarnajayanti Gram Swarozgar Yojana (SGSY) because there was no Self-Help Group (SHG) in the village.

Under IAY two houses were constructed in two years. No grant was received by the GP under IAY during 2004-2005. Grants received from the Eleventh Finance Commission and State Finance Commission have all been used for construction work.

The GP's main source of income is house tax. It could mobilise Rs. 1,110 in the recent years, which is not even half the amount of the total grant received by this GP from the State government. Recently the Panchayat has not received any funds from the State government as assigned/shared tax. There is no income from non-tax revenue.

According to the Panchayati Raj Act, six sub-committees are to be constituted at the Gram Panchayat level: (i) Education Committee; (ii) Planning and Development Committee; (iii) Construction Committee; (iv) Health and Welfare Committee; (v) Administrative Committee; and (vi) Water Conservation Committee. However, in Basunga GP, these committees exist only on paper, largely due to the lack of interest of the GP members and officials except for the Health Committee which has organized health camps with the help of the Health Department.

The State government has implemented the Right to Information (RTI) Act. Public Information Officers (PIOs) have been appointed as heads of the concerned departments. Presidents of GPs are performing the role of PIOs of the Panchayats. Sadly, most villagers are not aware of this Act. Many CBOs are also ignorant about it. This Act has not been used at the Gram Panchayat level here. However, replies to the villagers' questions have been given in GS meetings.

The Sarva Shiksha Abhiyan (SSA), a flagship programme of the Central Government, supposed to be implemented by the education committee of Panchayat, has not aroused much interest among Panchayat members.

Ganeshpur Gram Panchayat

Ganeshpur GP, which lies in Bhatwari Block, has a population of 900. Basic facilities like schools, sanitation, electricity and roads are available. Most villagers are involved in animal husbandry and agriculture. The Panchayat has the same set of CBOs as in Basunga.

Health camps have been organized in association with CBOs. In the financial year 2005-06, under SGRY, Ganeshpur received Rs. 98,000 from the government to give as wages to 53 persons. Under SGSY, an amount of Rs. 1,62,000 was received by one SHG in this village and under IAY an amount of Rs. 1,04,500 was received by four beneficiaries.

Under the Eleventh Finance Commission, the State government gave Rs. 1,18,249 as grant benefiting 35 persons during 2003-04. During 2004-05, 42 persons benefited from a government grant of Rs. 1,68,430. State government also gave an amount of Rs. 168,585 as grant to the GP during the year 2005-06, benefiting 42 persons.

The only source of income of this GP is house tax and it collected Rs. 1,695 during 2005-06. This is negligible compared to the total grant received from the State. This Panchayat has not received any funds from the State government as assigned/shared tax. It has no income from non-tax revenue.

Led Gram Panchayat

Led GP, which lies in Dunda Block of Uttar Kashi district, has a population of 1,100 persons. Out of the 140 households, 19 per cent live below poverty line. There is one primary school in the Gram Panchayat. Sixty per cent households have toilets. Here too, the villagers depend on animal husbandry and agriculture. This GP is well connected by road and the village has electricity. CBOs such as MMD, NKS and Bal Panchayats have been formed under the leadership of SBMA.

The GP's role in providing drinking water to villagers was limited to sending a resolution to the State government. Under SGRY, Led GP received an amount of Rs. 35,000 during the year 2003-04 benefiting 25 persons. During 2004-05, an amount of Rs. 36,000 was received as wages for workers. An amount of

Rs. 39,000 was received under this scheme during 2005-06 benefiting 35 workers. No grant has been received under SGSY since 2004. Under Eleventh Finance Commission and State Finance Commission, an amount of Rs. 89,532 was received during 2003-04 benefiting 35 persons. During 2004-05, an amount of Rs.1,63,383 was received under this scheme and in 2005-06 an amount of Rs. 52,344 was received benefiting 40 workers.

The GP collected Rs. 2,217 as house tax during the period under reference 2005-06. This worked out to be half of the total grant received by this Panchayat from the State government. It got no funds from the State government as assigned/shared tax. There was no income from non-tax revenue.

The government grant was used for construction of roads, Panchayat office and classrooms. Considering the high level of unemployment among the youth, the GP focused more on SGSY and similar schemes of NABARD and other organizations to create avenues of self-employment. At the time of our study the NREGS had not been implemented in Uttar Kashi. But the Panchayat representatives informed us that the scheme had been implemented only in three districts. Under the scheme, the members informed that the Panchayat does not have any role to play. It is the junior engineer who runs the show. Employment is given only for 14 days instead of 100 days with a minimum wage rate of 73 rupees. Only 300 job cards had been distributed.

People's participation in the development of the village has not been enthusiastic. Resource crunch apart, adequate powers have not been transferred to the Panchayats.

Micro Planning

Official micro planning through Gram Sabha basically involves implementation of centrally sponsored scheme by using Gram Panchayats. People's participation at such meetings was found to be weak—some meetings did not even have the minimum quorum. On the other hand SBMA has also conducted micro planning in 63 villages of Bhatwari and Dunda Blocks which is much more comprehensive. Although SBMA promoted the concept of Micro Planning in these villages, it did not meet with much success.

Funds and Functions

As per 243G of the Constitution of India, Panchayats are supposed to be autonomous institutions and are expected to prepare plans for economic development and social justice, including the 29 subjects listed in the Eleventh Schedule of the Constitution. Panchayats must have well-defined functions, adequate funds and personnel to carry out their work.

However, in the region under study, Panchayats have not emerged as autonomous institutions for they depend a lot on tied grants. They have also not been able to create their own resources. There is no system of tax sharing with the State government either. Out of the 29 subjects mentioned in the Eleventh Schedule, only 14 have been given to the Panchayats. Neither the elected representatives of Panchayats, nor the villagers are aware of the funds received by the GP. Awareness about the function of the Panchayat is also lacking.

Interlinkage Between Panchayats and CBOs

There is a close relationship between Basunga GP and the CBOs which is evident from the fact that people's participation in the Gram Sabha is far greater than in the other two GPs. In fact, CBOs have mobilized villagers for these meetings and in a way made the GP accountable to the GS. Due to the increased participation of the villagers, Basunga GP presented the statement of accounts and expenditure before the GS, thereby bringing in a transparent system of governance. The sanitation campaign, which brought accolades to Basunga GP, was largely due to the efforts of the CBOs.

Leadership has also played a prominent role in this regard. The President of Basunga GP is educated, well connected and can see the relevance of CBOs in strengthening the Panchayati Raj system and in development of the village.

In Ganeshpur and Led GP on the other hand, the relationship between CBOs and GPs is weak. TSC and other social mobilization campaigns have also proved to be ineffective in these two GPs. It was learnt from the focus group discussion that women never attend Gram Sabha meetings. Members of MMD say that the male family members as well as the chief of a Panchayat always discourage women from attending the Gram Sabha.

CBOs

Can CBOs sustain themselves? Sustainability factors noticed during research – (1) Cohesion, caring and sharing among different members and office bearers of the groups; (2) Activities like starting of library in the village, sanitation, social fencing for protecting crops from animals etc. give adequate evidence that the village communities accept CBOs as essential elements of their lives and consider it essential for the holistic development of the village; (3) External support from SBMA in monitoring activities of the CBOs strengthened the latter; (4) Regular training and capacity building courses sponsored for CBOs; (5) CBOs appeared confident, committed, concerned and dedicated. They seemed interested in changing things. They seemed capable of conducting meetings on their own, maintaining books, records etc.

The above mentioned sustainability factors relate to all CBOs except KSS. Based on interactions with KSS members and SBMA, it was observed that sustainability of the group was poor due to the following reasons:

- No monetary contribution was made by farmers to KSS indicating their limited involvement to the cause;
- It appeared that KSS members see SBMA's initiative as a routine government programme for getting subsidies;
- Proper social mobilization was not done before forming these associations in the village community; and
- It was also observed that KSS activities have not been properly monitored by SBMA.

Case Studies

A Victory for Women

Members of the Mahila Mangal Dal in Basunga, while discussing the importance of toilets with people, faced stiff resistance in the beginning. But gradually the women managed to convince the villagers about the importance of sanitation.

The President of Basunga Gram Panchayat said, "The credit for working hard to get the Nirmal Gram Puraskar for the Panchayat goes to the women of the Dal."

The women's strategy was simple they met the officials of PRIs and shared with them people's frustration regarding lack of proper sanitation in the region. It is the pressure put by women that forced the officials to improve sanitary conditions in the village.

Children Show the Way

Bal Panchayat of Ganeshpur village led by its young leaders Sangeeta and Raj Pal constructed a library in the village. The President of the GP supported their endeavour by providing them a room for the library. After getting the room, the children met the forest department officials and asked for some wood to build their racks. The officials allowed them to cut trees for this purpose.

The children also framed rules and regulations for effective functioning of the library. Children who had dropped out of school started coming to the library to read books. Some even returned to school. Parents too have inculcated the habit of reading books in the library.

Suggestions for Effective Community Governance

Although CBOs are capable of initiating community development, their linkages with Gram Panchayats, except in a couple of GPs, are weak. This is primarily because of lack of capacity building of CBOs and local bodies and to some extent reluctance of the implementing agencies of the area.

Also, the training of elected representatives of the PRIs and representatives of the CBOs has not been done jointly. A joint training needs to be organised by SBMA. Training modules may contain concepts of good governance, best practices, benefits of linkages and collaboration, social justice, leadership and team building, role of social capital in development and salient features of various rural development programmes.

Training of officials and non-officials needs to be made mandatory.

Creating awareness among people about various GP activities is necessary for ensuring effective community governance. Women's participation in the Gram Sabha is limited. SBMA needs to create awareness among people through folk media and puppet shows.

Further, the six sub-committees of the Gram Panchayat need to be activated.

SBMA needs to go beyond conventional training concepts for girls—tailoring and stitching—and organize computer classes for them.

The MMDs could organize themselves into SHGs.

The CBOs and the GP can work together on various socio-economic development programmes such as education, health, afforestation, disaster management and adult literacy.

The GP office bearers should be trained to implement RTI Act effectively. SBMA could organize interfaces between government officials, CBOs and Panchayat leaders at the Gram Panchayat level, intermediate and apex level.

Stern action should be taken against those officials who do not attend the meetings of the GS.

The experience of senior citizens may be harnessed for effective community governance.

Finally for the long term sustainability of CBOs, a strong linkage with the Panchayat is needed.

Conclusion

Linking up of CBOs with the GPs has made the village community far more conscious of its rights. Even children have become conscious of the importance of participating in the Gram Sabha to resolve local issues amicably. If Bal Panchayats are promoted well, they will bring greater accountability and transparency within the Panchayati Raj system.

Panchayats have not been providing any financial assistance to CBOs, which are either dependent on their own savings or on SBMA. The linkage between CBOs and Gram Panchayats is by and large weak.

On the other hand, the village community and CBOs lack an understanding of the working of local government bodies and their accountability. Although the Panchayats involve the CBOs and the community when they need their cooperation in implementing any scheme or when they need an assembly of people for a specific task, the former are not involved in any of the vital decisions taken for the community. In fact, the CBOs are not even aware about the rules and regulations governing the working of Panchayats.

According to the State Panchayati Raj Act, at least two meetings of GS should be held in a year, i.e 15th May to 15th June and 15th November to 15 December. All the villagers should be informed about these meetings at least 15 days before the scheduled meet. The meeting should be presided over by the president of the GP and must include government officials like the Block Development Officer (BDO) or Assistant Development Officer (ADO). But field research indicates that meetings often do not have the required quorum. In Ganeshpur GP, between 2003 and 2005, all meetings were held without the required quorum. In other words not many villagers attended the Gram Sabha meetings.

Government officials like BDO and Panchayat secretary are indifferent towards GS meetings. Members of Gram Panchayat also do not show any interest in attending the GS. Some members of MMD wanted to participate in the GS meetings but were not informed about it. The Panchayat president and his secretary feared the women may ask inconvenient questions.

CBOs could have formed pressure groups forcing Panchayats to adopt procedures. So far, CBOs have not been able to wield this kind of influence.

Undoubtedly, CBOs have been trying their best to strengthen community governance by motivating people to participate in GS meetings and other forums. SBMA has also been very active in imparting training to CBOs in this connection. SBMA has also been building the capacity of elected representatives regarding knowledge of the Panchayati Raj Act.

The community has benefited greatly from the exposure provided by CBOs. Ms. Kanswal, an MMD in Ganeshpur, has now been elected as the Vice President of the Gram Panchayat. It is heartening to know that in Dunda and Bhatwari Blocks, 24 members of MMD were elected at the Zila Parishad, intermediate and Gram Panchayat level.

However, SBMA needs to work hard to synergise the relationship between CBOs and Panchayats through proper social mobilization.

14

Orissa

K.K. Patnaik and *Puspa Asthana*

Objectives of the Study

The objective of the present pilot study is to document the experiences of Plan-partner NGOs in community governance processes and their interface with the Panchayati Raj system at the local level. It will look into the pattern of responsiveness, transparency and accountability of the Panchayati Raj Institutions (PRIs) and the role that CBOs/NGOs are playing in making them more responsive, accountable and transparent.

Study Area

The present study was carried out in two districts of Orissa—Keonjhar and Mayurbhanj—where Centre for Youth and Social Development (CYSD) works. It covered the Saharpada Block in Keonjhar district and the Thakurmunda Block in Mayurbhanj district. CYSD works in 17 Panchayats and 79 villages in two Blocks. 8 Panchayats from Saharpada and 6 Panchayats from Thakurmunda were selected for documentation.

Tables 14.1, 14.2 and 14.3 give the details of the Panchayats studied in both the Blocks.

Table 14.1: Blocks and Panchayats studied

Thakurmunda Block		*Saharpada Block*	
Name of the Panchayat	*Name of the Village*	*Name of the Panchayat*	*Name of the Village*
Digdhar	Patratola, Taramora	Dalpaka	Sunaposi, Gopinathpur
Saliabeda	Ranibhola	Badabil	Matiaguni

(*Contd.*)

Table 14.1 (*Contd.*)

Name of the Panchayat	*Name of the Village*	*Name of the Panchayat*	*Name of the Village*
Hatigodha	Dhirol, Kodapani, Jamudiha, Sarubil	Damahuda	Kumulabadi, Uchakanagar, Golakunda, Damahuda
Kendujuani	Kendujuani, Sunarposi	Digposhi	Godhinali, Asanabani
Khandabandha	Baliaposi, Badaposi	Khadikapada	Khadikapada, Purunapani
Talapada	Sarasposi, Chakuliya, Kaliposi	Saharpada	Gurandiposi, Radhapur
		Goras	Goras, Kantidiha
		Raidiha	Kotupada

Table 14.2: Community Health Posts

Sl. No.	*Health Post Location*	*Panchayat*	*No. of Villages Covered*	*Villages Covered*
Thakurmunda Block				
1.	Baliaposhi	Khanda-bandha	7	Baliaposhi, Nishaposhi, Khasakudara, Andharikhamana, Burudi, Badaposi (Tha), Mahulasahi (Padiabeda)
2.	Soraposhi	Talapada	4	Soraposhi, Gahandia, Talapada, Chakulia
3.	Kendujuani	Kendujuani	3	Kendujuani, Sarubil, Asanabani
4.	Nuagaon	Padiabeda	3	Nuagaon, Daulikila, Simidaha
5.	Dhirol	Hatigoda	5	Dhirol, Ranibhol, Asanakudar, Jamudiha, Ghadabindha
6.	Sunariposhi	Kendujuani	4	Sunariposhi, Padhiari Sahi, Bhairanibeda, Kaliajiani

(*Contd.*)

Table 14.2 (*Contd.*)

Sl. No.	*Health Post Location*	*Panchayat*	*No. of Villages Covered*	*Villages Covered*
7.	Akhapalan	Hatigoda	2	Aakhapalan, Chainbainsi
8.	Taramara	Digdhar	2	Tamara, Patratola
9.	Gobarjoda	Digdhar	3	Gobarajoda, Baliabeda, Goliajodi
10.	Nuapada	Khanda-bandha	3	Nuapada, Kucheikudar, Badaposi
11.	Tikarpada	Khanda-bandha and Talapada	5	Tikarapada, Burundi, Makundiapada, Kaliaposi, Dalapaka
Saharpada Block				
12.	Sunaposi	Dalapaka	5	Badaposi, Kendujoda, Kudabeda, Sunaposhi, Dalapaka
13.	Goras	Saharpada	7	Goras, Brahmanibeda, Gainsiri, Palaspada, Kantidiha, Asanbani, Nayajagannathpur
14.	Phulapahadi	Khadika-pada	10	Phulapahadi, Kundala, Bhulagharsahi, Purunpani, Talapada, Khadikapada, Khadibedsahi, Jaypur, Gohirasahi. Kotupada
15.	Damahuda	Damahuda	7	Gojapathar, Kumulabahali, Gopinathpur, Damahuda, Belsorai, Uchtangar, Gholkund
16.	Chadheibhola	Digposhi	9	Chadheibhol, Kesidiha, Sialijoda, Matiaguni, Radhapur, Pingupatna, Radhapur, Godhinali, Bhaliadiha

Table 14.3: Socio-economic Profile of Thakurmunda and Saharpada

Male		21,877
Female		23015
SC		4904 (11 %)
ST		28010 (62%)
OBC and others		11878 (26%)
Number of households		8350
Households with sanitary facilities		706 (8%)
Households with access to safe drinking water within a distance of 0.5 km		3775 (45%)
Number of households electrified		4365 (52%)
Number of households connected with all weather roads		6313 (76%)
Literacy		
Male		9812 (45%)
Female		5033 (22%)
Number of schools including primary and non-formal schools		80
Dispensaries		
Sub-centres		17
	Thakurmunda	8
	Saharpada	9
PHCs (2 in each Block)		4
Ayurvedic dispensaries (2 in each Block)		4
Health posts run by CYSD		16
	Thakurmunda	11
	Saharpada	5
Block health centres		0

Orissa is one of the major States in India with a population of 3.67 millions. Nearly 23 per cent of the population belongs to the Scheduled Tribes (ST) and they are mostly concentrated in Sundargarh, Keonjhar and Mayurbhanj districts. About 54.5 per cent of the total population belongs to ST category in Mayurbhanj district. On the other hand, Keonjhar has 47.8 per cent of its total population in the above category. At the Block level on the other hand, Thakumunda has 63 per cent of population under ST category. Interestingly these Blocks are well served in terms of all-weather roads and electricity but not in terms of drinking water. The female literacy rate is very low (22 per cent) as per Census 2001. The main economic activities of the area are agriculture and animal rearing.

Data Collection

Both primary and secondary data were collected for the study. Tools for data collection included Focus Group Discussions (FGD), interviews and field observations. Secondary data was collected from CYSD and other published sources.

The guidelines for the FGDs were developed and prepared beforehand in order to ensure that relevant information was obtained from the groups while discussions were in progress. Three different interview schedules were prepared. The respondents were members of CBOs, NGO partners and Panchayat representatives. Besides, personal and group interactions were carried out with BDO, Karanjia Block, selected Sarpanches, men's and women's groups and villagers. Some of the success stories and good practices were documented.

Centre for Youth and Social Development (CYSD)

CYSD works in three thematic areas—primary education, sustainable livelihood and participatory governance—with supporting themes of disaster management, women's empowerment, health and sanitation, drug abuse, HIV/AIDS prevention and child rights.

CYSD addresses these themes through three distinct but inter-dependent interventions. It has set up three wings—the Centre for Human and Sustainable Development (CHSD), Development Resource and Training Centre (DRTC), Centre for Policy Research and Advocacy (CEPRA).

CYSD Plan Project

CYSD became a partner of Plan in 1989. The project was started in the slum pockets of Bhubaneswar to work with the children of slum dwellers who had migrated from Mayurbhanj and Keonjhar. It was extended to the Saharpada Block of Keonjhar district in December 1995. Now, the project extends up to the Thakurmunda Block of Mayurbhanj district in Orissa, covering 17 Panchayats, 81 villages, 8,350 households and a population of 44,892.

Community Based Organizations

CYSD has promoted a large number of CBOs. It also takes up various capacity building programmes for these organizations through Training and Information, Education and Communication (IEC) activities. A profile of the CBOs of the study area is given below in Table 14.4.

Table 14.4: Profile of CBOs in the Study Area

Type of CBOs	*Total No. of GPs*	*Promoted and Supported*	*Not Promoted but Supported*	*Total No. of members*
Self Help Groups (SHGs)	16	292	31	4,392
SHGs (Swarna Jayanti Swayam Rojgar Yojana)	4	—	8	110
SHGs (Swayamshree)	11	—	80	258
Youth Club	16	31	26	1,839
Village Level Committees	16	55	25	1,823
Joint Forest Management Committee	5	—	05	403

CYSD has also promoted farmers' and children's groups. The activities undertaken by the CBOs include:

- Ensuring immunization of children,
- Popularizing breast feeding,
- Ensuring nutrition of children,
- Skill formation in managing diarrhoea,
- Birth registration of children,
- Empowerment of children,
- Mainstream schools/Alternative schools/Non-formal schools,
- Immunization of pregnant mothers,
- Nutrition of pregnant mothers,
- Pre-natal and post-natal check up of pregnant mothers,
- Personal hygiene,
- Universal enrolment of children,
- Eliminating drop-outs from schools,

- Health check up in schools,
- Anganwadi centres,
- PHC/Sub-Centre,
- Creating irrigation facilities,
- Creating social/farm forestry,
- Developing nurseries,
- Kitchen gardening,
- Smokeless *chulhas*,
- Skill training for farm and non-farm economic activities,
- Extending credit facilities,
- Encouraging savings,
- Grain Gola,
- Targeted public distribution system,
- Women's empowerment,
- Generating gender sensitivity among the people,
- Capacity building of citizens for enforcing their rights,
- Dissemination of information on various development activities,
- Capacity building for poor and other marginalized groups,
- Library/Information centres, and
- Helping to identify beneficiaries for different government schemes.

The post-Seventy-third Constitutional Amendment has witnessed confirmatory legislation establishing a three-tier system of Panchayati Raj in the State but adequate, satisfactory and complete doses of devolution of power and authority in terms of functions, functionaries and finance are still areas of concern. Orissa's Panchayats do not have adequate funds of their own. Resource raising effort seems to be very discouraging. Although 21 subjects of 11 departments are reportedly devolved to PR Institutions at various levels, these are more in theory than in practice. Complete and comprehensive devolution is yet to be practiced and followed. Elections to PRIs in Orissa have been conducted thrice after the 73rd Amendment, i.e. in 1997, 2002 and 2007 and two SFCs had been set up but no serious attempt has been made to build the capacity of elected representatives and strengthen the fiscal base of PRIs. PRIs continue to discharge functions as mere executing agencies rather than as institutions of self-government. Even though formation of DPC has taken place in different districts and preparation as well as assimilation of grassroots planning is supposed to be integrated with State plans, in reality, the convergence of plan inputs hardly gets reflected at the State level planning exercise. Involvement of elected representatives and the community in grassroots planning is absent by and large except sporadic interventions mostly by NGOs and CBOs. In these adverse situations of developmental governance, interventions of NGOs and CBOs can hardly be over-emphasized. The intervention of CYSD through Plan International initiatives is an encouraging development in the right direction. The convergence and interaction between plan-partners, governmental institutions, elected functionaries and the community members at large, is an encouraging attempt in the community governance process.

Status of Gram Panchayats

The tribal belts of Orissa have a lower density of population than the coastal areas. Therefore, each Panchayat covers more than one village. The project area has a concentration of scheduled tribes and more than 80 per cent of the people live below poverty line. Agriculture is the main economic activity and migration during the lean season is a common feature.

As per the Eleventh Schedule of the Constitution, Panchayats are supposed to implement the schemes relating to construction of roads, supply of drinking water, primary health care facilities like immunization and monitoring the activities of the Auxiliary Nurse-Midwife (ANM), implementation of Indira Awas Yojana (IAY), the Public Distribution System (PDS), the Integrated Child Development Scheme (ICDS) and the Annapurna and Antyodaya schemes. Recently National Rural Employment Guarantee Scheme (NREGS) has been routed through the Panchayats. But in most cases the officials of the Line Departments have control over implementation of schemes, leaving a minor role for Panchayats, except in IAY and NREGS.

The GPs generate a very small part of their revenue themselves. The schematic funds received from the government are their major source of funds. The revenue expenditure is mostly on salaries, honorarium, office expenses etc However, the members of the GP feel that the funds transferred under various schemes are not enough and to make matters worse, they come late. Much of the sanctioned funds are not transferred due to bureaucratic hurdles.

Ideally, Palli Sabha (Ward Sabha) should undertake planning for development of the village. Their proposals should then be placed before the Gram Sabha. Thereafter the plan is to be finalized at the Panchayat level and then sent to the Panchayat Samiti (PS). After it is passed by the PS, it goes to the Zila Parishad. Similarly, at the implementation level, attempts should be made to involve beneficiaries at all levels. In practice however, there is much deviation from this ideal. Meetings of the Palli Sabha and Gram Sabha are not held regularly and even when they are held, attendance remains low.

Panchayats in the study area are not functioning well because of excessive interference by the bureaucracy. Besides, there is shortage of staff and finances. People are unaware of the importance of attending Palli Sabhas and the Gram Sabhas. In many cases, even PRI representatives are not aware of development schemes.

There are various political and bureaucratic factors which hamper the performance of the Panchayats. Caste dynamics and factionalism are a major hindrance. There is also corruption in the implementation of schemes such as IAY. The PRIs have not been able to play a positive role as they are subservient to powerful socio-economic groups. The Panchayats do not even feel accountable for failure to deliver basic services like health and education. To make matters worse, the community does not demand accountability and transparency from the GPs.

Linkage between PRIs and CBOs

CYSD arranges training for PRI members. Besides, it also helps in organizing meetings on right to information, social audit and other social issues. CYSD has tried to build up a partnership with the PRIs. But the interaction between the CBOs and the Panchayat is either very limited or non-existent. Hence, community participation in decentralized governance is also limited.

SHGs are powerful forces in the Kendujiani Panchayat since 24 SHGs have formed a federation called Maa Ramadevi Anchalika Mahila Unnayana Sangha with support from CYSD.

The SHG members said that the GP constructs roads, maintains water bodies and runs the immunization programme and other health services. It also implements IAY and oversees the PDS. However, the Panchayat takes a long time to respond to problems in these areas. Palli Sabha and Gram Sabhas meet occasionally but generally women do not attend. SHG members said that the Panchayat does not do enough for the development of the village. The Sarpanch takes unilateral decisions to allot houses under IAY and is insensitive to the problems of the village. Most women are unaware about development programmes and the Panchayat's tasks.

CYSD on the other hand, has been working in this area since 1995 in the fields of health, education, formation of SHGs, training, awareness generation, formation of CBOs like forest management groups, watershed development committees etc. Women were found to be positively inclined towards CYSD and many were members of SHGs sponsored by it. The NGO has provided them with training and loans for their revolving fund. They take loans for repayment of debts, buying ration and medicines. A few women said that the services provided by CYSD are better than those of the PRIs and it has a more visible presence. This is because CYSD staff take an interest in the problems of the area and keep in touch through regular meetings. It has helped them learn about micro-planning too. It was clear that women had mixed feelings about the efficacy of Panchayats. They felt there was little interaction between the PRIs and the NGO or the CBOs.

With the help of CYSD, the Men's group Village Development Committee was formed in 2004 and it has 12 members in Hati Goda Panchayat. Members of the group said that the GP in their area was not functioning for the last two years because the Sarpanch had been suspended on account of corruption. The GP faced water shortage, lack of electricity and schools, and the Primary Health Centre (PHC) was far away. The implementation of ICDS, NREGS, and other development schemes was tardy. They had not received job cards under NREGS. The GP has no contact with CBOs or SHGs.

The forest department provided them with Rs. 90,000 for electrification, but that was not sufficient. They wanted to approach the Panchayat Samiti Chairman and discuss their problems with him.

CYSD, on the other hand, has conducted farmer's training, set up a grain bank, helped set up SHGs, organized AIDS and malaria awareness programmes. It also helped in the maintenance of roads, water bodies and check dams. They were heavily dependent on CYSD and did not want it to withdraw.

The youth group of Goras Panchayat said that lack of irrigation facilities restricted their income and forced people to migrate. They had developed a plan for water conservation but it had not been executed.

They said the Panchayat was working well in their area. It had undertaken construction of roads, small dams, school buildings, providing drinking facilities, immunization, distribution of IAY houses, job cards to unskilled labour. The GP was also trying to electrify the village. The Sarpanch was very cooperative and responsive to the needs of villagers. He regularly visited the Panchayat Samiti and was in touch with the Block Development Officer (BDO).

However, there was poor attendance in the Palli Sabha and Gram Sabhas and very few women attended the meetings. The Sarpanch and the Ward members made attempts to inform people through the *dakua* (messenger) and Ward members undertook house visits for the cause.

They said there was no discrimination or social exclusion and all the groups in the village were supported by the Sarpanch. The CBOs, NGOs and PRIs interacted regularly. They felt the Sarpanch should be given more power and finance and should be made more accountable. Committees could be formed to monitor activities of the Panchayats.

The youth group also acknowledged the role and support provided by the CYSD in their area. They said it would be difficult to carry on work if CYSD withdrew but they would strive to be independent and raise their own resources. They wanted further capacity building.

According to Mr. Nakula Jena, the BDO of Karanjia Block service delivery departments like Water Supplies, Food and Civil Supplies Department, Health, PWD and Irrigation had transferred some functions to PRIs. PRIs were now working effectively on PDS deliveries, rural development, construction of roads, providing social security, IAY, mid-day meal scheme, total sanitation and health programmes. The Sarva Shiksha Abhiyan was being executed by Panchayats.

The hurdles faced by the PRIs included shortage of manpower, lack of proper infrastructure and training, political pressure and bureaucratic intervention, poor attendance in Gram Sabha meetings and corruption and financial irregularities. For strengthening the

PRI system, increasing accountability and transparency, every GP should have an accountant or Rozgar Sevak who should be computer literate. All accounts should have joint account signatories.

PRIs members took time to understand their role and his office undertook training and IEC activities for them on various government schemes. CBOs like SHGs, mahila mandals, youth groups played an important role in rural development, he said. He also acknowledged the role of NGOs like CYSD, Gram Vikas etc. He observed, "In my opinion, if PRIs, NGOs and the CBOs work together, it will make the community governance process more strong, viable and participatory".

Ramrai Murmu, the Sarpanch of the Goras GP in the Saharpada Block, Keonjhar district was a teacher before he became the Sarpanch. He said that the GP implemented the mid-day meal scheme, sanitation and health programmes, constructed a permanent water-body, took up tree plantation and training of the Panchayat members. However, its work was hampered due to lack of unity among the members. There were 11 Ward members, 1 executive officer and 1 secretary in his GP.

The functioning of the GP could be improved with support of the people and greater commitment on the part of the Sarpanch and Secretary. There should be more transparency among and training for PRI members.

He also informed that more men than women attend Palli Sabhas and Gram Sabhas because women do not like to go out. There were many CBOs including SHGs, farmer's groups and youth clubs that worked with the Panchayat. CYSD had conducted training for PRI members, IEC activities, organized SHGs, worked for women empowerment, provided health services and set up ECCD centres for children.

Case Studies

Panchayat Digaposhi

Panchayat Digaposhi is very active because of a dynamic Sarpanch, Panamani Marandi. She is a graduate and is very articulate. She is familiar with government programmes. The people in this GP are mostly tribals and the sex ratio favours women. There are 560 households, mostly agricultural labourers. More than 75 per cent of the families were from the BPL category. Since the village is inhabited by Santhals, the composition of Gram Sabha in quite cohesive. Hence Panamani has the advantage of convening the Gram Sabha (wth full quorum) quite regularly. Interestingly her decisions are also respected by the members of Gram Sabha.

In the last four years, the Panchayat has executed projects like construction of tube-wells and ring-wells for drinking water. The other activities undertaken by the Panchayat are micro-planning for the village, renovating the village pond and implementation of the Employment Guarantee Scheme.

The Sarpanch attended the Village Education Committee (VEC) meetings and checked if primary schools were functioning. She also monitored as well as facilitated immunization and other public health care facilities, widow and old age pension scheme, Annapurna and Antyodaya schemes, infrastructure creation, especially roads, social forestry, soil conservation etc.

Panamani Marandi said the GP was also working on disaster management, and maintained close contact with the ICDS centre on the functioning of the mid-day meal scheme, Anganwadi Workers (AWWs), etc. She monitored the functioning of PHCs and the visits of the ANMs. She talked about the implementation of 'Janani Suraksha Yojana' under NRHM. She said there was a shortage of funds to undertake developmental activities. Full-fledged implementation of NREGS would take some more time.

The GP has an annual expenditure of Rs. 5 lakh and received Rs. 6,55,000 under NREGS in 2006. For transparency and accountability, the money received and expenditure incurred under each scheme was written on a wall notice board. The GP generated little revenue of its own through house tax and other non-tax sources.

Out of several CBOs, the most active are the SHGs and the youth clubs. PRI representatives cooperated and maintained close contact with these organizations. The GP worked with the local people for the delivery of basic services such as health and education and felt accountable when a programme was not implemented. The Sarpanch has taken up implementation of schemes with the collector.

The CBO members said CYSD was doing a good job in areas of health and education. It has regularly organized capacity building programmes. PRIs and civil society organizations cooperate for the development of the village.

The role and functioning of PRIs could be improved by educating them, capacity building to familiarize them with the PR system, extending the term of Panchayats for more than five years, building awareness on Right to Information (RTI) and social audits and ensuring greater participation of women.

Maa Gauri Federation

The SHG Federation, Maa Gauri Mahila Unnayan Sangha (MGMUS), was established on January 2, 2001, comprising 39 SHGs with 362 members from 10 villages. Nearly 67 per cent of the members belong to the STs, 13 per cent belong to SCs and the remaining 20 per cent belong to the OBC categories. The membership fee for each SHG is Rs. 5 per month.

CYSD helped set up the federation, select the office bearers and the primary members. The General Executive Body consists of seven members and was assigned the task of taking decisions of the Federation. The Federation had 39 members, one from each SHG.

The aims and objectives of MGMUS are:

- Monitoring the functioning of the SHGs affiliated with the Federation;
- Providing financial assistance in the form of loans to the needy SHG members as and when required;
- Providing training for capacity building;
- Increasing literacy levels of the members;
- Helping in the formation of new SHGs in the villages;
- Taking up new business activities like purchase and renting of cooking dishes; and
- Managing health insurance schemes.

MGMUS Federation has generated a loan amount of Rs. 1,95,000 from internal sources and Rs. 70,000 from CYSD. The General Body members decide who gets loans depending on the need and repaying capacity of the person concerned. The interest rate is 1.25 per cent per month. The ratio of credit utilization is fixed at 75 per cent for productive and 25 per cent for domestic purposes.

The Federation informed people in villages of awareness and training programmes and helped with logistics. It mobilized parents to send their children to the Early Childhood Care and Development (ECCD) Centre, motivated pregnant mothers to go for immunization and pre-natal, peri- and post-natal care. It also helped identify malnourished children and worked with CYSD in its micro-health insurance programme.

MGMUS has contributed immensely to the empowerment of women. It helped women increase their earnings by providing loans at lower interest rates than the local SHG. However, the loan was given only for productive purposes and interest was imposed after two months of disbursement, facilitating repayment.

The Federation plans to get involved in more activities through the Panchayats. However, they are not even informed about the meetings of the Palli Sabhas and Gram Sabhas. As a result, they are not involved in government programmes. The women are kept out of Panchayat Committees.

Community Health Financing Programme

There was a distressing lack of access to basic health care and sanitation in the remote areas where CYSD works. It organized regular health camps, training sessions and awareness campaigns to provide both preventive and curative health care services. CYSD had started a Community Health Financing Scheme (CHFS) for sharing of the burden of medical treatment.

CHFS was a combination of management representation and community ownership. While the management model would largely be used at the supply end, community ownership would reflect the role played by the community in resource pooling and effective monitoring of the programme.

It included three types of coverage: primary health coverage at the village level through a network of professionally managed health posts; secondary level hospitalization at Karanjia in collaboration with a local nursing home and tertiary level care coverage through institutionalized health insurance and death benefits.

Healthcare expenses were the second most common cause of debts in rural areas. This scheme helps its members by charging a premium only to the extent of total cost incurred and diversifying the risks from the individual to the community level. Because of this health plan, more and more members are getting involved in SHGs and the federation.

Chandrakala Yuvak Sangha

The youth club "Chandrakala Yuvak Sangha" was started in 1985 with 30 members. The age group of the members varies between 18 and 35 years.

The Sangha was set up to meet the financial needs of its members and work for village development. The President, Secretary, and cashier are elected every year. Monthly meetings are held on the 5th and 20th of every month.

The objectives of the Chandrakala Yuvak Sangha are to work for the development of the village, check migration, and create awareness among the villagers about various socio-economic issues and work collectively for solving various problems of the village. According to them, illiteracy, electricity, water, lack of good roads and migration are some of the major problems faced by the villagers.

The Yuvak Sangha set up a grain bank in 2003 to store 20-25 quintals of grain and 8-10 quintals of rice for emergencies. It promoted fish cultivation, distributed NREGS registration forms and provided information on NREGS, helped in the construction of roads and motivated villagers to attend Palli Sabha and Gram Sabha meetings. They interact with SHGs, address social issues like child marriage, dowry, etc., facilitate health committees and publicize the health insurance schemes of CYSD. They also set up a forest protection committee.

CYSD has helped them in their activities by setting up health posts and an ECCD Centre. They said after CYSD withdraws, they would earn by taking up work like contracts for road construction and fish cultivation.

The Sami Brikshya Samanuya Sanchaya Samiti

The Sami Brikshya Samanuya Sanchaya Samiti (SBSSS) is an SHG Federation consisting of 53 SHGs from two Panchayats in the Thakurmunda Block. It was formed in 1996-97 to protect members from the exploitation of moneylenders.

Earlier, members took loans for personal/family purposes but they had now started taking loans for productive work such as agriculture and financing small businesses like animal husbandry, mahua, honey, jhuna, badi, turmeric powder, chicken and goat rearing. Nearly 562 members had taken loans for business purposes.

Earlier, the interest rate was 3 per cent per month but this had been reduced to 1.5 per cent. SBSSS had savings of Rs. 5,55,145 and loans from banks of Rs. 4,44,855 in 2006.

The SHGs and the Federation meet PRI members regularly. Many SHG members had contested Panchayat elections and won. They regularly attended the Palli and the Gram Sabhas. The Sarpanch of the Panchayat, who is also a woman, also attended meetings of the Federation.

SBSSS supervised the construction of the village road under the scheme "Pradhan Mantri Sadak Yojana". It maintained a close association with CYSD and supervised the health posts. It was also involved in the community health-financing scheme. CYSD helped the Federation to start a revolving fund to support the health-financing scheme.

ANMs and AWWs also attend the federation meetings and talk about the immunization programme, institutional delivery, care of pregnant mothers, child care etc. They also talk to adolescent girls about personal hygiene. The AWWs spoke about ICDS programmes.

Some members said that in the beginning, their family members and husbands protested against their going out for meetings. They were confident that after CYSD withdrew, they would be able to carry on with their programmes.

Synergy between PRIs and CBOs

Successful development implies that local communities take the lead in ensuring accountability and transparency of governance. LGIs bring local communities into the development mainstream in a very significant way. NGOs and CBOs play an important role in the process of bringing about a culture of local governance, which is accountable, permanent, sustainable and people-centric.

This study showed that there had been some positive changes, albeit slow, in these areas due to the government's socio-economic programmes and the introduction of the PRI system and the presence of NGOs and CBOs.

One of the strongest CBOs in the area are the SHGs and their Federations. They had been successful in generating awareness among the villagers about socio-economic aspects and contributed to women's empowerment. Their loan consumption pattern showed that they spend a major amount on investment, consumption needs, health and medicines. They, however, faced challenges in marketing products. Sometimes money spent on productive lines did not yield good profits and sometimes, they incurred losses though they try to minimize the loss by the use of revolving fund. Some SHGs had been able to venture into new economic activities. SHGs also got assistance from the government and the banks apart from being sponsored by CYSD.

Due to limited interaction among the CBOs, the SHGs cannot perform well. Gender dynamics prevents them from playing an active part in the PR system and this also affects their status and competence. More training on capacity building was needed to make them effective.

The health project of CYSD-Plan was another important intervention in the project area. The SHG federations were actively engaged in implementing the health post- programmes and the health-financing scheme. Youth clubs also played an active role and provided support to the implementation of CYSD-Plan programmes.

The grain banks developed by the CYSD and run by CBOs were also commendable. They provided food security and had also checked outmigration to some extent in the area.

However, there was also some skepticism about the opportunities offered to the PRIs. There were fears about the effective devolution of decision-making powers to the PRIs. Also, the bureaucracy did not extend much support, as it was uneasy about being accountable to an elected body. Moreover, there was a general apprehension over the existence of Panchayats dominated by a particular caste, with the possibility of conflicts between the haves and the have-nots.

At the grassroots level the NGOs, CBOs and PRIs should be involved in the implementation of development programmes and strengthening community governance. Greater accountability and transparency will be possible if these institutions work harmoniously at the grassroots level.

Training and capacity buiiding programmes for elected representatives, government officials, CBOs, community leaders and NGO partners should be undertaken at regular intervals. Community members, men and women, should be trained to access services provided under different Government programmes and thosc by private charitable institutions.

There was need for a platform for elected representatives, CBOs, NGOs and community leaders to interact on local development issues and sources of finance. On the issue of sustainability of the CYSD-Plan project, steps should be taken to withdraw in a phased manner. This would provide people and CBOs enough space and time to build up their own capacity, face challenges and also work towards their sustainability.

To conclude, the democratic governance process necessitates full participation of the PRIs, NGOs and the CBOs at the grassroots level. In the event of withdrawal of the NGOs at some point of time, it is the PRIs, which are supposed to deliver results and play a more positive role in collaboration with CBOs. It was important that the PRIs be strengthened through training and capacity building. Devolution of administrative powers, financial powers and infrastructure facilities should be provided to them.

15

Rajasthan

Pamela Singla

Introduction

The 73rd Amendment to the Constitution recognizes Panchayati Raj Institutions (PRIs) as important tools for effective and sustained development of rural India. Seventy-two per cent of India's population lives in villages and PRIs, as democratically elected bodies, are responsible for their well-being.

Besides the PRIs, there are other organizations that work towards the welfare and development of rural areas. These include Non Governmental Organizations (NGOs), also known as the voluntary organizations, and Community Based Organizations (CBOs).

Although the three bodies work with similar objectives there is a structural difference between them that makes PRIs less flexible in their dealings, while the CBOs and voluntary organizations can afford to be less rigid in their approach. Nevertheless, studies have revealed that only if these bodies work in collaboration, can any change be effected and sustained.

Methodology

The study is a pilot study sponsored by Plan International and carried out by Institute of Social Sciences (ISS), Delhi. It was carried out in the Udaipur district of Rajasthan. The partner organization networked within Udaipur is Seva Mandir. The geographical area for data collection was assigned by Seva Mandir. The study was conducted in Jhadol Block of Udaipur district in the Chandwas Panchayat and Madla Panchayat.

Data Collection

The data was collected in two phases. The focus of the first visit was to pre-test the schedule and to finalize the methodology for the study. The three schedules were pre-tested on 40 respondents and necessary changes shared with the concerned authorities back in Delhi.

The second visit was meant to orient the two investigators identified by Seva Mandir for data collection and to conduct Focus Group Discussions (FGDs). Besides, interviews were held with the BDO, Secretaries, Panches and Sarpanches to get a complete picture. The data collection in the FGDs was facilitated by employing an interpreter.

Seva Mandir

Seva Mandir (SM) is located in the city of Udaipur and is currently working in 472 villages in the districts of Udaipur and Rajasmand. It believes that citizens and their associations should engage separately and jointly with the State in matters of governance and development. The organization has been active since 1969.

History

For over a decade until 1980, SM conducted adult education programmes in the districts and villages of Udaipur. Interacting with the community through these classes, the NGO was also able to heighten the villagers' awareness of social and environmental concerns. Gradually the community started to express their everyday concerns which the adult education programmes were unable to resolve. From mid-1970s for nearly a decade, droughts in Rajasthan had caused innumerable hardships for the villagers. With no relief coming through the State machinery, the villagers turned to NGOs like SM for help. SM now adopted a "Group Approach" strategy whereby women and men's groups would sit together to identify the problems in the villages and find ways to resolve them. Unemployment, lack of pastures for grazing cattle and depleting forest cover were some of the crucial issues which were identified. To start with, SM initiated some experimental projects in agriculture and water harvesting. These essentially aimed at making the community aware of two things—(1) the resources available and (2) how to use them.

Work Strategy

The group approach helped identify core issues such as health, livelihood and women's status. The present units were formed on the basis of the issues identified. Livelihood came up as a major issue and several measures were taken to create sustainable livelihoods. One of them was a non-farm initiative for employment, 'Sadhna', formed by tribal women. Since 1990, SM has been working under a Comprehensive Plan that essentially makes the village its focus; encourages people's participation and looks upon the community as partners and assigns responsibilities to villagers. Apart from 'Sadhna', SM has undertaken district poverty alleviation programmes and has also started a People's Management School. The other ongoing programmes are related to natural resources, education, health and women and child development.

Seva Mandir is active in five Blocks in Udaipur district—Badgaon, Girwa, Jhadol, Kherwara and Kotra. We have studied two Panchayats in Jhadol Block.

Jhadol Block

The 1991 census for Jhadol Block indicated poor literacy rates. Only 13 per cent of the male population and 2.8 per cent of the female population is literate. But in the year 2001, the total literacy rate had increased to 59 per cent. Even though the gender division of literacy rate is not available, in all probability, the female literacy rate would be much lower than the male literacy rate if the district rates are an indication. In the district as a whole, male literacy rate is 60 per cent and that of females is 35 per cent as per the Census of 2001. Health status of the people particularly that of women is low. Traditional division of roles has also ensured that men have greater access to resources and institutions.

CBOs

The CBOs are known as the Gram Vikas Committee (GVC). The GVC members are elected from the 'Samuh', where household is the unit. To become member of the 'Samuh' a household has to contribute Rs. 5 as lifetime membership fee. One GVC is formed for each village.

Under the banner of GVC, all development issues of the village such as health, education, formation of SHGs, watershed, forest management etc. are taken care of. In some areas, the GVCs have emerged as powerful entities and are approached by political parties.

Status of Panchayati Raj System

Rajasthan's Panchayati Raj Act was passed in 1943 but came into effect in 1994. Certain important amendments were made in 1999, 2000 and 2004 to make these institutions more effective. The State has a three tier system of government, namely Gram Panchayat, Panchayat Samiti and Zila Panchayat. The Act provides for holding two Gram Sabha meetings per year. There is also a provision of having a Ward Sabha as in Orissa and Kerala. The State enacted Panchayat Extension to the Scheduled Areas Act (PESA) in 1999. But the Gram Panchayats have not been activated to work in conformity with PESA. Out of 29 subjects, functions of 18 subjects, functionaries and funds have been transferred to Panchayats. In 2004-05 the State government constituted a district sector/Panchayat window in its budget and funds are given through own source revenue through octori, agricultural land, primary education, water and stamp duty. But own source of revenue constituted only two to three per cent of the entire amount. The rest is borne by the State government.

Working of Gram Panchayats

The Panchayats in the tribal belt of Udaipur have a low population density in comparison with Panchayats in other areas. On an average, a Gram Panchayat (GP) comprises 4-5 villages. The name of the GP could be on anyone of the village names or independent.

Most villagers work as agricultural labourers and the area is dominated by the Scheduled Tribes. The GP is involved in providing drinking water facilities, primary education and immunization. It implements the various poverty alleviation schemes of the government such as Annapurna, Antyodaya as well as Indira Awas Yojna (IAY) and National Rural Employment Guarantee Scheme

(NREGS). Maintenance of infrastructure such as roads, Anganwadi Centres and the Primary Health Centre is the responsibility of the Panchayats. Panchayats have also funded construction of wells as part of other development schemes and have also implemented the widow pension scheme.

Revenue

Since people are poor and unable to pay taxes, Panchayat does not collect any tax. Funds are obtained from the Centre and the State. The Zila Parishad was also mentioned as source of fund. The Gram Panchayat spends Rs. 60 to 70 lakhs in the form of establishment expenses/office expenses per year besides grants and subsidies. With the implementation of the NREGS, this was expected to rise to over a crore.

Planning of Village

The Gram Sabha is supposed to make the Annual Plan for the villages in consultation with Ward representatives. It is a democratic process as the villagers, who constitute the Gram Sabha, attend these meetings. Issues concerning the villages are taken up for discussion. Based on these meetings, a draft agenda is prepared by the GP and sent to the Panchayat Samiti. Once approved by the Samiti, the Plan is sent to the Zila Parishad. Schemes and projects are normally implemented with the knowledge of the village community.

An Analysis

The topography of the Jhadol belt itself seems to make the Panchayats' work difficult to coordinate. The elected members belong to different villages. The villages are scattered over a large area and this makes it difficult for the members to attend to the needs of the villages, other than their own or those she/he can reach easily. On an average a GP comprises 4 to 5 villages.

Political and caste factors have also prevented Panchayats from functioning effectively. Panchayats were often seen as playing into the hands of powerful lobbies, i.e. those who are wealthy or belong to the upper castes. Also, the Panchayat was often regarded as a corrupt body. This was repeatedly pointed out by villagers at the FGDs.

This is in agreement with Poonam Abbi's report for Seva Mandir, which says, ..."Panchayats presently (*sic*) provide only 'presence without empowerment' of those who are marginalized... Panchayats are subservient to the State and powerful socio-economic groups. The socio-economic conditions at the grassroots level also make it difficult for village communities to hold their elected leaders responsible and to take advantage of the spaces provided by such initiatives."

Status of Panchayats in the Study Area

The four FGDs were conducted in two different Panchayats, namely Madla Panchayat and Chandwas Panchayat. Separate discussions were held with women and men from the two Panchayats. Focus was on the key features that are important to community governance. Hence response was sought for:

- Tasks taken up by the GP;
- Role performed by the Panchayat in development of the village;
- Role performed by CBOs or Gram Vikas Committee (GVCs) as they are known here;
- Collaboration between Panchayats and CBOs;
- SHGs and their functioning; social initiatives taken by SHGs;
- Sustainability of CBOs in the absence of the supporting NGO; and
- Ways to improve the functioning of Panchayats.

Panchayat: Chandwas; Village: Talai

As mentioned earlier, Panchayat Chand comprised six villages. The percentages of ST and SC are 69 and 0.64 respectively. The population of males is 65 per cent and that of females is 39 per cent. It is worthwhile to note that 71 per cent of total population are cultivators and only 12 per cent are engaged in agricultural labour.

Role of GP in Village Development

Most respondents, women and men deemed the Panchayat as an insignificant body, working only for influential people. They accused the Sarpanch of favouritism and partisan attitude. Thus for instance, the village had electricity but only in areas where the upper caste and wealthy people lived.

The beneficiaries of the welfare schemes for housing and employment were those who had voted for the Sarpanch, the villagers at the FGD claimed. Only those close to the Sarpanch were allowed to use the electric *chakki* (to grind wheat) installed at her house.

The men at the FGD were of the opinion that it was the Sarpanch's husband who took the real decisions. Only one woman present at the FGD said that she attended the GS meetings. She said that the few women who did attend did not speak at the meetings.

There were a few tasks, though, that had been undertaken by the Panchayat over several years. These were:

- The construction of the school building, village road and several small dams. The programmes and initiatives had been taken by different Panchayats over a period of time. The respondents were not clear which of these were Panchayat initiatives and which were begun by the NGO,
- Work was given under NREGS but no payment had been made in the last seven months,
- Immunization programme, and
- On Public Distribution System (PDS), the women unanimously said that ration supplies were timely and adequate.

Role Performed by CBOs/GVC

Seva Mandir, the Udaipur based NGO working in this Block, is treated as a father figure by the villagers. SM is the only NGO working at Talai Gaon. The women unanimously felt that SM was better than the Panchayats.

Many women were members of the SHGs formed by the above NGO. The SHGs helped them with loans. Women took loans to buy rations or to clear off debts.

The women compared the functioning and the role played by the NGO and the GVCs with the Panchayats. They said that while the former delivered what was promised, no one could be sure of the Panchayat.

Apart from forming the SHGs, SM was also engaged in forest management and making small dams. The work carried out by SM also provided employment to a number of villagers. Unlike Panchayats and NREGS, the wages were paid by SM on time. The villagers have also been able to start a dairy farm and a fishery enterprise as well as marketing *safed musli* (medicinal plant) with the help of the NGO.

Collaboration Between Panchayats and CBOs

The unanimous opinion was that the Panchayats and the CBOs/GVC did not work together. The members of CBOs did not meet the Panchayat members and *vice versa*. The villagers felt that unlike the SM, where the community seemed to be involved in the decision-making process, the programmes and projects of the Panchayat were already planned before they reached the village. They said, '*SM ki rooprekha ham banate hain. Panchayat mein aisa nahi hain. Panchayat ki rooprekha upar se aati hain*' (We the people participate in planning the programmes in SM while in the case of Panchayats the programmes were already planned before they reach us). People's participation was to be seen in SM's programmes and not in the Panchayats, where everything was already planned by the top officials.

Since members of GVC and the Panchayat belonged to the same village, there was some social interaction between them. But these were never formalised and rarely ever was work discussed. The group was also of the view that the Panchayat members including the Sarpanch looked at the GVC members as a threat to their position. The respondents did not seem to be aware of cases where a GVC member was elected as a Sarpanch or a Panch member and then tried to make the Panchayat more responsive.

Most respondents at the FGD were of the opinion that political clout and money influenced the Panchayat. The Sarpanch of Chandwas belonged to the Scheduled Tribe community as did most villagers. However, among them it was the economically weaker sections which seemed to be excluded from the development processes and it was the wealthier people who were beneficiaries of the government programmes and projects.

SHGs and their Functioning

Around 10-12 women present were members of the SHGs formed by SM. One group per *mohalla/phalan* was formed. They deposited Rs. 20 per month. The women members deposited money on time. Loans up to a maximum of Rs. 500 could be sanctioned by the group. It seems that most loans were taken for consumption purposes. Thus, the money often helped in paying school fee or marriage or even buying household goods.

Apart from functioning as a credit and thrift cooperative, the SHG had not involved itself in any issues affecting the village community. Although child marriages were common here, especially among the Gariya tribe, the group had not voiced any opposition to it. They, however, did intervene if a woman was ill treated by her husband, but such interventions were rarely done with any planning.

Withdrawal of SM

On being asked whether the SHG could continue if SM withdrew from the village, the unanimous reply was 'no'. The women trusted the NGO and often sought its advice and guidance. It was the NGO that informed them of the new schemes and helped them approach the bank for loans. Recently, SM helped some of the women with paper work and negotiations in acquiring a loan from the bank to open a dairy business.

The men were also uncomfortable with the idea that SM could withdraw from the village. '*SM to hamara sahara hai. 1982 se SM yahan kaam kar rahan hai. Iske bina to rehna mushkil hai*', they said. (SM is our life line/support. It has been working in this village since 1982. Life without SM will be difficult).

Ways to Improve the Functioning of the Panchayat

Opinion differed on ways to make the Panchayat an effective tool for the development of the entire village. While some felt that the situation was hopeless with the present Sarpanch, others felt that they must approach the Panchayat more often to press for their demands. "Why should that be necessary? The Sarpanch and Panch belong to the same village; they should know what needs to be done?" asked a respondent.

Some of the men felt that there should be Committees at the level of the Panchayat with representatives from villages so that villagers could monitor the working of the Panchayats

Panchayat : Madri, Village : Madri

Panchayat Madri consists of four villages. As per the census of 2001, the Panchayat has 78 per cent ST population and 3 per cent SC population. In so far as the literacy rates are concerned 69 per cent of the total males and 37 per cent of the total females are literate. 66 per cent of the total population comprised cultivators and 41 per cent comprised agricultural labourers.

Separate discussions were held with girls and boys in the age group of 12-17. Response was sought for queries pertaining to the same issues raised with the groups in village Talai of Chandawas Panchayat.

Role of Panchayat in Village Development

The respondents were vocal about the fact that no work had been carried out by the present Sarpanch and services provided were of poor quality. There were allegations of corruption and partisan attitude. The villagers alleged that even BPL cards had not been made. Construction of anicuts or small dams and school building had been done by the Panchayat in the last few years. The present Panchayat had apparently taken up construction of roads but these were of such poor quality that the road was full of potholes after one rain. Further under the universal sanitation scheme, the Panchayat is supposed to provide subsidy to construct toilet which it was unable to do. At the same time they reported that the NGO (Seva Mandir) had built 130 toilets for the poor households.

The group alleged that the Sarpanch had stopped construction of the Anganwadi centre but the work was later resumed owing to pressure from the villagers. The group said that the Panchayat was inefficient because the Sarpanch as well as some of the Ward members were completely illiterate and were thus mere puppets in the hands of the rich and powerful. In fact, in the present case, it was the Sarpanch's son who took the decisions.

Role of CBOs

Two NGOs including Seva Mandir were active in the village. Seva Mandir was a better known organisation. They had constructed toilets for villagers as mentioned above and had also started computer classes for the youth.

Several SHGs had been formed with the help of the NGOs. The SHGs had taken up matters concerning rights of women. More importantly, the NGOs had instilled a certain confidence in the villagers who were not hesitant to speak up any more. It was more so in the case of women who had been coaxed to come out of their veils and voice their concerns.

Collaboration between Panchayats and CBOs

Panchayats and CBOs worked separately. The villagers thought the CBOs/NGO could not work with the Panchayat as the latter was inefficient and corrupt.

Withdrawal of NGO/SM

Seva Mandir has been working in the village since 1982. The women felt that SM could withdraw because some of the persons from village who had been trained by SM had been doing quite a good job. However, SM needed to have a representation in the village as it provided a certain moral support.

Ways to Improve the Functioning of Panchayat

The women said that earlier when they approached the Panchayat office individually, no one would listen to them. This was often the case when individuals went to collect their pension. However, they now go to the Panchayat office in large groups. This seems to put some pressure on the authorities to deliver the service they were supposed to. Therefore, collectively the villagers could get the Panchayat to function in a proper manner and respond positively to their demands.

Voices from the Field

Opinion of the respondents was sought on aspects such as work being done by the Gram Panchayat in their respective villages and programmes implemented by the Panchayat for its people; how they were administered; role being performed by the Ward Panch and their level of awareness of government schemes; ways to strengthen the working of the Panchayat; their understanding of the work of NGOs; kind of interface between NGO and the Panchayat; and which was better in functioning Panchayat or NGO.

Shrimati Gattar Bai, Ward Panch of Madli Village

Unwilling to reply to our queries, Gattar Bai repeatedly said she was an illiterate and, therefore, could not understand us. She was assured that a translator would help us interact.

Despite being a Ward member of the Panchayat, Gattar Bai said she was not involved in any of the activities of the village. She was neither called for the Gram Panchayat meetings, nor was she fully aware of what was happening in the village.

Regarding the work being done by the Panchayat, she was able to mention the construction of the roads and setting up of the hand-pumps. (None of these hand-pumps, as the villagers showed us, functioned).

When asked about her awareness of the government schemes for the people she replied that she was illiterate and could barely sign her name. On being asked about how to strengthen the position of the Ward Panch she replied that it could happen only if any of the work was done properly.

She said she was not aware of SM's work in the village; neither did she understand the importance of collaboration between the two agencies. However, she did understand the importance of education. She said her daughter was studying in class X and she wanted her to study further. She felt concerned that the school in the village was not a senior secondary school.

Shri Shiv Ram, Ward Panch, Chandawas Panchayat, Chandawas Village

Shiv Ram's house had been washed away in the floods and at the time of the interview he was living in a temporary shelter. The Panch responded to the questions genuinely. He replied that the only government programme that was in progress was the Rural Employment Guarantee Programme. Regarding Mid-Day Meal

Scheme, projects on sanitation and health etc., he said that the Panchayat had taken no initiative. As for the functioning of the Panchayat, he said that all the Ward members worked separately. The GP hardly held a meeting.

To make things worse, those who had worked under the Sadak Rozgar Yojana had not been paid. The GP secretary was held responsible and had thus been suspended. However, the new secretary appointed in his place was also inefficient, Shiv Ram said.

He said the Panchayat in the village was corrupt. The Sarpanch did not attend the Panchayat Samiti meetings and hence had little knowledge of the different schemes and projects of the government. He said a good Gram Sevak/Secretary could also help in making the Panchayat a more effective body.

Ram Lal Chandawas, Ward Panch, Chandawas Panchayat, Jhadol Village

The Panch, Ram Lal, said that there was too much infighting among the Panchayat members. The Sarpanch and the Panchayat secretary did not want to share any information with the Ward members. The two held the meetings as per their convenience. The Ward Panch did not come to know of the government schemes as nothing was shared with them by the Sarpanch. Regarding the work that was being done by the Panchayat, he said that it was mainly providing villagers with employment through Sadak Rozgar Yojana. The Panchyat had also undertaken construction of small dams. He was of the opinion that the villagers should be able to monitor the Panchayat. SM, as the NGO, was doing well in Jhadol and had benefited people. However, there was no collaboration between the NGO and the Panchayat.

BDO, Ghansyam Veerwal

The BDO, Veerwal said although the workload of the Panchayat had increased considerably over the past couple of years, there was no increase in manpower. This shortage often resulted in inefficient service.

The BDO said it was true that often the Panchayats resented the NGO presence in the community. This was mainly because the latter needs the Gram Sabha's permission before starting their work in the village. Now the government has taken a policy decision that no financial aid will be given to anyone including NGOs, without approval of the Gram Sabha.

The BDO said that as many as 65 NGOs were registered in Jhadol Block. Of these only 12 were working effectively. Seva Mandir, which employed local people as staff, was present in most villages in the Block. The NGOs seem to have more manpower than a Gram Panchayat. However, now the Zila Parishad, Udaipur has sent a proposal to the government to provide the required manpower to the Gram Panchayats.

Veerwal said they are working towards generating awareness among the Panchayats about the various schemes and programmes of the government. He said that from 16th May to 16th June 2006, a month long programme was organised on behalf of the Panchayati Raj department with the primary objective of creating awareness among the people about various government schemes. This programme was meant for everyone. The programme was known as the 'Jal Chetna Rath Yatra'. Under this a proposal for constructing 100 toilets at the GP level has been made. For creating awareness 15,000 pamphlets about the work of various departments were distributed. The Block officers talked to people in person about the various schemes. In order to ensure effective delivery of information, folk songs and dances were used as the medium of communication during the one month programme.

He also said that they had recently organised a training programme for the Panchayat Samiti (PS) members which was well attended. Proper publicity of the meeting, good logistic arrangement like boarding and lodging and a sense of accountability of the members led to good attendance, he said.

To ensure better transparency, the GP is supposed to report its work to the Gram Sabha meetings. Social audit is done and programmes are implemented once they are approved by the Gram Sabha. He also informed that a vigilance committee at the level of villages had been formed to check the working of the Panchayats. It is not, however, working very effectively at the moment and needs to be strengthened soon.

Bheru Lal Sharma, Manager – LAMPS (Cooperative Society), Bhagpura Panchayat

Although Bhagpura Panchayat was not part of the study plan, we interviewed Mr. Sharma just to see how any other GP in Jhadol

Block functions. Sharma said the Panchayat functioned well and the credit for it went to the Panchayat Secretary. Left to the Sarpanch, nothing would ever get done, he said. "The government is spending crores of rupees on the development of the villages but only those who are close to the authorities can get their benefit. The poor who have no voice are getting poorer", he said. Regarding Panchayat CBO/NGO interface he said that the two agencies wanted to work independently as both seemed to have something they could not disclose. However, ideally, the two agencies should come together to work for the welfare and development of the people. Regarding the Gram Sabha he said that less than a handful spoke at these meetings and the rest were mere listeners. No one came to the Sabha with the objective of sharing anything. The majority attended the meetings just to know what they would get. Those who speak at these meetings gain and those who are quiet do not get benefits, he said.

Interaction Between CBOs and GPs

Youth Clubs, Self Help Groups, Mahila Samitis and Joint Forest Management Committees are some of the CBOs that have been formed with the help of Seva Mandir in the areas where the latter is active. Since members of the Gram Panchayats and the members of the GVCs belong to the same areas, often of the same villages, there is adequate social interaction between them. However, there is no formal interaction or any collaboration amongst them for any of the development work. In fact, in several places, as seen in the Gram Panchayats covered in this study, there is mutual suspicion and the relationship between GVC and GP members is fraught with prejudice and bias.

Community Governance or the Lack of it in the Areas Under Study—Brief Summary

During the FGDs and interviews with Panchayat members and officials, several issues concerning community governance were raised. The important points made were:

- In both areas under study (village Talai in Chandawas Panchayat and village Madli in Madli/Madala Panchayat), the Sarpanches were suspected to be corrupt, inefficient and pawns in the hands of the rich and powerful.

- The Panchayat (especially the Sarpanch) was perceived to be partisan and it was suspected that the benefits of welfare schemes went to those who they personally favoured.
- The presence of women in the Panchayat or even as Sarpanch was of no help as very often it was the husband or son of the Sarpanch who took the decisions. It was worse in cases where these women were illiterate.
- Ward members, especially the women, were often extremely ignorant of the functions of a Panchayat.
- There was little interaction between the CBOs or GVC and the Gram Panchayat members.
- Villagers had faith in the supporting NGO (Seva Mandir, in this case) and were appreciative of the work done by it. The NGO had helped in making the people more confident in voicing their demands. Villagers were apprehensive of the withdrawal of the NGO from their area.
- The Gram Sabha meetings were sometimes attended by a few women but they rarely spoke up at these gatherings.

Index